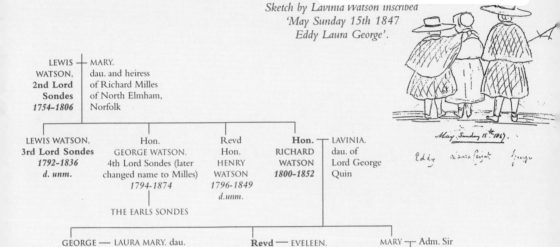

Sketch by Lavinia Watson inscribed
'May Sunday 15th 1847
Eddy Laura George'.

May Sunday 15ᵗʰ 1847.
Eddy · Laura George

LEWIS WATSON, **2nd Lord Sondes** *1754-1806* — MARY, dau. and heiress of Richard Milles of North Elmham, Norfolk

LEWIS WATSON, **3rd Lord Sondes** *1792-1836 d. unm.*

Hon. GEORGE WATSON, 4th Lord Sondes (later changed name to Milles) *1794-1874*

THE EARLS SONDES

Revd Hon. HENRY WATSON *1796-1849 d.unm.*

Hon. RICHARD WATSON *1800-1852* — LAVINIA, dau. of Lord George Quin

GEORGE LEWIS WATSON *1841-1900* — LAURA MARY, dau. of Revd Sir John Culme-Seymour, 2nd Bt.

Revd WENTWORTH WATSON *1848-1925 d.s.p.* — EVELEEN, dau. of Revd Sir Frederick Stopford

MARY GEORGINA *d. 1912* — Adm. Sir MICHAEL CULME-SEYMOUR, GCB, GCVO, 3rd Bt.

Vice-Adm. Sir MICHAEL CULME-SEYMOUR, **KCB, MVO, 4th Bt.** *1867-1925* — FLORENCE, dau. of Albert, 3rd Baron Nugent

Cdr. Sir MICHAEL CULME-SEYMOUR, **5th Bt., RN.** *1909-1999* — Lady FAITH MONTAGU, dau. of 9th Earl of Sandwich

ELIZABETH — Capt. LESLIE SAUNDERS, DSO, RN.

Cdr. MICHAEL SAUNDERS WATSON, **CBE, RN.** *b. 1934* — GEORGINA, dau. of Adm. Sir William Davis, GCB, DSO.

JAMES SAUNDERS WATSON *b. 1961* — ELIZABETH, dau. of Dr. Christopher Brown

FIONA *b. 1965*

DAVID SAUNDERS WATSON *b. 1968* — TABESIM, dau. of Mr. Karamat Khan

ELEANOR *b. 1995*

BEATRICE *b. 1997*

LEWIS HENRY *b. 2002*

YASMIN *b. 2008*

Cdr. Michael and Georgina,
James and Elizabeth,
Eleanor, Beatrice, and Henry
Saunders Watson

I am given a
Castle

I am given a
Castle

The memoirs of Michael Saunders Watson

FOR GEORGINA

ISBN 978-1-899163-88-5

First published 2008

Published by
JJG Publishing
Sparrow Hall
Hindrigham
Norfolk NR21 0DP

Designed by Graham Hiles

Printed in China through Colorcraft Ltd., Hong Kong

Contents

Foreword

by Tam Dalyell

Michael Saunders Watson is a man of interesting and varied incarnations. As a sailor, his contemporaries and competitors, in a position to make an informed judgement, tell me that, had he stayed in the Service, he would certainly have reached Admiral's Rank. As Chairman of the Trustees of the British Library, he was a midwife and nurse, during the most difficult period of that Institution's troubled birth. As a Health Service Mandarin, doctors, again in a position to know, tell me that by a combination of drive and tactful patience, he helped to achieve significant improvements in an important General Hospital.

But, above all, Saunders Watson will be in the Pantheon of those who alerted opinion-formers in Britain to the pressing problem – all too often dire straits – facing swathes of the heritage. Indeed, I do not recall anyone using the term 'heritage', now in common parlance, before Saunders Watson. I think he introduced 'heritage' to the language, a concept reinforced by his creating of the Heritage Educational Trust.

Among many memories for me one will always stand out. That of two youngish-looking middle-aged men, turning up punctually at 4pm on a Tuesday, Wednesday and Thursday afternoon at Committee Room 10 on the Committee Floor of the House of Commons sitting in chairs allotted to "strangers", and staying put until 7pm when my parliamentary colleagues and I on the Finance Bill Committee stage, would break for dinner. Usually, it was a matter of greasy steak and chips in the Members' Cafeteria, during which they would explain any notes or whispered information which they had given to us during the proceedings upstairs. We would mull over the relevance of forthcoming numbered Amendments, likely to be taken in the next session of the Committee. The evening stint would re-commence at

8.30pm, and the two "strangers" would remain until the small hours of the morning, when the Committee packed up. The "strangers" were the late, and sorely missed, Jeremy Benson, architect and owner of Walpole House on the Thames, and Michael Saunders Watson.

Joel Barnett, in charge of the Labour Team, most professionally competent of all shadow and actual Chief Secretaries to the Treasury in my 43 years in the Commons, asked me, a little concerned,

'Tam, are you sure you are not allowing yourself to be used by these guys, Benson and Saunders Watson, grinding their own financial axe?'

'Joel,' I said, 'I've come to know them, and I believe their prime motivation is a passionate concern to preserve the British Heritage. Rockingham is incidental.'

A week later, Barnett said to me,

'Bob Sheldon' – his great friend, fellow Treasury Minister, later long-serving Chairman of the Public Accounts Committee, and Vice-President of the All-Party Heritage Group – 'shares your highly favourable opinion of Benson and Saunders Watson.'

What is certain is that by dogged and informed persistence, with a lacing of charm and humour, Benson and Saunders Watson transformed political and fiscal attitudes to the treatment of the Heritage.

This book is not ephemeral. It is a required text for any historian of the attitudes of the British towards our past.

Tam Dalyell
The House of the Binns

Introduction

My mother had a form of second sight and amongst other associated interests, a rudimentary knowledge of palmistry. She read my hand when I joined the Navy, and announced that my lifeline was very disjointed, which meant that I should be doing many different things in my life. I have to confess that I did not find that an encouraging start to my naval career but how true it turned out to be.

I was in two minds whether to publish this memoir. On the one hand I have been lucky enough to have had an interesting and varied life which just occasionally provided me with a minor walk-on part on the national stage, but I am no celebrity, thank goodness, and does my life really merit recording in the public domain? Am I simply succumbing to the deadly sin of vanity?

I wrestled with this dilemma for a number of years until I was encouraged by various friends, notably the late Richard Ollard, Professor Jack Spence, Neal Ascherson and my cousin by marriage, David Hart Dyke, who had recently published a book of his own experiences in the Falklands War, to go ahead; publish and be damned.

There have been two threads which have run through my life, each as it were opposites, each elemental, and each in its way compelling. Without doubt my element is the sea. Ever since my earliest memories I have been fascinated by the sea, its constant movement, changing colour, its moods – the grandeur of a gale the peace of a calm. There are times when I have hated it, been frightened by it, but always drawn by it. By and large I enjoy being on it and I get a real thrill out of handling a small boat in the sea, be it a dinghy in the shallows with that myriad life about and below you or punching into a brisk south-westerly, watching the curve of the sails against the sky and feeling the boat powering through the waves. I love the freedom of the sea.

Paradoxically, much of the latter half of my life has been spent against the background of a building, Rockingham Castle, which could not be further from the sea. It has its own fascination, its moods, its changing colours; as far as I was concerned it gave me a sort of freedom, but above all it offered a challenge, an opportunity to make sense of a historic building in today's world. As the fifteenth member of my family to have the responsibility (one can hardly call it ownership) for Rockingham my task as I saw it was to identify and develop a role for Rockingham in contemporary society not just as an interesting relic of the past, but as a vital part of the present. My training for this task was twenty-one years service in the Royal Navy.

Within a few years of my arrival at Rockingham I found myself having to defend this concept against the threats of punitive taxation which, if implemented would have spelt the end of private ownership of heritage property. I thus became heavily involved in the politics of preserving the 'heritage' in private hands through the Historic Houses Association. While my inspiration and example for this activity came from Rockingham the techniques I employed and the experience on which I drew were strongly influenced by my naval career.

My work for the Historic Houses Association in turn opened up further avenues of service in areas as diverse as the Royal Botanic Gardens, Kew, the National Heritage Memorial Fund, the National Curriculum History Working Group, the British Library and the National Health Service. All the while my wife and I were running Rockingham and playing our part as best we could in local affairs.

Rockingham Castle is unusual if not unique in that if one discounts one or two periods when the Castle briefly changed hands between kings and queens, when it fell into disrepair under Henry VII in the late fifteenth century, and when it was occupied by the Roundheads in the Civil War, it has been continuously inhabited for at least 900 years, 450 of which have been in the ownership of the King and 450 in the Watson family. As the years have passed so the building has been adapted to meet the successive requirements of a royal fortress and hunting box, a modest Elizabethan family home, a fortress again in the Civil War and post war restoration to a family home once more, this time coupled with the active management of an agricultural estate, a role which it has played at varying levels of activity throughout the eighteenth, nineteenth and first half of the twentieth century. As we move towards the end of the twentieth century and into the twenty-first century the requirements change once more. The combined pressures of politics and economics demand a new approach. The family home may remain the first priority, but in addition Rockingham has become in common with many other country houses, an important tourist attraction, an education resource and, more latterly, a venue for corporate entertainment.

My siblings and I were all born at Rockingham and it was our base throughout the latter half of the thirties up until the end of the War when my uncle, Sir Michael Culme-Seymour married and we moved out into a house my parents had bought in the valley below. I can still picture the day we left; I was sitting on my bicycle in the garden aged thirteen feeling deeply sad to be leaving this wonderful happy home, reflecting that this was the end of an era; the first major milestone of my life. I was neither the first nor the last to feel so strongly about Rockingham. It has this effect on almost anyone who visits it; the longer they stay, the more Rockingham becomes embedded in their lives. Little did I realise that 24 years later I was to return and once again Rockingham would become the centre of my life, my home, and my inspiration.

Many people have helped me with this book and I am deeply grateful to them all for their interest and support. In particular I should like to thank Jenny Worsfold and her husband Roger Hennessey who edited the chapters on the History Working Group; Andy Stephens, Secretary to the British Library Board, who checked the chapter on the British Library, Norman Hudson who helped me with the chapters on the Historic Houses Association and Dr Brian Silk, my mentor as regards the NHS. I am indebted to Andrew Norman, Operations Manager at Rockingham, and his staff for their practical support, to Basil Morgan for his noble effort at improving my text, to Jo Winterton for gripping the project so enthusiastically and to my patient publisher, Jeremy Greenwood for taking on this book in the first place and making it a reality.

My thanks, too, to my son James for the use of his office, and to my daughter Fiona, and second son David for sorting out my computer snags. Finally to Georgina, my wife of almost fifty years who has advised criticised and actively supported me in all my various activities (provided I never became a politician), and without whom there would be no story to tell, my undying love and thanks.

While I have drawn on contemporary diaries and notes much of the detail of what I have written is based inevitably on my increasingly fallible memory. I was also concerned with the length and the relative speciality of the various matters. I have tried to keep the narrative in the mainstream, but if, in doing so, I have omitted some important individual or event, then I apologise to those concerned.

Many people mentioned in these pages have subsequently been honoured, enobled or promoted. For simplicity, I refer to them in the rank and title that they held at the time the event described took place.

Michael Saunders Watson
The Manor House, Stoke Albany
1st January, 2008

CHAPTER 1

'Will you take Rockingham?'

It was a bright sunny morning in March 1967. Spring was in the air and the scent of garlic wafted through the open windows of the car as we drove down through the narrow Dorset lanes. We were to lunch with my uncle Michael and his wife, Faith, at Sort, the cottage to which they used to escape from the responsibilities of running Rockingham Castle, their home in Northamptonshire.

The invitation had come at rather short notice and no reason was given, but it was an easy drive from Dartmouth where I was serving as a lieutenant commander on the staff of the Royal Naval College, and we were looking forward to one of my aunt's alfresco lunches where the food might be sparse but the salads delicious, the wine superb, and the conversation wide ranging.

Michael and Faith greeted us warmly and we sat down to drinks on the terrace while the children played in the stream nearby. Then Faith went off to 'prepare lunch' which the family used to joke meant putting on an apron, opening a tin of sardines and tossing the already mixed salad.

Lunch over, Faith somewhat pointedly suggested that she should take my wife Georgina and our two children off to look at the farm while Michael and I sat down for a chat. This was unusual, as normally we would all go for a walk and I wondered what was coming next. Michael went straight to the point.

'I have spent the last forty years of my life paying off death duties and putting Rockingham into some sort of order so that it can pay its way. I believe that the present Labour government, with Roy Jenkins as Chancellor, could well introduce a tax on gifts which would take Rockingham back to where I started from and undermine all I have been trying to do. There is a window of opportunity for me to hand it on now under estate duty and, if I live for five years, no tax will be payable. It is a window which will not be open for very long, however, and I must act quickly. I should therefore like to give you Rockingham now, freehold and without restriction. It will mean that you will have to give up the Navy and learn to farm, and I shall want you to change your name to Watson but these are details. My central question is: Will you take Rockingham?'

It came like a bolt out of the blue. While Michael had adopted Gemma, Faith's daughter by her first marriage, as his late and only sister's eldest son, I was his nearest blood relation living. Tragically, he and Faith had a rhesus negative problem and had lost three sons, one of whom was still-born and the other two survived only briefly. Right from the beginning, however, he made it quite clear that he had broken the entail and could do anything he liked with the castle and estate. If ever the subject arose between us, which was seldom, I was firmly told to think no more about it and apart from one unforgettable moment when my future father-in-law was pressing me on my financial prospects and in desperation I played the Rockingham card, I never gave it a thought.

I was therefore totally unprepared for this extraordinary and generous offer which I knew at once would completely change our lives.

The first thought that entered my head was that this meant financial security and that I should be able to educate the children. We had no resources to speak of other than a small cottage in Hampshire which Michael had bought for us and my naval pay. Then I thought about my naval career which I was really beginning to enjoy, but these thoughts were quickly overtaken by one of awe at the scale of the challenge and the generosity of the offer.

I must have hesitated because he then said:

'If you don't want it then I can pass it on to your son but that would inevitably delay matters, and I should much prefer to hand over to you now.' He went on to say, 'There is another reason why I wish to act now, and that is our relative ages. I want to hand over Rockingham while we are both young enough to start new lives. I want to see your young family growing up at Rockingham.'

After that there was only one reply: 'What a wonderful offer. Of course I'll take it on. When do you want the actual handover to take place?'

Anticipating my acceptance, Michael had had all the documents prepared for the handover to take place immediately so that everything would be in place before the April budget. The plan was that he and Faith would go on living there for five years to see out the period required to clear estate duty. They would then move to a new home somewhere in Dorset, and I should leave the Navy and make my home at Rockingham.

This timescale suited me admirably as I had just been appointed Staff Officer Operations to the Senior Naval Officer, West Indies, based in Bermuda. It was an appointment I had long coveted and one it would have been a pity to have to give up. Besides, it was not unhelpful to Michael that I should be out of the country for the next two years.

By this time Georgina and Faith had returned from their walk and we talked more over tea. It was clearly as much a major decision for them as it was for us, and made particularly poignant as they should have been handing on to one of their three sons.

We drove home to Dartmouth in silence. I was balancing up in my mind the relative merits of the financial security and the social challenge offered by Rockingham as against my naval career which had just started to take off. Five years seemed a long way away, however, and my chances of promotion and command hung on the thread of fate. Georgina was coming to terms with the loss of her beloved garden and family home that she had built up in Hampshire and the potential responsibilities involved in running Rockingham.

The die was cast and the deal was struck. Michael was true to his word. I went up to London and spent a morning signing papers at the lawyers'. By the end of the month Rockingham was mine absolutely, and Michael my tenant.

If one has to give up one's professional career for a building, Rockingham is a good candidate. While it is big, it is a friendly and liveable house. Its rooms are of a human dimension and Faith and Michael had made it very comfortable. Steeped in 900 years of history, it stands on a promontory of land commanding the valley of the river Welland. A fine defensive position which enabled it to withstand at least three sieges, the latest of which took place in 1985 when the castle and park were the principal location for a BBC TV series on the Civil War *By the Sword Divided*.

The site goes back before recorded history. The *Domesday Book* records that it was inhabited by the warlike 'Bovi' when King William ordered a castle to be built there, primarily as a hunting box. While William the Conqueror never visited the finished castle, his son William II, better known as William Rufus, held a Council at Rockingham in February 1095. It was one of a number of Councils which William held in various parts of the country in an early attempt at Parliament or perhaps the House of Lords, since the barons who attended represented no one but themselves.

For the next 400 years the castle was used by the kings of England and their queens for brief periods until the middle of the 15th century when the affairs of state had become too complex to be conducted on this itinerant basis and the King established himself in London. The last recorded royal visit to Rockingham was by Henry VII in 1485 when he found the roof had fallen in and was forced to camp in the park.

Rockingham languished for some fifty years and would no doubt have disappeared almost without trace like many other royal castles of this period were it not for a local entrepreneur named Edward Watson. His father had connections at Court and through these the young Watson obtained a lease of the castle and park and spent the rest of his life turning the gaunt medieval castle into a comfortable Elizabethan home. This is substantially the house my family lives in today, and we are very grateful for Edward's practical sense and modesty.

The Watson family continued in residence at Rockingham, enjoying a smooth pattern of increasing prosperity until the Civil War cast a dark shadow over their lives. The story is well chronicled elsewhere but, very briefly, the family's loyalties were split. Sir Lewis Watson stood for the King while his wife's family were for Parliament. Rockingham Castle was taken by the Parliamentarian forces early in the war and heavily fortified against frequent but ineffective forays by ill-disciplined Royalists. The Watson family meanwhile were arrested by the King and imprisoned for losing the undefended castle. Ultimately Sir Lewis was released and created Lord Rockingham by way of compensation but the King was doomed and Watson returned to Rockingham to find the place in a shambles. He at once set about restoring the much damaged castle and claiming compensation from the government.

The post Civil War reconstruction was followed by a period of relative inactivity as far as the castle was concerned. The family had taken to marrying heiresses, the most notable of whom, Miss Catherine Sondes, inherited a substantial house and estate in Kent where they made their home. Rockingham was used purely as a hunting lodge. Early sketches by the Tilleman brothers in 1721 give it the air of an overgrown farm steading with the great round towers obscured by stable and other buildings added on outside the walls.

The 18th century may have been a quiet time for the castle but it was a period of development for the estate. The agent, Mr Walker, lived in the house across the forecourt which bears his name and while the present village of Rockingham has houses dating from 1670 and earlier, many of the existing cottages date from this time.

Rockingham became once again a family home in the mid 19th century when the Honourable Richard Watson, youngest son of the third Lord Sondes, was given the castle by his brother. He and his wife Lavinia retained the architect, Anthony Salvin, to modernise the essentially Tudor house by adding passages outside the bedrooms, and creating two new staircase halls. Salvin also added a small flag tower to the long gallery wing which, while modest in scale, nevertheless perfectly balances the long low roofs on either side of the great hall.

Richard Watson suffered from consumption and the family used to pay regular visits to Lausanne where he found the air easier to breathe. On one of these visits they met Charles Dickens and liked him very much. Both Richard and Lavinia kept diaries and there are frequent references to 'Boz'. Their friendship grew and Dickens used to be a frequent visitor to Rockingham, of which he became very fond. He used it as a model when describing the imaginary Chesney Wold in *Bleak House*, though he was at pains to explain that there was no resemblance whatever between his host and hostess and Sir Leicester and Lady Dedlock. The two families used to act his plays in the great hall and, as a tribute to their friendship, he dedicated *David Copperfield* to Richard and Lavinia Watson.

Richard was succeeded by his eldest son George who married Laura Culme-Seymour, sister of his brother-in-law, Admiral Sir Michael Culme-Seymour. George had plans prepared for building on to the castle by enclosing the inner courtyard with cloisters, adding a tower and converting the old brewhouse into a chapel with a billiard room underneath. Mercifully for his successors, George ran out of money and had to be satisfied with the square tower designed as bachelor quarters with access to the main house only on the ground floor.

There is nothing stately about Rockingham. It is no great architectural masterpiece. Its unique interest lies in the way successive generations altered and modified it to suit their changing lifestyles but, in doing so, did not totally destroy what was there before. With a little imagination it is possible to demonstrate how domestic lifestyles changed over time from the open plan system of the medieval hall in which everyone lived, ate, loved and slept in the same space, to the Tudor period when separate rooms were required for eating, living and sleeping; but privacy in the latter was confined to a curtain round the bed. The Victorians dealt with this by adding on corridors, but it is under the Edwardians, whose lifestyle required rooms for every conceivable use, that the country house reached its apogee. A hundred years later as we enter the 21st century we find most of the house is open to the public or used for other purposes and the owner and his family have retreated to the kitchen, where they do everything but sleep.

George Watson had no children. His second brother, Edward, had one son who died training to be a soldier, and twelve daughters. His youngest brother, Wentworth, married late in life and had no children. In his will George passed over the twelve Miss Watsons, only one of whom married, and left the estate to his brother, Wentworth, for his lifetime and then to his sister's eldest son, Vice Admiral Sir Michael Culme-Seymour, 4th Baronet, my grandfather. Wentworth Watson died in 1925, and his heir, Sir Michael, died three weeks later. My uncle Michael, who was about to go to sea as a midshipman aged nineteen, thus found himself succeeding to a baronetcy and a castle with a double amount of estate duty to pay but nothing with which to pay it.

The castle was by contemporary standards very old-fashioned with no central heating and only one bathroom. It badly needed modernising but there was no money. As so often happens when the British landed families are in difficulties, the Culme-Seymours looked across the Atlantic and let the castle to an American businessman, Victor Emanuel, for five years. Part of the arrangement was that he would pay for the installation of central heating, bathrooms, lavatories and some splendid cupboards for all his hunting gear. He hunted locally and gave many unforgettable parties.

Unfortunately Mr Emanuel's tenure of Rockingham came to an abrupt end in 1932 when his wife went off with a local Master of Foxhounds, leaving the castle empty once more but at least habitable. My grandmother, Florence, Lady Culme-Seymour, moved in together with various members of her family and ran the house on a shoestring throughout the 1930s and 1940s while my uncle Michael continued his naval career.

The 1930s were a difficult time for anyone concerned with the land. Agriculture was in the doldrums as the country lived off cheap imports from the Commonwealth, and farm tenants simply could not afford to pay the rent. Michael struggled to run the estate by remote control through agents, some good, and some not so good. All the time he was faced with the enormous burden of the double death duty. It was a fight for survival.

Meanwhile his naval career blossomed. After serving as ADC to the Governor General of Canada, Lord Bessborough, he commanded the destroyer *Brazen* which was employed on escort duties in the English Channel during the early part of World War II. The *Brazen* was frequently bombed but Michael manoeuvred his ship in such a way that for a long time they escaped serious damage. He was a very good tennis player and he used to say that it undoubtedly helped in judging where the next stick of bombs was to fall. Finally *Brazen* succumbed, but the ship's company were so impressed with their Captain that to a man they requested they should all serve under him in his next ship.

This was not to be, however, and he was sent to the Mediterranean to serve on the staff of the Commander-in-Chief, Mediterranean, Admiral Sir Andrew Cunningham, one of the great war commanders. The Admiral had a fiery temper and Michael's office was at the bottom of some stairs leading up to the Admiral's office. He used to relate how he would have to pick up and dust down senior officers forcibly ejected down the stairs to the accompaniment of some rich language, only to find the victim saying what a wonderful person the Admiral was. It was a very small staff, the workload was horrific and ultimately Michael's health broke down. After a period of sick leave he was promoted Commander and saw out the remainder of the war in the Pacific as Executive Officer of the aircraft carrier, HMS *Ruler*.

The war over, it was clear that Rockingham needed his attention. He retired from the Navy in 1947, married Lady Faith Nesbitt (née Montagu) ,daughter of the Earl of Sandwich, and together they made their home at Rockingham while my grandmother moved into the square tower. In due course when she died they converted the square tower and library wing into comfortable private quarters.

Having paid off the death duties, Michael's first priority was to modernise the tenant farms followed by the cottages in the village, few of which had indoor sanitation. He was assisted in this by the expansion of the new town of Corby which, while he fought to keep it as far as possible from encroaching on the castle, nevertheless produced some welcome development capital.

With the tenant farms properly equipped and the village scheme complete, he turned his attention to the castle roof on which the death watch beetle had been feasting for some years. This together with dry rot had brought the roof and certain other parts of the castle into a perilous condition. The whole two acres of roof needed to be renewed and also a good deal of stonework. It was a major undertaking phased over five years, involving much disruption, discomfort, and expense, in spite of a generous grant from the Historic Buildings Council.

As a result of all this work both the castle and the estate were in very good order when Michael handed them over to me on that spring day in 1967. The only problem was that the estate was running in deficit which had been made up by sales of land to Corby. This had to stop and my task was to use the assets Michael had set in place to turn the economic situation round so that the estate could generate sufficient income from its own resources to fund both its revenue and capital costs.

With the castle came 4000 acres of land, 500 of which was farmed in hand round the castle, 400 were in forestry, and the remainder let on agricultural tenancies. The village comprised some 45 cottages and farmhouses, and there were numerous outlying properties. This was what I was given, outright, with no trust or any arrangement to tie me down, just a letter which said that if I felt that the house was becoming too big a burden for the estate to bear I was not to hesitate to make some other arrangement including sale. At all events I was to hold onto the land. It was far more important to keep that in the family than the house. If, as occurred in a number of cases, the land was sold off first, the house invariably followed. No great house can survive without its supporting estate unless there is a substantial income available from another source.

These were very wise words which made a profound impression on me and which I remembered in later years when I found myself in the forefront of the political battle to save privately owned historic houses from the devastating effects of capital taxation.

CHAPTER 2

The early years – from Rockingham to Sea

I was born at Rockingham Castle on 9th October 1934, and much of my childhood was spent there up to the age of thirteen. I therefore know every nook and cranny of the castle and the garden in a way that only a child can.

The house was large, rambling and shabby. In contrast to its tidy appearance today, the rooms and corridors were crammed with furniture, books, piles of old magazines and all kinds of junk. Nothing was ever thrown away. The stone passage, which divides the main house from the square tower on the ground floor, provided a home for, amongst other things, an old bath chair, a pedal-driven harmonium, and an exercise bicycle, and was virtually impassable. Outside, the stables and outbuildings contained a number of horse-drawn vehicles including a 'shooting brake' and a fire engine, but no carriages. Then there were several elderly motor cars; I remember an open Austin Twelve of 1920 vintage, an old Rover dating from the early thirties and the estate lorry, a Model A Ford which my mother used to drive at harvest time.

In those days, before and during the war, Rockingham was run on the lines of a family commune by my grandmother, Florence, Lady Culme-Seymour, known to everyone as Florrie or Aunt Fof. She was a redoubtable lady of mixed European ancestry. Her father was an Austrian baron with Irish connections while her mother came from a prosperous family of Greek traders called Baltazzi in what was then Constantinople. Her relations were scattered all over Europe and included a cousin, Maria Vetsera, who was the central figure in a major scandal involving Crown Prince Rudolf of Austria, when they were both found dead together in the hunting lodge at Mayerling.

My grandmother loved having people about her, and the house was almost always full. We stayed there whenever we were not following my father and at any one time there could be at least two families of cousins plus various other guests, some paying and some not, living in different parts of the castle. Everybody came together for lunch in the great hall.

Tea would be taken in the library or panel room and afterwards the children were expected to play games with the grown-ups, some of which might have been calculated to make a diffident child feel even more insecure and would surely have appalled a modern child psychologist. There was one called 'Sit by me' which involved us leaving the room while the grown ups decided who they would have beside them. We were then called in one by one to be greeted by cries of 'Darling come and sit by me'. Tentatively you chose your favourite aunt only to be booed and hissed out of the room for getting it wrong. Then there was the 'Penitent Stool', in which you sat in front of the assembled company while a catalogue of your supposed misdeeds was read out and you had to guess who had said them.

Rockingham was a wonderful place for children. The garden with its great trees, rolling lawns and ancient elephant yew hedge, and the wild sunken grove, its pathways long overgrown with laurel, provided endless opportunities for childish imagination. My younger brother Alasdair and I used to play war games in the yew hedge. As the eldest I was invariably Montgomery, and Al had to make do with being Rommel. The humps in the hedge which were meant to be elephants served as the turrets of our tanks as we manoeuvred our respective armies into battle. Poor Walpole, the gardener, thought the hedge would never recover but yew is a tough old plant.

Every so often we were brought into direct contact with the real war. My mother had a skylight above her bed and we could hear, and sometimes see, the bombers flying overhead heading to or from the Midlands. The German aircraft had a pronounced whine while ours were characterised by a deep throb.

There was no formal air raid shelter at Rockingham, but what was known as the 'telephone room' under Salvin's tower was thought to be the safest place and its walls were piled to the ceiling, not with sandbags but with old reference books such as *Who's Who* and *Debrett's Peerage*. There was also a stock of 'iron rations' (barley sugar, and other such goodies). Alasdair and I prayed for an air raid so that we could go down there and sample them. One night we were attacked but there was no time to go down to the 'shelter' and it was all over before we had even got out of bed. A stick of bombs was dropped at the end of the drive but did little damage other than making a large hole and killing a cow.

A neighbour, Sir Arthur Brooke, woke up the next morning to find a huge crater outside his front door and most of his windows smashed. He was rather deaf and had not heard it. The story went about that he rang his agent and said: 'Those damned Germans have dropped a bomb in my drive. Tell them I won't have it.'

At the beginning of the war my father was serving on the duty Captain's roster at the Admiralty, while my mother was driving ambulances in the blitz in London. She related how once she went to the garage where she kept her bicycle to find the whole place in smithereens except for the bicycle standing unharmed in the middle of the chaos. My mother was not a great driver, believing that the gear stick was a means of making the vehicle go faster and the sooner she had it in top gear the better, but her driving skills were nothing to those on a bicycle. The mind boggles at the thought of Liebe, as she was known to everyone, wobbling about amongst the ruins of wartime London in total darkness. At least the ambulance would have been so low-geared as not to mind being driven everywhere in top!

In the summer of 1941 my father was appointed to command the new colony class cruiser, HMS *Trinidad*, completing in Plymouth, and down to Devon we went for three months 'standing by' the new ship. *Trinidad* joined the Home Fleet after a brief period of trials and work up in January 1942 and was straightaway sent on Arctic convoy escort duty. She survived her first convoy despite persistent enemy air attacks and appalling weather conditions. On the second she was not so fortunate. In an engagement with three German destroyers, one of which was sunk, *Trinidad* received a direct hit by a torpedo which turned out to be one of her own. The gyro had jammed, the torpedo had reversed course, and, in a million to one chance, hit *Trinidad* zigzagging at full speed. She managed to limp into Murmansk for repairs only to be sunk by German bombers on the passage home. My father and most of the ship's company were rescued but he was shattered by the loss of his ship and came home expecting a court martial. Instead he was awarded the DSO.*

His next appointment as Captain 'D' Greenock took us, augmented now by my sister Elizabeth, north to the Clyde where he was responsible for looking after the escort vessels engaged on the North Atlantic convoy routes. They would come in rust streaked and exhausted and father would go out in his barge to meet them. Alasdair and I used to stow away in the sternsheets, scramble up the gangway after he had gone below, and cause havoc by running round the ship much to the amusement of the sailors.

We lived in a very grand modern house equipped with a ballroom and a most magnificent air raid shelter. We could not wait to use it but the

---

* This epic story is related in *The Ship that Torpedoed Herself* by Frank Pearce, Baron Jay Ltd. 1975.

bombers concentrated on the Glasgow docks and we had only one air raid. I was sent off to school at the Greenock Academy. I remember little about it except that I had some trouble with a girl called Tracey Waters who, supported by her friends, gave me a hard time. At my mother's suggestion, I collected some creepy crawlies off the beach and took them to school in a matchbox. When Tracey was not looking I emptied the matchbox down her neck. There was a frightful scene and I had no more trouble from that quarter.

After two years with the family at Greenock, my father was sent to Ceylon in the temporary rank of Commodore in command of the naval base at Trincomalee, unsuitably named HMS *Highflyer*. We returned to Rockingham where my mother, with her usual enthusiasm and flair, converted the old servants' quarters cum nursery wing into a self-contained apartment. The estate carpenter put in a staircase and we were to do the rest. My mother fancied herself at decorating. Unfortunately her choice of materials was restricted to cream, green, or pink distemper. So cream it had to be – 'a warm colour anyway,' she said, seizing a paintbrush. Her technique was to slap paint on anything she could see which meant that the back of windows and cupboard doors missed out. Everything went well until she decided to strip the oak beams which had been coated in centuries of paint, and that was not so much fun.

In the spring of 1943 I was packed off to preparatory school, The Old Malthouse, near Swanage. The headmaster, Victor Haggard, was an inspired teacher, particularly of music and amateur dramatics. His powerful personality pervaded the school which was friendly, but tough. For instance, to be beaten was regarded as an honour almost on a level with winning colours at games. You were not considered to have 'arrived' until you had 'broken your duck'.

From there I was sent to Eton in the spring of 1947. The pass mark for Eton in the common entrance exam was 32%. I must have done quite well as I found myself in Upper 4th which was above average for new boys. I boarded with Wyndham Milligan, a delightful man who went on to become Warden of Radley. The first year was pretty miserable. As a rather shy and awkward thirteen-year-old, I was a prime target for the house bullies. At Eton you had a room to yourself from the beginning which, while it had the advantage of privacy, meant that you were trapped there when the bullies arrived. Things improved in the second year and I began to enjoy the freedom which is such a feature of Eton life, but by now I had decided that I wanted to make the Navy my career.

I was also aware that my Eton fees were becoming a severe strain on my parents' finances. In those days, while I could have taken the entry exam for

Dartmouth when I was thirteen, this was changed to sixteen by the post-war Labour government to conform to the state school leaving age. Failing that there was a further opportunity at seventeen which was the normal public school entry. The thought of a week off school in the middle of the summer of 1950 was too good to miss, so I sat the very simple entrance exam, and was called for interview the first part of which took place in Queen Anne's Mansions. We were then taken down to Exbury House in Hampshire where we were put through a number of tests including 'evolutions' designed to demonstrate our ability to think fast and take charge. My team had to remove an unexploded bomb from a street above which it was suspended by its parachute. To my astonishment, I passed.

At one point during the interview we had to complete a questionnaire, in the course of which we were invited to indicate our interests from a list which included the word 'people'. I ticked a number of what I thought would be popular items such as sport, music, sailing, walking, painting, but it never occurred to me that 'people' might be a legitimate interest. The Admiral President of the Board focussed on this omission and asked why I had not ticked it.

'Are you not interested in people?'

'Well, I suppose if you put it like that, the answer must be yes,' I answered.

I have never forgotten his reply which has guided me all my life.

'You cannot be a good naval officer unless you have an interest in people. To lead your men you must understand them and relate to them so that they have confidence in you as their leader and you likewise know their capabilities.'

I thus left Eton somewhat unexpectedly at the age of sixteen to don my cadet's uniform and report to the Britannia Royal Naval College, Dartmouth. My sudden disappearance gave rise to rumours that I might have been expelled and for a few brief moments my totally undistinguished career at Eton acquired a modest degree of notoriety, but it soon died when the more mundane truth emerged.

In retrospect, whatever I thought of them at the time, both Eton and The Old Malthouse served me well. The latter gave me a love of painting, music and drama, while the former taught me independence of view and the ability to express it.

On his return from Ceylon, my father was given command of the cruiser HMS *Liverpool*, in my view and his, one of the best looking ships in the Navy. It was to be his last appointment and in 1947 he retired, came home and took a job in the training division of Stewarts and Lloyds, the steel and tube manufacturer in Corby.

My uncle Michael also retired from the Navy at about the same time, married, and came to live at Rockingham. This was the signal for us to move out of the castle. It was a sad moment saying goodbye to that old house in which I had grown up. I never thought that I should ever return.

My mother then discovered the west coast of Scotland. She loved the sea and boats and my father, a Scot, revered his home country. For once their interests coincided and the spring of 1948 found us bound for Tayvallich, a landlocked harbour at the head of Loch Sween – the most perfect place for young children to play around in boats. Thus started an annual pilgrimage which, in those days of petrol rationing, involved travelling by public transport. Almost invariably my father found some reason why he could not accompany us to Scotland and would join us later. I can understand why. The party consisted of my mother, nanny, Mrs Rhodes, our very fat cook, three children, and a dog or two. Together with our bicycles and luggage we were driven to Rockingham station where we caught a train for Rugby at about 3pm. At Rugby we transferred to the night sleeper for Glasgow. At Glasgow Central station we transferred to the Gourock boat train. At Gourock we caught the steamer for Ardrishaig where we were met four hours later by Mr McLaughlan in his little red bus that drove us to Tayvallich. The whole trip took not far short of 24 hours.

One year Alasdair and I were playing on the pier when an elderly gentleman came alongside in his dinghy. We had been admiring his 42-foot blue ketch *Kanwara* and fell into conversation with him whereupon he invited us on board and began a friendship which lasted to his death twenty years later. Mr Brown, or HAB as we called him, would arrange to bring *Kanwara* to wherever we happened to be and remain throughout our holiday. We would play with his two boats, go for day trips in *Kanwara* and even short cruises of two or three nights. Then as time passed, we moved to Crinan where there was more scope for sailing.

Kanwara was exchanged for a motor cruiser as HAB grew older. For many years he lived in Crinan harbour in a leaky old houseboat known as the *Foray* which was reputed to have once been the Dutch royal yacht, though I found that hard to believe. Eventually *Foray* sank beneath him and he was forced to move ashore and spend his last years in a caravan on the pier. He was a wonderful mentor and gave us some unforgettable experiences. I owe to him practically all I know about sailing, seamanship, and that particular piece of water between the Sound of Jura and Mull, with its fast currents and scattered rocks, on which I have sailed all my life.

The area enclosed by Loch Crinan, Loch Craignish, the Sound of Jura, and the Dorus Mor, the great door in the islands through which the tide runs at up to eight knots, continues to have a very special fascination for my family. As soon as I left the Navy I put the proceeds of the sale of our cottage in

Hampshire into a small wooden bungalow at Ardfern by the water's edge. Subsequently we bought fifty acres of land bordering the lagoon where I keep my boat and were able in due course to build a small house of local stone facing down the Sound. My brother Iain bought the farmhouse next door, and my other brother, Alasdair, has also recently bought a house at Ardfern. The adventure, happiness and fun of our childhood has thus continued into adulthood and, now, old age!

After the freedom of Eton, Dartmouth was like returning to prep school. We were made to double everywhere and sleep in great dormitories called 'chest flats' with compulsory cold baths every morning. We were given four shillings and sixpence a week pocket money which we could only spend in the canteen and generally treated as small children, or so we thought.

In a term of over forty cadets only about six of us had been to public school; the remainder all came from grammar or other schools. Many of them had never been away from home. The rigours and proximity of our life drove us together and a camaraderie developed between us in a way I never experienced at my previous two boarding schools. While I was dead keen on the Navy and never regretted my decision to join it, I did find the Dartmouth regime irksome and showed it. As a result I was not made a Cadet Captain and left Dartmouth with an undistinguished third class pass.

My particular friends at this time were Robert Chitham who subsequently became an architect, and Peter Kemp. He contracted rheumatic fever lining the route at the Coronation and became a civil servant rising to be Second Permanent Secretary at the Cabinet Office. At one point our second professional lives crossed; when I was President of the Historic Houses Association, Peter was the Treasury Officer responsible, amongst many other things, for heritage matters and Bob, Head of Conservation at English Heritage.

We passed out of Dartmouth in the presence of HRH Princess Margaret, and after Christmas leave reported on board the training cruiser HMS *Devonshire* at Devonport. She was an old three-funnelled county class cruiser which had had three of her four eight-inch gun turrets removed to make way for classrooms. She rolled like a bucket, and her quarterdeck comprised a huge expanse of teak which we had to scrub at crack of dawn every morning. Delicious smells used to waft up through the wardroom skylight giving a foretaste of a life of ease and luxury to come, but for the present we lived the life of not exactly ordinary seamen, mixing hard practical ship work with a certain amount of classroom activity. I loved it. It was wonderful to be at sea at last.

We sailed in January 1953 for Bermuda and the West Indies and steamed at once into a full blown Atlantic gale. During our first night at sea I had the middle watch (0001-0400) as boatswain's mate. This entailed sitting in a small 'caboosh' behind the bridge which contained the ship's broadcast. My duties involved making 'ki' for the officer of the watch and bridge staff. 'Ki' is a substance along the lines of cocoa which is made by slicing pieces of unsweetened chocolate into a tin mug (preferably with a rusty knife to give it flavour) and applying boiling water, condensed milk and sugar to taste. The ship was rolling 20 degrees or so in a beam sea, and of course the movement was accentuated high up at bridge level. Endeavouring to make ki under these conditions would try the toughest stomach and mine was not in that category. Luckily I did not have many takers and spent most of my watch sitting miserably in my little caboosh with an equally miserable rat squatting on a nearby cable run.

We endured a week of this discomfort; then one morning all was still and we woke to find ourselves gliding through an azure sea with a brilliant white island close at hand to port as we steamed down the narrow channel which led to the dockyard in Bermuda. It was like entering paradise.

The highlight of our second cruise, *Devonshire*'s last, was the coronation of HM The Queen at which we were to line the route in Parliament Square. This involved practising standing in one place without movement for six hours. We worked up gradually on the quarterdeck at sea before proceeding to Bantry Bay on the south-west corner of Ireland where we stood on the pier for the full six hours, during which I passed out. It was one thing to stand on the quarterdeck heaving in the swell, but quite another to stand perfectly still on the shore.

A couple of days before the event we were sent to Sandhurst, for a final polish under the command of the fabled RSM Brittain, known as 'The Voice'. Voice he certainly had, but used to the relatively quieter tones of the naval gunnery instructors, the naval contingent could not understand any of his orders and chaos ensued which raised The Voice to even more unintelligible heights.

On the great day, we left in darkness for Vauxhall barracks where we were fed, watered and invited to empty ourselves in the rows of elsans provided for the purpose. It was a gloomy damp misty morning and we must have presented a sorry bunch fallen in in our best No.5 uniforms at 5.30am. To cheer us up, the Gunnery Officer, who was the parade commander, appeared in front of us rather more red faced than usual.

'Joke of the day, chaps, just dropped me medals in the bog!'

We had to be in position four hours before the procession which would itself take about two hours. My billet was directly opposite Big Ben in Parliament Square. At least I knew the time but the danger was that whenever there was a gap in the procession, Big Ben would move in the opposite direction. I had to concentrate extremely hard on something else to prevent falling over.

We returned to *Devonshire* to take part in the Spithead Review. Led by the battleship *Vanguard* it was a most impressive affair. Over 120 ships were moored in four columns several miles long. It was the last time the Navy would ever field a fleet of that size. Aboard *Devonshire* however we were more concerned with our new appointments which had just come through. I found myself appointed as a Midshipman to HMS *Ceylon*, a colony class cruiser on the East Indies Station.

With my friend, Bob Chitham, we took passage in the troopship *Empire Windrush* sailing from Southampton in September 1953. We were meant to do some work but I do not remember anything very arduous. There was a rather attractive colonel's wife and daughter going out to join him in Singapore. In accordance with seniority the sub-lieutenants competed for the wife while the midshipmen fought over the daughter. Then one night both ladies were discovered by the Captain in compromising situations under respective lifeboats and were summarily put ashore at Port Said.

Empire Windrush was a dreadful ship; she had diesel engines which wheezed along with sparks flying out of her two funnels. Our cabin was amidships with no ventilation other than a fan and the heat passing through the Red Sea was stifling. We eventually made it to Colombo after a series of breakdowns but it was to be her last voyage. She sank off Gibraltar after an explosion in her engine room.

We disembarked at Colombo and were driven across the island to the naval base at Trincomalee, a huge natural harbour on the east coast of Ceylon (now Sri Lanka) to find our ship *Ceylon* swinging round a buoy. For some reason we were not expected and our first night on board was spent under 'Y' turret on camp beds. I was woken by a flapping noise to find a flying fish trying to jump into my sleeping bag.

The following morning we were issued with hammocks and a space to sling them outside the gunroom where we messed. We were then allocated various ship's duties. Mine was to be midshipman of the pinnace, a long open boat, the principal function of which was to ferry 'liberty men' between ship and shore. Grossly underpowered, it manoeuvred like a mini container ship and when filled to the gunwales with 'jolly jack' going ashore in his best kit, it took some stopping.

Running the last boat from Pepperpot Jetty in Trincomalee was an instructive operation. There were always one or two sailors the worse for wear and it was the midshipman's job to keep order in the boat. An inclination on the part of the returning liberty men to burst into song as they approached the ship meant that we would be sent round the ship until

17

they sobered up. This was generally an effective process as it encouraged the more sober to sit on their mates and shut them up. The local spirit was pretty lethal. On one occasion a certain notorious seaman returned onboard apparently sober and was allowed to go forward only to return a few minutes later, pick up a large armoured hatch and pursue the officer of the watch round 'Y' turret.

Our life on board revolved round the gunroom which was presided over by the Sub-Lieutenant, Ronnie Stevenson, who ruled us with a light touch and a gentle self-deprecating manner which endeared him to us all. We were looked after by Goanese stewards who used to prepare wonderful curries for our Sunday lunch which were invariably followed by a dessert known as 'goulamalaka'. Consisting of tapioca in coconut juice liberally laced with black treacle it was meant to extinguish the fires lit by the curry.

Looking back on my days in *Ceylon*, it was an extraordinary period; quite unique in my time in the Navy. The Korean War had just ended, and while the Cold War overhung Europe, the East Indies station was at peace. India and Pakistan were now six years into independence, still suffering somewhat from the trauma of partition; Ceylon had been independent for a similar period but East Africa was still coloured red on the map and administered by the Colonial Office. The British Empire was dying but not quite dead yet.

The British naval presence was based on Trincomalee and consisted of two cruisers, *Ceylon* and *Newfoundland*, with two frigates operating mainly in the Persian Gulf. Our movements were strictly limited by a severe fuel shortage, and we used to spend weeks swinging round the buoy, in between cruises to the Indian sub-continent, East Africa, and, on one unforgettable occasion, Australia. Apart from the odd and rather farcical 'night encounter' exercise with any ship that happened to be around, we did no serious exercising other than taking a rather sedate part in joint exercises with the Indian Navy which occurred once a year. It was a leisurely existence; no one seemed to be very concerned with our operational efficiency, and for the whole time I was aboard, the after six inch 'Y' turret was never fired for fear of damaging its glistening enamel paintwork.

Visiting India and Pakistan for the first time I was appalled by the conditions in which people lived. I could not have imagined that humans could sink so low. Going ashore from our berth in the commercial port of Bombay meant running the gauntlet of the docks area before reaching the city. My first impressions of India were therefore drawn from this very poor area. Children clustered round me as I walked the streets; some were suffering from awful deformities, some were covered with sores.

'One anna, two anna, no mama, no papa,' went the cry.

People defecated on the pavement, their mouths red with the betel nut juice they chewed, hawked and spat. The smell was overpowering.

Returning to India thirty-five years later, on a 'round the world' flight, the place had not changed much but I had. By comparison with the human ant heaps that we encountered in Japan and Hong Kong, India, with infinitely more people, had a social system which gave each individual their pre-arranged place in society, and there was therefore much less pushing and shoving.

The highlight of our year on station was to visit Australia as escort to HM The Queen on her post coronation Commonwealth tour in the RMS *Gothic*. We did not in fact see much of Her Majesty or the *Gothic* until she left Australia but we had a splendid cruise all on our own to Fremantle, Hobart, Sydney, Melbourne and Adelaide. In every port we were looked after like lords, with invitations for, picnics, weekends, and every sort of function, including a Queen Charlotte's Ball in Hobart.

I had a particularly interesting time in Sydney, as a neighbour near Rockingham had a sister who was companion to Lady Slim, wife of Field Marshal Lord Slim, the Governor General. I was at once asked up to Government House where the Slims were extraordinarily hospitable, taking me on picnics in their official vehicle, an ancient Rolls Royce, and having me to stay for the weekend. Bill Slim had a rather gruff manner but off duty was kindness itself and like all really great men was able to make you feel that all he was interested in was what you had to say. For a nineteen-year-old midshipman, this was quite an experience.

Ceylon was due to 'pay off' on return to Portsmouth and in August 1953 we left Trinco for the last time, flying a very long 'paying off pennant'. Traditionally this was the length of the ship plus so many feet for every month on station. It was not an easy flag to fly gracefully and on this occasion we had to tie balloons to the end in an effort to keep it out of the water. As we made our progress home via Aden, the Suez Canal, and Gibraltar, the ship gradually assumed the look of a superior junk shop as the ship's company stocked up on 'rabbits' (the sailors name for presents brought home from overseas). There were parrots by the hundred, cane furniture, carpets, and all sorts of exotica. We reached Portsmouth on a gloomy September morning, damp and miserable. A dark cloud hung over Portsmouth and Southsea as we lay at anchor off Spithead to clear customs, but it was the best sight we had seen in the last eleven months.

At the end of the year my group of midshipmen were promoted to acting Sub-Lieutenants and for the first time wore one solid gold braid stripe on our sleeves. We were now due to go to a small ship for six months still under training. I was sent to HMS *Tumult*, a 'T' class war emergency destroyer converted into an anti- submarine frigate. She was one of the first such conversions to have an enclosed bridge. She had also had her after gun mounting replaced with an anti-submarine mortar. Otherwise she still had those graceful looks which seduced me into the Navy during my time at Greenock.

Tumult was based at Londonderry where our principal role was to carry out anti-submarine exercises with the RAF Coastal Command Shackleton aircraft based on RAF Ballykelly. We were berthed, some twenty miles up the river Foyle. This meant an early start and at 0500 we would emerge from our bunks bleary-eyed to slip and proceed quietly down the winding river in pitch darkness. The pilot left us at Moville and we headed out to sea.

The Atlantic swell hits the continental shelf off the north-west coast of Ireland and produces some of the sharpest seas I have ever known. How well I recall even now the sickening moment when we rounded the headland and the ship took that first beam sea, lurching over to starboard then back again to port. It was a horrid motion and I have never been so ill. Eventually I became used to it but it was always most uncomfortable.

When we berthed alongside in Londonderry we used to put the ship's armoury under special guard, but apart from the odd minor incident the IRA had been totally quiescent since before the War and they might well not have existed as far as we were concerned. *Tumult* was a happy ship and I left her in the spring of 1954, a firm convert to the informality and camaraderie of small ship life.

Still under training, I rejoined other members of my Dartmouth term that summer at the Royal Naval College, Greenwich, for two terms of academic work followed by nine months touring the various specialist schools and training institutions. I am not quite sure what we were supposed to be doing at Greenwich as I have only the haziest recollection of doing any actual work. I spent most of my time in a white tie and tails going from one party to the next and trailing back down the Old Kent Road in time to catch a couple of hours of sleep before the morning lecture. There were no exams and I regret to say that I completely wasted a golden opportunity to learn from some of the best naval historians in the country.

Instead I enjoyed an intensive social life 'doing' the London Season. I am not sure that the experience thus gained was worth it but I am absolutely sure that at that stage in my life I was simply not prepared to return to school. I wanted to be out there living life and if I was to have to sit behind a desk I wanted to learn about the Navy. I was therefore rather relieved when Greenwich came to an end and we set out in our cars for the various specialist schools.

One day towards the end of May, when we were in Portsmouth, one of our group, Rodney de Chair, asked me if I would like to take his place at a tennis party at the Admiral Superintendent's house in the dockyard. To sweeten the pill he added, 'Georgina Davis is going to be there.' Georgina Davis was the daughter of Admiral Sir William Davis, the Vice Chief of Naval Staff, and reputed to look like my favourite film star, Jean Simmons. Her reputation had preceded her from Malta where she had been the toast of the gunroom in her father's flagship. At the prospect of meeting this paragon any misgivings I may have had about my ability to play tennis disappeared and I accepted with alacrity.

Luckily the tennis was cancelled due to rain and we went for a walk instead. Georgina not only lived up to and indeed exceeded her reputation for good looks, she was enormous fun and we hit it off straightaway. We arranged to meet the following week in London and at once I knew that this was for real. So close were we that all I had to do was to ask her what stone she would like for her engagement ring. Without hesitation she said, 'Sapphire.'

An interview with her father the following year did not go so smoothly. We paced the tennis court at his home in Gloucestershire.

'I understand you want to marry Georgina. What are your prospects?' he asked.

'Well, sir, since you have access to my confidential reports you will know better than I what my prospects are,' I replied, missing the point.

The Admiral, testily: 'I mean your financial prospects.'

'I have a lieutenant's pay and will have a sergeant major's marriage allowance until I reach the age of twenty-five.'

'Is that all?'

I thought hard. 'There is an outside chance of a castle in the course of time.'

The Admiral was unimpressed. Indeed I do not think he registered what I had said.

'You are both much too young. Go away and come back in two years' time.'

Not long after this discussion, I received an appointment from Their Lordships instructing me to report to HMS *Messina* at Christmas Island in the Pacific where she was acting as guardship for the British nuclear bomb tests. Whether there was any connection between this appointment and my interview with my future father-in-law I shall never know.

All this is leaping ahead, however, and in the autumn of 1956 I was appointed to HMS *Jamaica* as Sub-Lieutenant of the gunroom. *Jamaica* was a colony class like *Ceylon*, the flagship of the Flag Officer Second-in-Command of the Mediterranean fleet, Vice Admiral Sir Robin Durnford-

Slater. I was now a commissioned officer in the Royal Navy, and all those years of being 'under training' were over.

Drawing from MSW's midshipman's journal

CHAPTER 3

Traversing the Oceans

Watchkeeper, Fighter Director and Navigator

Reflecting on the fifteen years I spent as a commissioned officer in the Royal Navy, I think I must have been extremely lucky to have had such an interesting and varied time. I served in ships of many different types and ashore in appointments ranging from divisional officer at the Royal Naval College, Dartmouth (which is the equivalent to being a housemaster at a public school) to running military operations in the Caribbean. I do not suppose my career was very different to that of any other seaman officer of my age, but to me it provided an experience of extraordinary depth which I drew on constantly in the equally varied and interesting things I was called upon to do in later life.

I went to sea at a time when the Navy still enjoyed an Imperial role; Britain was a major world power with naval and military bases all over the world. Visiting Malta, Singapore, or even Trincomalee, felt like being on home ground. It was an unreal situation as Britain's international responsibilities could not justify, nor could she afford to maintain an international military presence on this scale. My time in the Navy was therefore characterised by a general contraction both in the Navy's size and in its scope. By the time I left, Britain had no permanent military presence east of Suez other than in Hong Kong, and the great Mediterranean fleet was no more.

The ships also changed, and I saw a generation of new ships take over from those which fought the Second World War. Out went the great gun platforms, the battleships and cruisers; ultimately they were nearly followed for a short and potentially disastrous time by the aircraft carrier. The new ships were smaller, lighter, not much faster, less well armed – but more versatile. The emphasis was very much on the underwater and air battle rather than the surface. Equipment was becoming more sophisticated; the guided missile was replacing the gun. In my specialist field of communications, I just saw the introduction of satellite links which would totally transform communications between ships and shore across the world.

My ships echoed these changes. My first appointment was as Sub-Lieutenant of the gunroom in the cruiser HMS *Jamaica* which had reached the end of her life and was destined for the breaker's yard. The gunroom, an ancient naval institution where the officers under training lived, but now also obsolete, died with her.

My last sea appointment was as Signal Communications Officer of HMS *London*, a brand new guided missile destroyer, equipped with the Navy's first medium range surface-to-air missile known appropriately as SEASLUG. It took so long to develop that it was obsolete by the time it came into service. In between I served in a landing ship tank (LST), two destroyers converted to frigates and a number of aircraft carriers.

My appointment to *Jamaica* had an inauspicious start. It was November 1956 and the Suez invasion had just taken place. I said goodbye to Georgina against a background of newspaper hoardings yelling 'RUSSIA THREATENS NUCLEAR ATTACK', with the country split on whether or not we were doing the right thing.

I flew to Malta and took passage in the destroyer HMS *Comet* to join *Jamaica* off Port Said. There was no space and we had to sleep on the upper deck. The Mediterranean is no tropical paradise in November and it was bitterly cold. I must have had a touch of flu when I left London which was not helped in these conditions, and by the time I reached *Jamaica*, I was feeling like death. I lasted twenty-four hours before passing out in the middle of the three minute silence at the Remembrance Day service.

I came to in my bunk to find the surgeon commander looking at me with a worried expression on his face.

'I think I am going to have to send you ashore,' he said. 'You have a temperature of 104 and I do not know what is wrong with you.'

I thus became a casualty in a war zone. I was parcelled into a Neil Robertson stretcher like a cocoon, transferred to the flagship HMS *Tyne*, alongside in Port Said, and then taken ashore to the casualty clearing station. This was a squalid building with overflowing lavatories, and a ward in which Florence Nightingale would have felt at home, though I am sure she would have had something to say about its cleanliness. I was feeling pretty groggy by this time and really did not care much. My neighbour had a box over his feet.

'What's your problem?' I asked.

'I was shot down by the gyppos and lost both my feet,' he replied nonchalantly. 'What's yours?'

'I haven't the faintest idea; I think I must have flu or something.'

In fact I was suffering from glandular fever complicated by pneumonia.

Eventually I rejoined my ship in Malta by which time the excitement of Suez was over and life in the Mediterranean fleet had settled back into its normal peacetime regime with the usual programme of exercises interspersed with foreign visits.

A visit to Villefranche afforded the opportunity of a chance meeting with the novelist Somerset Maugham. I was walking on the hillside above Cap Ferrat when I met a group of people led by an elderly man whom I at once recognised as Maugham. We exchanged pleasantries and he asked me to lunch the next day.

I was met on the jetty by his secretary, Alan Searle, in a large black Rolls Royce, who greeted me warmly, a little too warmly I thought as I edged over to my corner of the back seat. My concern deepened when he explained that the guests for lunch were to be Jean Cocteau, the poet/painter, his boyfriend, and his wife plus her girlfriend. I began to wonder where I fitted into this party.

At the Villa Mauresque the great man was sitting on a sofa surrounded by his wonderful collection of contemporary paintings. He was very relaxed, talking about his student days at Heidelberg while we drank the strongest martinis I have ever tasted. I asked him about his writing. He told me that he wrote regularly every day and that sometimes it was very hard work faced with a clean sheet of paper and a blank mind – 'But you must write even if you cannot think of anything to say.' Sometimes he would spend many hours with only a sentence to show for it. Those clear clipped phrases which in a few words give the reader such a vivid description did not come naturally but were worked at over again and again.

After lunch Alan suggested that I might like to see the Picassos in 'Willie's bathroom', I took this is as a warning to make my escape as elegantly as I could and found my way back to the ship on foot.

Jamaica was not a particularly happy ship. Three times the size of a destroyer, and the fleet flagship, inevitably life on board was more formal and lacked the camaraderie of a smaller ship. My gunroom consisted mainly of national servicemen, who were good company but naturally did not have the commitment to the Navy of a regular officer and were inclined to regard hallowed naval traditions with less than due reverence. One tradition they excelled at, however, was the acquisition of trophies. Having cleaned up the remaining gunrooms in the fleet including the much prized 'barber's pole', they then proceeded to denude Valetta of street signs and petrol pump tops. The place looked like Steptoe's yard.

The spring of 1957 saw *Jamaica* serving out her last few months in the Home Fleet now commanded by Georgina's father. After a happy summer during which Georgina and I were able to see a lot of each other, I found myself on a bitterly cold October morning standing on the tarmac at RAF Northolt with a draft of sixty sailors who were flying out to recommission HMS *Messina* at Christmas Island in the middle of the Pacific.

We boarded the aircraft, an ancient twin-engined DC4 chartered from an American airline, which to my relief and the sailors disappointment was dry, and lumbered off down the runway. It was to be the beginning of an horrific fifty-six hour flight halfway across the world with fuel stops at Keflavik in Iceland, Goose Bay, Labrador, Winnipeg and San Francisco, by which time the freezing cold darkness had given way to increasing warmth. It was a long night not improved by delicious smells of frying from the galley turning out to be fried apple.

Finally we reached Honolulu, where the heat was overpowering but at least there was a bar of which my sailors took full advantage. All too soon for them we were called back to our aircraft to find the cabin at oven temperature. They closed the doors; we stripped off our collars and ties, strapped ourselves in and waited. Eventually an engine started but the aircraft did not move and the cabin grew even hotter. Then an announcement came that they could not start one engine, and would we please alight onto the tarmac while they tried to start it by running the aircraft up and down the runway.

We all disembarked in various states of undress whereupon after a minute or two the authorities, having failed to start the second engine, wheeled the aircraft away to the maintenance area, and bussed us back to the terminal. Pleas to be allowed to return to the aircraft so that we could dress properly fell upon deaf ears. 'Don't worry, it will only be a few minutes,' they said.

This was pretty serious. There was I, the sole officer in charge of this bunch of sixty half-dressed, already semi-inebriated, sailors heading once more for the bar of the international terminal at Honolulu airport. Luckily I had salvaged my collar and tie so I still looked reasonably respectable in my best blue uniform, if that is possible after some fifty hours in the air.

The airport was used by the military as well as civilians and I looked around to see if I could find some military authority that could help – at least by providing an alternative, less exposed area for us to wait until our aircraft was ready. Then I felt a hand on my shoulder and looked round to see a smart young lieutenant USN in a glistening white uniform draped with the gold aiguillettes of a flag lieutenant.

'Are these your men?' he asked.

'I am afraid so.'

'In that case you had better get them out of the way pretty fast as C-in-C Pacific Fleet is due by in five minutes.'

Jolly Jack[*] was by now living up to his name and one or two had decided that some vocal music would enliven the scene. The prospect was dire. No way could I shift these men. There was nowhere to go, and many of them were too far gone themselves. I could visualise signals from CINC Pacific Fleet to CINC Home Fleet, Admiralty, the World; my naval career would be in tatters.

Then, mercy of mercies a US naval patrol appeared on the scene, no doubt summoned by the helpful flag lieutenant. Together we managed to herd the men behind a curtain and sit on them while the Admiral and his entourage went by. Shortly after that we were allowed back to our aircraft and, with both engines functioning, took off on the final leg to Christmas Island, where we arrived without further incident.

Christmas Island is a coral atoll of approximately fifty square miles, situated in the middle of the Pacific ocean. It has an imported population of around 1000 Gilbertese Islanders who worked in the phosphate mines (now closed) or on the copra plantations. The nearest land is well over one hundred miles away. A series of tests had been conducted over the years and the programme was now nearing its conclusion with the development of the ultimate nuclear weapon, the hydrogen bomb. The Navy's task was primarily to support the scientists monitoring the tests on the outlying islands, and to keep the area clear of strange shipping during the test period.

The test programme was run by the Atomic Weapons Establishment (AWE) at Aldermaston and the next and final test was not due until the following spring. By way of a shakedown for the new commission therefore, we sailed from Christmas Island to visit the two islands which had been selected as monitoring sites for the next test. It was my first experience of the great Pacific ocean and I can quite see how it earned its name. Where the Atlantic is primarily green, rough and cruel, certainly in the northern latitudes, the Pacific is a deep blue with a great rolling swell. It can be rough as we were to find out but for this short voyage it was utterly benign, and dolphins danced round the bow hissing at each other as we ploughed along at ten knots.

We had no sophisticated satellite plotting system in those days and were dependent for our navigation on the sun and the stars. Our destination, an island called Malden, was little more than a raised beach about five miles across and four hundred miles from Christmas Island. We were following in the paths of those fine Polynesian navigators, whose instrument was a

---

[*] 'Jolly Jack', short for 'Jolly Jack Tar', is a term traditionally used to describe a sailor in the same way as a soldier is known as 'Tommy'

coconut pierced at either end with a hole. Water was poured into the coconut to a certain level and the navigator observed the reflection of the heavenly body in the water. They would identify the low lying islands by observing the cloud formation and heading for the lowest. We did likewise.

The great Pacific rollers pounded onto the beach at Malden with a roar and a cloud of spray. There was no natural harbour, and finding a suitable landing place was not easy. The landing craft which we carried on the foredeck was a robust craft, however, and capable of landing in some pretty rough water but it weighed thirty tons and the simple act of lowering this huge craft into the water in the swell was itself a perilous operation requiring a high degree of expertise and seamanship.

I hitched a lift ashore and the first thing I noticed were the enormous cowrie shells on the beach, the size of a man's fist. Beautifully polished and coloured in delicate shades of brown and blue, it was quite amazing that they survived in this pounding surf.

The island was completely flat, treeless, and uninhabited. There was, however, a small wooden building and one or two gravestones including one to a small child. The building itself seemed in good condition; there were kitchen implements and bedding inside and it was as if someone had just walked out of the door. We reported this to the Foreign Office who informed us that it had been a German guano colony, and, on the outbreak of the First World War, the islanders from Raratonga, who worked the guano and were loyal to the British, killed the two German supervisers and made off in their canoes back to Raratonga.

The other island, Fanning, was a beautiful coral atoll with palm trees and bright, almost silver, beaches in an azure sea; it was man's idea of heaven on earth. There was a small community of engineers employed by Cable and Wireless to maintain the trans-Pacific cable which surfaced at that point. They lived in a group of comfortable houses set in a square about a mile from the landing place. They were immensely hospitable and straightaway we were invited to 'Have a beer'. The beer drunk, the can was consigned to the square and bets were being taken on when the pile would reach the first floor window sills.

On the day of the test we embarked the entire civilian population of some two hundred Gilbertese with the district officer. They were incarcerated in the spacious tank deck where we kept them amused with a series of old Western films. I took up my position as ship's radiation officer on the bridge with my Geiger counters and we waited for the countdown. The bomb was to be released from an aircraft with a parachute, and was programmed to explode at a sufficient height to ensure that there was no radioactive fallout and certainly none of my machines registered any radioactivity throughout the test.

As the minutes ticked by we crouched below the bridge screen, with our hands clasped behind our necks, our eyes closed, and our backs towards the explosion. There was a brilliant flash accompanied by a searing blast of heat and we all stood up to see a shimmering wave coming rapidly towards us. The shock wave struck seconds after the flash, with an almighty bang and we all fell over. What the Gilbertese down in the tank deck watching cowboy films must have thought I cannot imagine.

We recovered in time to watch the mushroom cloud, a brilliant orange at first turning to pinkish white as it billowed up into the heavens. It was an incredible sight; one could not but be aware of the awesome power that created it.

Our task completed, we set course for the long passage home across the Pacific, and through the Panama Canal. The tank deck was full of vehicles and we were carrying three LCMs on the upper deck which, while well within the design specification, made the ship feel rather top heavy. The voyage was not uneventful.

In addition to being the ship's correspondence officer, I was also the forecastle officer which meant that I was responsible for the forward end of the ship and the seamen who worked there. The construction of an LST was similar to a car ferry in that there was a ramp which, when closed, created a watertight seal which in turn was protected from the force of the sea by two bow doors. These were operated hydraulically, and once closed were then secured by horizontal girders called strong backs, which were bolted to the frame of the doors. The area thus enclosed was free flooding. We had been aware for some time that all was not well with the strong backs and that the bolts appeared to be working while the doors themselves were not watertight. Were they to open in a seaway, they could unroll the ship's side like a sardine tin. The chief shipwright and the chief engine room artificer, the two principal authorities on such matters, descended into the space to inspect the situation. They tightened up the bolts and received a dunking for their pains.

Two days out from Christmas Island, we hit a gale, and after a day or so ploughing into the heavy seas, it was clear that all was far from well and that major repairs were required. This involved steaming astern into the sea while each strong back was unshipped in turn, and hoisted up out of the space to allow the door frames to be reinforced and new holes drilled. While the gale had subsided, there was still a heavy swell and every time the stern went up on a wave, the bow plunged into the sea and the space between the doors flooded, covering the lower two strongbacks.

Finally the bow doors were pronounced fit, we turned round and resumed our passage. Panama seemed a very long way away. It was even further away next day when the engine room reported that one of the two engines had broken down and that it could only be repaired if the ship was stopped in the water. For the next three days we wallowed in the Pacific swell. With that huge amount of top weight created by three LCMs it was not only unpleasant, it was downright frightening. The 'Chief'* refused to be hurried, the weather was kind, and we resumed our passage once more. Then the weather really did turn against us, and we were driving into a Force 9 gale with a sea to match. As I looked out of my cabin scuttle, I was convinced I could see the deck buckling.

We finally reached Panama rust streaked and looking like some old tramp. We still had the Atlantic to cross however and there would be plenty of time to clean the ship before our arrival in UK. Not so; as we steamed into the Panama Canal we received a signal ordering us to proceed forthwith to Trinidad and act as guardship for the granting of independence to the West Indies Federation. Panic ensued. This meant painting the ship overall and training up a guard consisting of sailors who had not seen a parade ground for months, if not years. Somehow we managed it; but we need not have bothered as no one came to visit us.

While in Trinidad, I bought a ring, a very small sapphire with two diamonds which I presented to Georgina when she met me on return to Chatham; shortly after we announced our engagement.

Terrified that I might be left with the rusting hulk as it prepared for refit, and keen to widen my experience, I volunteered for a Fighter Direction course and found myself one of a dozen or so direction officers in the aircraft carrier HMS *Eagle* in the Mediterranean. *Eagle* was due home for Christmas, so the wedding was planned for December and my old friend and term-mate, Rodney de Chair, who was my future father-in-law's flag lieutenant, agreed to be our best man. With these important details in place, I flew away to join my ship in Malta and left the arrangements in the capable hands of Georgina and her mother, Elizabeth.

By any stretch of the imagination *Eagle* was huge. With a ship's company of over 2500 including the aircrew, she was equivalent to a small floating town. A feature of life in an aircraft carrier is that when at sea they are always fully operational. A conventional ship might go to 'action stations' from time to time in exercises, but in peacetime this was a fairly rare event. When a carrier was flying aircraft, it was a matter of life and death and, while the ship's company might not be at action stations as such, all the key personnel connected with flying would be at their posts. This sense of danger gave an added flavour to life on board which kept everybody on their toes.

---

* The Chief Engineer Officer

The Captain, John Byng Frewen, appeared on first acquaintance a cold hard man. He set himself the highest standards of competence and efficiency and expected them of everyone else. At the same time he could be immensely human. He kept photographs of all the ship's company in his cabin, and before visiting any part of the ship would memorise them so that he could address the sailors by name. As a junior officer amongst many I may have seen him more than most, as he used me as a sort of supernumerary flag lieutenant, but I did not come to know him really well until, as a rear admiral, he became William Davis's Chief of Staff when his charm and dry humour became apparent. He was one of my heroes and should have been First Sea Lord.

It ought to have been a happy time but I was becoming restless. I am not particularly interested in the air or aircraft, and I did not want to spend the rest of my naval career sitting in a darkened room directing aircraft on a radar screen. I wanted to follow my father and become a signal specialist but there was a shortage of Direction Officers and I did not know how to break out of the net.

One day I was sent for by the First Lieutenant, a cheerful officer known as Basil Parish. 'I should like you to take on the ship's laundry,' he said. 'It is in a bit of a mess at the moment and it needs sorting out.'

I have to confess that running the ship's laundry was not one of my greatest ambitions. Indeed it seemed like a kiss of death and, coming on top of my other professional misgivings, I felt it was almost the last straw. There was no question, however; I had to do it.

I went down to visit my new command and after some difficulty. I finally found the laundry, as one might imagine, in the bowels of the ship; a low steam-filled space, with men in dirty singlets and boxer shorts perspiring over boilers and primitive ironing machines. Looking down the records of the staff, it appeared that most of them were old lags who had been sent to the laundry for punishment. The laundry had an appalling reputation in the ship and most people preferred to do their own or send it ashore if possible.

Talking to the stoker petty officer in charge I realised that, given the materials and the right encouragement, we could turn the whole thing round. The key was money. The laundry charged a pittance for its services which was used to maintain the equipment and pay the staff some pocket money. There was in fact quite a lot of money in the fund. I went ashore to visit the local laundry and see how they did things there and they kindly agreed to give my staff some training. I mustered the staff and told them that we were going to have the best laundry in the fleet. I was going to invest in new ironing machines, and they were to go ashore for three days to learn how to use them. Finally I told them I was doubling their pay, introducing a bonus scheme, and upping the price of our product.

The transformation was extraordinary. Within a few days the whole attitude of the staff had changed. Everyone was coming forward with ideas on how we could improve the service. We learned how to press shirts and trousers and to serve them up on hangers or in bags with 'Your shirt Sir from the Eagle Laundry' on them. People who had never dared use the laundry before sent their washing, and our output and income doubled. Whereas before it had been regarded as a punishment, now I was being swamped with volunteers. The final accolade was a visit by the Captain who spoke to each member of staff personally by name and congratulated them on their achievement. For me personally it underlined the truth of that old adage – 'Look after your men and they will look after you'.

Eagle returned to UK in the late summer and joined the Home fleet. The month of December found us in Gibraltar wearing the flag of the Commander-in-Chief, Admiral Sir William Davis, my future father-in-law. The ship was scheduled to take part in a major NATO exercise before returning to Plymouth on 10th December. Our wedding was due to take place at Gloucester Cathedral on the 13th. The already tight timing became rapidly tighter when the exercise was delayed due to weather and a 'buzz' went round the ship that our return date might also be delayed. The implications of this went far beyond my personal domestic problems and involved the Christmas leave arrangements for the entire ship's company – a matter of considerable concern to everyone on board.

The weather abated and the exercise took place. I was sitting on my radar tube in the aircraft direction room, controlling a combat air patrol, when I became aware of a presence beside me. I glanced round and saw a sleeve full of gold lace leaning on the display; I looked up and up went the gold lace till I counted one thick ring and three thin ones. It was the Commander in Chief.

'It's all right, Mick,' a voice said, 'we'll make it on time.'

We did, and the wedding was magical. My mother-in-law, who was something of an expert in these matters, mustered two bishops and a dean and it was one of the happiest days I can remember.

Georgina had taken a cottage called 'The Dell' in the Cornish village of Crafthole, five miles south of Torpoint and we headed straight there. It had one room downstairs, one and a half bedrooms upstairs, and an Elsan at the bottom of the garden from which the occupant could enjoy a marvellous view across the Tamar to Princetown on Dartmoor. It had other charms which we were shortly to discover. The walls were constructed of mud and wattle, and the roof was of large very old slates which had been repaired over the years with generous helpings of cement. As a result the roof had become so heavy that the walls could barely hold it up and the process had come to a halt. It was raining when we arrived to be greeted by a plastic basin in the middle of the double bed catching the drips. There was no space to move the bed but it would take more than a few drips to cool our newly married ardour and we loved The Dell. Sadly we were its last occupants as it was condemned and is now a pile of rubble.

After a happy six months living in Cornwall and preparing *Eagle* for refit, I was appointed to HMS *Broadsword*, a weapon class destroyer commissioning at Chatham for service in the Mediterranean.

The ship herself was built at the end of the war, very much in the traditional destroyer design. Her conversion to a radar picket involved certain modifications above deck including the fitting of a large mast to take the huge aerial of the long range early warning radar, but it did not affect the accommodation below decks which was decidedly short on modern comforts. The officers shared cabins in the bowels of the ship. The ship's company fed under a system known as broadside messing which meant that the food had to be collected from the galley in trays and carried down to the mess deck where it was eaten. If your mess was in the after part of the ship then your supper could easily be diluted by a wave as the 'cook of the mess' struggled down the iron deck in an Atlantic gale.

Naval tactics in those days revolved round the large aircraft carrier group which would act in support of an amphibious operation on either the northern or the southern flank of NATO's area. Our job in this grand concept was to be positioned between the fleet and the enemy to give early warning of air attack. We were thus somewhat exposed out there transmitting our radar for the enemy to intercept while everyone else remained silent. If we were lucky we might be given a CAP (Combat Air Patrol) which it would be my job to control, but more often than not the carrier preferred to keep them under her own control which left us feeling pretty lonely and me with little to do.

We sailed for the Mediterranean in March 1960 to join the 7th Destroyer Squadron based on Malta. While we were not officially supposed to be 'accompanied', Georgina flew on ahead, courtesy of the RAF. She was followed rapidly by our car which was shipped out on a Royal Fleet Auxiliary. Looking back on these days it was really rather remarkable how easy it was for wives to move about the world in pursuit of their husbands. Today things are not nearly so straightforward; the wife probably has her own professional life which takes priority and in any case the facilities for such movement are not available. We were really very lucky to live when we did.

Operationally the Mediterranean was quiet, but the aftermath of Suez still pervaded the atmosphere and quite a lot of the southern and eastern littoral were 'no go' areas for British warships. The two highlights of an enjoyable, but otherwise uneventful, year were a period of six weeks as Cyprus guardship, and a three month refit in Gibraltar, during which I was loaned to the Spanish Navy as a liaison officer during exercises.

All too quickly our time in the Med was over. We returned to UK almost exactly a year after we had left, finally paying off in Chatham in May 1960. I called on my appointing officer and received a sympathetic response to my request to specialise in Signal Communications. The Long Course was not due to start until the following spring, however, and I therefore had nine months to kill. I angled for command of a minesweeper but it was not to be and I was sent out to the Far East to join HMS *Rocket* as navigating officer.

Rocket was built as an 'R'class war emergency destroyer. She was then converted in the 1950s into what was called a Type 15 frigate. This involved stripping off everything down to the upper deck and rebuilding the superstructure so that as much of the ship as possible could be worked under cover thus reducing the risk of exposure to radiation in the event of a nuclear attack. The effect was to make the ship look rather like a large single decker bus perched on the graceful hull of a destroyer. The enclosed bridge was only marginally above the forecastle and the visibility both forward and more particularly astern was rather less than that available to the average bus driver.

I joined in Singapore and almost immediately we sailed for the east coast of Borneo on anti-piracy patrol. There was no satellite navigation system in those days and we had to rely on the sun, moon and stars for our position fixing.

Not only were we reliant on my astronavigation skills for our position when out of sight of land, but the charts we were using had been drawn by some intrepid C19 navigator who had great faith in nature. Landmarks were few and far between and he had been reduced to using a 'palm tree conspic' as a mark for a passage through the coral. Needless to say the palm tree had long since disappeared and the coral reef, with a depth of six feet or less, extended well out of sight of land. Luckily in the daylight it was fairly easily identified by the marked change in colour of the water.

Our mission was to pursue and arrest Filipino pirates who had been making 'hit and run' raids on the plantations along the east coast of Borneo. These people were said to be tough ex-commandos who had been trained up as shock troops by the US in the Pacific war. Bored by peace they had found a new, exciting and lucrative outlet for their energies. They used traditional dugout canoes to which were strapped two or three high powered outboard motors on either side giving them a speed well in excess of 30 knots, and of course drawing practically nothing at all. We drew 17 feet and could just about manage 28 knots flat out. We were thus at something of a disadvantage in the chase and our only hope was to catch them 'on the job' which was easier said than done.

The area was still very primitive and the only radio link was shore based run by the police. This would give us information of raids that had taken place but by the time we reached the site it was too late. The Celebes Sea in which we were operating abounded with small sailing traders who had as much to fear from the pirates as the plantations. They proved a more useful source of information than the local police and with their help we did eventually capture a boatload of pirates. They were a brutal looking lot, and it was with relief that we handed them over to the civilian authorities.

We brought *Rocket* home through the Suez Canal which had only recently been opened following a major mine clearing operation by the Royal Navy. The canal was now being run by the Egyptians and there was some concern as to the competence of their pilots. These fears proved groundless. Our Egyptian pilot was a naval officer who had been trained by the Royal Navy. He exuded confidence and took us through in great style.

Before leaving Singapore, I had received a telegram announcing that Georgina had given birth to a baby boy four weeks premature. James weighed only three-and-a-half pounds at birth but he was a tough little chap and he thrived. We had bought a tiny cottage in Soberton with some help from uncle Michael. The principal rooms were twelve feet square, and the ceiling barely over six feet in places, but it had staggering views over the valley and we loved it. On arrival in Portsmouth I spent a week redecorating it from top to bottom, after which I never want to see a paint brush or roller again, and moved my small family in.

A flying visit to the West Indies followed, during which we spent twenty-four hours trying to salvage a burning tanker. At considerable risk to our men and the ship itself we managed to douse the fire, using our own power, but her master refused to accept our offer of a tow, and it was agonising watching the vessel slowly sinking, and with it our hopes of salvage money as we waited for the tugs to arrive.

Signal Communications Specialist

I left *Rocket* on our return to UK and found myself once more behind a desk in a classroom. This time in the Naval Signal School, in a very different state of mind to the previous occasion six years earlier when I was coming to the end of my Sub-Lieutenant's courses. Then I was twenty-two, as yet untried and burning with frustration to get to sea and do a proper job. At the same time I was not entirely sure that the Navy was what I wanted to do. One of the questions my future father-in-law asked me when we were pacing his lawn was whether I was flat out for the Navy. My honest answer, which did not impress him, was that I was not sure. Now at the age of twenty-eight I was married, mature, and experienced. I knew where I was going and I was most certainly flat out for the Navy.

The subject was radio theory. In the past it would have been a complete turn off, but this was different. I lapped it up, and if personal motivation was not enough, Instructor Commander Tom Foster was one of the most inspiring teachers under whom I have sat. His ample form attired in magnificent braces, he embarked on potentially the dullest subjects with a compelling enthusiasm, which was quite irresistible. From a quick reminder of schoolboy mathematics we delved immediately into electrical circuitry, electronic theory, and radio waves, ending up with satellites and computers. I found it fascinating and what is more, understood it. The rest of the course was mainly practical, learning to type, read Morse, tune radio sets and so on. The ambience was greatly helped by being based on Laydene House, set in the country near Petersfield.

Signal communications is historically a service as opposed to a tactical arm. In the military world it is regarded as a technical matter, and its specialist officers are technicians first and foremost. The Navy has always taken a different approach and its specialists are primarily operational staff officers very much in the main stream. Traditionally the naval communicator saw himself as the admiral's right-hand man; an essential link with the fleet, on the one hand, and organiser of his personal affairs as flag lieutenant, on the other. In the late 19th century, he did indeed have considerable authority. Lest any contemporary communicator gain too high an opinion of his sub-specialisation, however, he should read Andrew Gordon's excellent book *The Rules of the Game*[*] which indicates clearly how over-reliance on an outdated signal system contributed to the confusion and inability to achieve a decisive victory at the battle of Jutland.

In the Navy in which I served signal communications embraced electronic warfare which gave it a tactical capability alongside its traditional service role and was becoming more and more important. As the developments in radar were increasing the detection range of the fleet and the accuracy of its weapons, so the interception of these transmissions by the enemy was giving him a clearer idea of the fleet's position and its capabilities. Electronic Warfare (EW) could be used either in the passive role of interception, intelligence, identification and position fixing of the enemy or it could be used actively by jamming his transmissions. Just as the

---

[*] *The Rules of the Game* Andrew Gordon (John Murray)

fleet had to have a tactical policy for each weapon system, missile, gunnery, antisubmarine and aviation, so it had to have an EW policy to control the electronic transmissions in order to minimise the chances of detection.

I found the course fascinating and enjoyed almost every minute of it. Georgina became fed up with seeing me hidden behind what she called SO (Stationary Office) books as I swotted up my notes. To my, and everyone else's, surprise, I came top of the course winning the Jackson Everett prize. This gave me £30 to spend which was meant to be used to purchase practical things like binoculars, but I spent it on three marvellous art books by Skira with superb illustrations on Italian, Impressionist and contemporary art, which I particularly enjoy now in my retirement when I have time to develop my interest in art and painting. The other more serious effect of coming top was to single me out as a potential communications 'boffin' which I was very far from being, and which would have had disastrous consequences for my naval career.

I was now anxious to get to sea to put my new-found knowledge to good use. When the appointments were announced I opted for an operational staff and was sent as Deputy Signal Communications Officer on the staff of the Flag Officer Aircraft Carriers (FOAC). My immediate boss, Ronnie Graham-Clark, combined the job of Signal Communications Officer with Flag Lieutenant, and I was supposed to deputise for him on both counts but because, to his chagrin, the domestic requirements of the Admiral took up much of his time, the emphasis of my work was very much on the communications side which suited me very well.

The carriers were always the focal point of any operation in which they took part, so we were right at the forefront of naval tactical thinking at a particularly interesting time. One of my first tasks on joining the staff was to plan a major fleet exercise which for the first time included the brand new nuclear hunter/killer submarine, HMS *Dreadnought* in a defensive role, and also for the first time the brand new guided missile destroyer HMS *Devonshire*. Not only was the latter fitted with SEASLUG, but she had the latest EW interception equipment and the first ship-borne radar jammer.

I was responsible for drafting the communications plan which was straightforward enough until it came to communicating with *Dreadnought*. We were unable to use the traditional sonic underwater telephone for some reason, and had to resort to letting off hand grenades which was not the most satisfactory way to communicate with a submarine capable of moving at speeds in excess of 30 knots. Then there was the question of emission control which required a plan and a means of signalling it. In all these issues we were moving into new territory. I devised a special code for signalling various states of emission control which with some modification was subsequently adopted as standard practice.

At this time the Admiral was flying his flag in HMS *Ark Royal* in home waters. She was a large ship, and the whole of his staff were accommodated without difficulty. She was due to go into refit as soon as the exercise was over, and the plan was for the Admiral to transfer his flag to HMS *Centaur*, then in the Mediterranean. *Centaur* was not big enough to accommodate the whole staff and some of us were therefore preparing to form a shore-based 'rear link' at Portsmouth which would have suited me domestically.

As we were about to embark on the exercise however, the situation in East Africa deteriorated and a carrier presence was needed east of Suez. *Hermes* was in the Far East, and *Centaur* was sent through the Canal to stand by off Aden. The one remaining carrier, *Victorious*, was undergoing trials following a major refit. It was decided that the Admiral and his operational staff would fly out to join *Centaur* while the rear link would be set up in Singapore rather than Portsmouth. I was to form part of the latter. Everything happened rather quickly. One minute we were conducting a complex live exercise which broke new tactical ground in a number of areas. The next, we were packing our bags and office files for immediate transfer by helicopter to RAF Lyneham and on to Singapore.

One of my responsibilities was to hold the secret codes and Top Secret intelligence material which I kept in a large safe in my office. The material turned over fairly regularly and the obsolete material had to be destroyed. Above all it should not be seen by any person not specially cleared by security. My practice was to place the material for destruction on the bottom shelf pending the next burning session. In preparation for the move, I jammed a shelf down on the material scheduled for destruction, securing the current material in a similar way. On arrival at RAF Lyneham, I was informed that my safe was too big to be carried on the aircraft, and I found myself sitting on the perimeter track of RAF Lyneham in a strong wind, trying to transfer the contents of the big safe into a much smaller one. I just managed it, having kept everyone waiting for a quarter of an hour.

About three weeks later an ominous signal arrived from the Superintending Naval Stores Officer, Portsmouth to say that a certain amount of Top Secret intelligence material had been discovered in a safe returned by FOAC. Of course it was my material scheduled for destruction and hidden from view under the bottom shelf. This material might have been for destruction but it was still of a very high classification and it had found its way into unauthorised hands. There would be hell to pay, and there was.

A court of enquiry was convened and of course I had not a leg to stand on. What would happen next, I wondered. A friendly secretary in the Commander-in-Chief's office showed me a copy of a letter to the Admiralty recommending that I should receive an 'expression of Their Lordships' displeasure'. I visualised these distinguished personages taking time off from matters of naval policy to express their displeasure at the minor misdemeanours of a very junior officer. In the event I heard nothing further and since, as subsequent events proved, the incident seemed to have no effect on my career, I can only assume that some kindly soul, finding this document on his desk, realised the extenuating circumstances and consigned it to the bin. I was not to know this, however, and it was a worrying time.

This aside, the Rear Link was not overburdened with work and our boss, the staff planning officer, Commander 'Tubby' Fraser, took a fairly easy-going view of life. The two junior secretaries and I acquired an elderly Ford Consul which enabled us to see something of the Island and we had a lot of fun. The Naval Commander-in-Chief was Admiral Sir Desmond Dreyer, whom I had known in Malta when I was serving in *Broadsword*, and whose son, Jeremy, had been on my Long Course and was a great friend. Jeremy's mother had tragically died and the Admiral married his second wife, Marjorie, just before taking up his appointment as Flag Officer Flotillas Mediterranean. She was a charming, unconventional lady, quite unversed in matters of naval etiquette and a constant source of embarrassment to her husband's flag lieutenant. All the young officers loved her sense of fun and lack of pomp.

It is customary for officers arriving on a new station to sign the Admiral's book, and one weekday lunch I stopped work half an hour early in the hope of being able to drive up to Admiralty House, sign the book and get away before the Admiral arrived for his lunch party. Admiralty House in Singapore Naval Base was an impressive building on top of a hill with a large classical portico over the front door. I pulled into the portico in my shabby motor car, dashed in and signed the book. When I turned to leave, however, the car was not there; the portico was empty. How extraordinary, I thought, someone must have moved it. The truth was soon apparent when I spotted the rear end of the Ford Consul upended in a monsoon ditch about 100 yards down the drive with the rear wheel slowly turning.

The situation was interesting. Any minute C-in-C would be returning for lunch, followed no doubt by a phalanx of VIP guests, all to be greeted with a battered old heap stuck in a monsoon drain virtually blocking the drive. Once again my career was in the balance. I ran into the pantry where the Chinese staff were preparing for lunch and hustled them out into the drive – 'Quick Quick Chop Chop Pull car out of ditch.' I remember the mystified expression on their faces as in their pristine white uniforms they pulled and pushed at this wretched car. 'Come on, I shouted, trying to keep the panic out of my voice, 'One last heave, Two Six Ha Ha!'

It rapidly became clear that we were not getting anywhere, and in desperation I turned round to find the chief steward at my elbow with a silver tray in his hand containing an ice cold bubbling 'horse's neck' (brandy and ginger ale to the uninitiated).

'Her Ladyship thought you might need this.'

Before leaving the UK I had called on my appointing officer at the Signal School, HMS *Mercury*, to find that it was confidently expected that I should return to do the advanced signal course and become a communications boffin. This was apparently thought by those in authority to be a great feather in my cap, but I did not see it like that. I was not an intellectual and only too well aware that once you allow yourself to specialise too deeply, no matter what anyone may say to the contrary, your career focuses on research and opportunities for general service and the experience required for high command are accordingly limited. Luckily I had an ally in my old Captain, Tony Morton, now Commander of the Signal School. 'Don't touch it with a bargepole,' he said. I didn't and it was not popular.

By way of retribution I received an appointment as First Lieutenant of HMS *Messina*, the old rust bucket in which I had served in the Pacific, which was commissioning for service in the Gulf. I wriggled and squirmed. It was not at all the sort of job I wanted at this stage in my career. If I could not command a minesweeper, then at least I wanted to be able to work with the fleet and put to good use some of the experience I had gained in my present job. The authorities were adamant however and I left for Singapore somewhat gloomy about the future. Altogether in retrospect this brief period in Singapore was a low point in my career. Things could only get better.

They started to improve when I received a signal cancelling my appointment to *Messina* and sending me instead to HMS *London* as Signal Communications Officer (SCO). *London* was the last of the first four Guided Missile Destroyers (DLG) to be built. She was just completing builder's trials and I was to join in Plymouth as she sailed for her work up at Portland. To be SCO of a brand new DLG fitted with the latest state of the art electronic warfare equipment was an appointment beyond my wildest dreams and I could not wish for anything better, short of command. I flew home on a high.

My appointment had come about because my predecessor, Warren Gilchrist, had contracted TB and was on protracted sick leave. I went to see him in the sanatorium at Midhurst where he gave me an excellent briefing, not so much about the ship as about its Captain, Jozef Bartosik, whose reputation was a byword in the Fleet.

Jozef Bartosik had had a remarkable career sailing from his native Poland in the Polish Navy training ship, never to return, as war broke out while they were in South American waters. He transferred to the Royal Navy and devoted himself to it with an intensity which went far beyond that of the average British officer, and ultimately achieved flag rank. He drove himself hard, and expected others to do likewise. He had no time for someone whom he felt was not pulling his weight and it was important not to allow oneself to be beaten down.

It did not take long for me to put this advice to good effect. A few days into the work up, we were ordered to send the landing party ashore to deal with an exercise involving a civil unrest situation. For some reason the command post was set up beside a large aircraft hangar and as a result the small portable radios failed to communicate with men on the other side of the hangar because VHF radio waves do not like travelling through metal. The exercise was a disaster and at the wash-up the Captain blamed it on the communications which failed and let the side down. I pointed out the problem but my intervention was not appreciated and I was sent for shortly afterwards. Jozef was at his coldest; his eyes bored into me like lasers.

'Signal Officer, next time you contradict me in public, I shall send for your relief.'

There was only one response, 'Aye aye sir.'

He then made some dismissive gesture, but I felt that this was a test and I stood my ground.

'Well, Signal Officer, have you something to say?'

'Just two things, sir. Firstly, I am sorry if I appeared to contradict you in public but I felt it important to put the record straight for the sake of my men. Secondly, you may send for my relief, but I fear you will not find one. They scraped the bottom of the barrel to produce me.'

'That will be all, Signal Officer.'

I feared the worst when, at lunchtime, I was sent for again. This time however my greeting was different.

'Come in, Michael, what will you drink?'

Life with Jozef Bartosik was never easy, but I like to think that we got on pretty well after that. My department and I let him down on numerous occasions but once the justifiable fury had abated, good relations were resumed and he gave me an excellent report. I learned a lot from him, mainly about self control, and standing up to authority when I felt I was in the right.

The work up completed, we sailed in September for Houston, Texas, the first port of call of a memorable cruise which took us through the Panama Canal and round South America, en route to the Far East via South Africa.

We continued our progress down the west coast of South America with a visit to Callao in Peru where we met up with the rest of our squadron, led by the cruiser, HMS *Tiger*, flying the flag of Admiral Sir Fitzroy Talbot, Commander-in-Chief South Africa and South America. This was followed by Valparaiso in Chile. We then steamed for three days at 17 knots through the Trinidad channels, those mysterious inland waterways on the west coast of Chile with hardly a sign of life. I thought of those early navigators and wondered how many blind alleys they went up before they found a way through.

Finally we emerged into the Magellan Straits in a snowstorm. As we approached the port of Punta Arenas out of the murk appeared the outline of three or four clipper ships at anchor. For a moment it was as if we had passed through a time warp and were back in the days of sail, but the truth was more mundane. They were in fact coaling hulks.

In due course we parted company with *Tiger* and *Penelope*, and Admiral Talbot transferred his flag to *London* for passage to Simonstown. He was an admiral of the old sort, a true gentleman, a friend of uncle Michael's and a keen foxhunter. The passage proceeded without incident until we reached the island of Tristan da Cunha which the Admiral wished to visit. This is the largest of a group of islands about 1500 miles west of Cape Town. It is of volcanic origin and it rises steeply out of the sea with its peak shrouded in mist. In 1961 the volcano erupted and washed away the harbour. The islanders were evacuated and housed in a camp at Calshot. Most of them preferred their island life, however, and an advance party returned in 1963 with the remainder joining them shortly after. Today they number around 300.

With no sheltered landing area, the Admiral had to go in by helicopter and he kindly invited some of the officers to accompany him, including me. As it was an official call by the Commander-in-Chief, we all had to wear formal tropical uniform which consisted of a plain white tunic with shoulder straps and long white duck trousers (known as the ice cream suit). Whatever the islanders must have thought when we descended from the sky equipped with swords and medals, they kept it to themselves and went quietly about their business as we wandered through the village. They were a strange looking people with thickish lips, a dark swarthy complexion and deep-set eyes. They were said to be descended mainly from a member of the British garrison, Corporal Glass, who volunteered to remain with his wife and two children when it was withdrawn in 1817. He and five others formed the first settlement subsequently augmented by five women from St Helena in 1827 and no doubt the odd passing sailor.

Their manner of speaking seemed to come from centuries past. We were greeted with expressions like 'How thee are?' It must have been a hard life living under the continuous shadow of that threatening volcano with its peak almost continually shrouded in mist. At that time they had no proper harbour and launching one of three large longboats straight into the Atlantic surf would have been a major operation. There were small plots of corn and flax here and there looking as if they had been tilled by hand and the houses were reminiscent of the Hebridean Black House.

All thoughts were now directed to our next port of call, Simonstown, the South African naval base on the eastern side of the Cape. South Africa, before the days of apartheid, was generally acclaimed as one of the best 'runs ashore' such was the hospitality of its people, and the charm of its environment. We were due to spend three weeks there including Christmas. I was particularly excited as Georgina was flying out to join me with James, aged three. She was to stay with old friends of her parents, Noel and Dennis Newton King who had a fruit farm at Somerset West, about 30 miles east of the Cape.

True to form, Georgina was there on the jetty to greet us with a number of other enterprising wives. There was some concern in certain quarters that the welcoming party might be augmented by one or two passing acquaintances from South America as indeed happened on one occasion when a colleague was met by two ladies, one of whom he had met during a previous visit, and the other his wife.

Kings Kloof was a heavenly place. The small town of Somerset West lies at the foot of a large volcanic crater comprising a semicircle of what seemed like perpendicular cliffs bounded on one side by the sea. The Newton Kings' farm was halfway up the western side of the crater looking across the valley to the eastern cliff with the sea on the right. Every afternoon the clouds would form over the eastern cliff, and pour over it like a giant waterfall into the valley below. Outside our bedroom window was a tree with the biggest avocados I had ever seen. The house seemed to be set in a Garden of Eden, so lush was the vegetation.

The Newton Kings lent us their holiday cottage by the sea in Gordon's Bay. For Georgina and me, it was a second honeymoon (we never really had a first!), marred only occasionally by loud howls from a bored James next door. There were parties all over the place, and a splendid ball at Admiralty House. Christmas came and went; I invited my communications department over to Gordon's Bay on Boxing Day which was a great success, with James as the centre of attention. All too quickly the date for our departure came upon us and on 29th December we sailed for Singapore with heavy hearts. Georgina returned to the United Kingdom in the *Windsor Castle*, and nine months later produced Fiona, who in adult life has always had a special feeling for the country in which she was conceived, and at the time of writing has just returned from seven years there.

It was now four months since we had left UK and, apart from a few basic exercises with our small squadron on passage from one port to another, our time had been spent visiting foreign parts and enjoying ourselves. We had not seen an aircraft or a submarine and the ship's company were thoroughly bored. There were rumblings on one of the mess decks which, while they never approached the level of mutiny, were sufficient to indicate that morale was not what it should be. The Captain threw the ship into a complex series of exercises and kept the hands in two watches for the remaining passage to Singapore. There was no more trouble. Another lesson was learned. People are really only happy if they are given plenty to do with reasonable breaks in between.

Our six months deployment to the Far East was dominated by the Indonesian confrontation. Faced with abject poverty and economic disaster in his own country, President Soekarno had designs on Malaysia and had been actively supporting rebel movements in the region. His threats were almost meaningless and really designed for his home market to divert his people's attention from their miserable condition. We had to take them seriously at the time, however, as the Indonesians had a Navy of sorts which included a number of KOMAR class fast motor-boats equipped with guided missiles supplied by the Russians. In the busy Straits of Malacca, with their high speed and low radar profile, these could have caused considerable havoc if they had been properly used. We were also concerned for our security alongside in the Singapore naval base where there was always a possibility of attack by underwater saboteurs. From time to time an appropriately named exercise 'Operation Awkward' which involved searching the ship's bottom with divers, would be ordered, generally in the middle of the night, in response to some over-enthusiastic sailor sighting a 'suspicious object' in the water.

There were one or two comic moments, however. From time to time intelligence used to be received that the Indonesians would be infiltrating agents into Singapore. Their means of transport were low-lying high speed craft such as the dugout canoes we used to chase off Borneo in *Rocket* five years before. HMS *London* was equipped with guided missiles designed primarily to protect a carrier group from air attack and it had no weapons other than the standard rifle which would bear on such craft. We had therefore to be fitted with a pair of Oerlikon guns of World War II vintage.

One night we were on patrol in the straits in response to some intelligence report. Everything was quiet until suddenly we heard the sound of gunfire. Shortly afterwards a signal was received from HMS *Ajax* to the effect that, on the anniversary of the Battle of the River Plate, *Ajax* was engaged with the enemy again. Not only was it a rather different sort of enemy, but there seemed to be something wrong with the dates as the original action took place in December and it was now March. We never in fact discovered who the enemy was and the whole thing could easily have been a hoax. It was not far off 1st April.

We left Singapore for UK at the end of July arriving in Portsmouth a month later. I had now been serving in *London* for almost fourteen months and it was time to move on. I heard that the appointment as SCO and Divisional Officer at Dartmouth was becoming available. Not only would it look good on my service record but it would be a fascinating experience to return to Dartmouth as the equivalent of a housemaster. I made discreet noises and in due course my appointment was confirmed to take effect from 13th December, our seventh wedding anniversary.

Schoolmaster

The process of training junior naval officers at Dartmouth had undergone a number of changes since the days when I felt that I was being treated like a prep school boy in the early '50s. The arrangements now in force known as the 'Murray Scheme', required successful candidates of the Admiralty Interview Board to join Dartmouth at the age of seventeen and carry out a year's training as a cadet, comprising three terms. Two terms, the first and one other, would be spent at the college while the third would be spent in the training squadron. They would then go to sea for a year as midshipmen, returning to Dartmouth for a further academic year as acting sub lieutenants before carrying out specialist courses and finally going to sea as commissioned officers in the rank of sub-lieutenant.

There were thus two principal streams at Dartmouth, the cadets who were undergoing their initial training, and the acting sub lieutenants whose course was more geared to a first year at university. Intermingled with these streams were junior officers from foreign and commonwealth countries who provided a colourful cultural input to the general scene.

The cadets arrived as raw recruits and were at once plunged into a tough initial seven weeks new entry training designed to weed out the hopeless and instil some sense of discipline into the rest. The remainder of the first term was taken up with mainly seamanship and leadership training with some basic technical input, while in the second term the emphasis was more on the technical side. Underlying the whole course was the requirement to convert a motley crowd of new entry trainees of differing backgrounds and abilities into open minded, civilised naval officers who could maintain and enhance the fine traditions of the Royal Navy, and be a credit to their country.

The sub-lieutenants had an easier time, albeit considerably more rigorous than that which I enjoyed at Greenwich. Their course was principally an academic one, though they were required to keep their hand in on professional matters and, of course, the parade ground was never far away.

The college was divided up into divisions which reflected the 'houses' of my day, and the same familiar names remained: *Blake, Grenville, Exmouth, St Vincent* and *Hawke*. The sub-lieutenants formed the senior division and the cadets the junior division. Both the senior and the junior divisions would have a lieutenant commander in charge as the divisional officer, and while the senior divisional officer had one lieutenant as an assistant, the junior divisional officer had two. Paradoxically the junior DO was the bigger and more interesting job of the two, not only because there were more cadets than sub-lieutenants but, because their course was more practical and professional, he was necessarily much more personally involved in their individual development.

I wore two hats. As the Signal Communications Officer I was responsible for all professional training in Signal Communications. This ranged from daily signal exercises in semaphore and morse, to picket boat manoeuvres off the mouth of the Dart, to classroom lectures in ship formations and how to operate a fleet at sea. I had a small and splendid staff to help me, who also ran the main signal office. This was strategically placed right by the front door of the college so we always knew what was going on.

My second hat was my divisional one. The normal procedure was to spend the first term or two as an assistant DO before being given a division of one's own. In my case I worked as assistant DO to Lieutenant Commander Mike Casement in *Grenville* Senior Division for my first term before taking over as *Blake* Junior Divisional Officer in the spring of 1966. This enabled me to concentrate on my department and the professional aspect of my job before becoming almost totally involved in the running of my own division.

A major issue area of policy in which I was involved during my time at Dartmouth was the question of whether naval officers should receive a university training and if so where and at what stage in their career. The issue had been brought into sharp focus by what had been known as the 'carrier battle'. Briefly, the Navy had set its heart on building a new aircraft carrier which would be fitted with every possible piece of equipment that the state of the art and long experience of operating aircraft at sea could offer. When I was serving on the Flag Officer Aircraft Carriers' staff we had been very much concerned with this project. As everyone fed in their latest idea in a rapidly developing area, so this ship took on the proportions of a monster costing huge sums and the Navy could only afford one of them. This made it an easy target for the Secretary of State, Denis Healey, whose incisive mind was concerned above all with cost cutting. If it was essential for the Navy to have this new highly sophisticated aircraft carrier, what would take its place when it was being refitted?

At the same time, the RAF was fighting for its survival and particularly that of Bomber Command. They pinned their hopes on an aircraft known as the TSR2 which could, according to the RAF planners, attack any target in the world, operating from existing bases at home and overseas. To sceptical naval planners it sometimes appeared that their RAF counterparts, in their anxiety to prove the range of their aircraft, had forgotten that it would be useless in ground support operations unless it could spend at least some time in the target area.

The battle echoed round Whitehall and both services looked on in alarm because so much was at stake. For the Navy it meant the future of the Fleet Air Arm, and all the experience that we had accumulated over the years in the importance and techniques of operating aircraft at sea was in question. I am sure our colleagues in the RAF were equally concerned. In the event they won, but it was a pyrrhic victory as a few years later the contract for the TSR2 was cancelled, and a new Conservative government reinstated the aircraft carrier under the guise of the 'through deck cruiser'.

The point of this digression is that in the agonised wash up that took place in the Navy after this debacle, it emerged that the advocacy of the RAF under their barrister trained Chief of Air Staff, Marshal of the Royal Air Force Sir Charles Elworthy, had won the day and that furthermore every member of the Air Board had been to university. Indeed it was rapidly becoming clear that the RAF were altogether far better trained for Whitehall warfare than the Navy. The latter had always worked on the basis that the best training for a naval officer is at sea, and shunned the idea of in-depth academic training. It had been a policy of proven success over the years until now. The writing was however clearly on the wall. If the Navy was to hold its own amid the intellectual battles of Whitehall, then officers' training should be geared to this, which meant university training, at least for the potential stars.

By the time I had arrived at Dartmouth there was a system of late entry for those who had been to university and there were one or two bright officers who had secured a place at university before coming to Dartmouth and were now taking it up as sub-lieutenants. The Navy had no control over the courses they took or any influence. A committee was therefore set up under Professors Michael Howard and David English to look into the possibility of a dedicated service university. They duly came to Dartmouth and we had some interesting debates.

There was general agreement for broader based training along university lines for those officers who would benefit by it and from whom the Navy would have a return on its investment. The arguments focussed on how long the course should be and when and where it should take place. The academics were keen, once they had the young officers under their control and in a learning mode, to keep them that way for a further three years. In other words they would like to see the sub-lieutenants' year at Dartmouth extended to three years and take place in a university environment. My naval colleagues and I favoured a longer period at sea before embarking on the university course. I was very influenced by my own experience as a frustrated teenager longing to get to sea and do a proper job. By the end of my sub-lieutenant's course aged twenty I had had enough of sitting behind a desk and wanted to go out and prove myself. Then, some years later, aged twenty-six, married, and with a much clearer idea of what I wanted to do, and confidence in my ability to do it, I embarked with enthusiasm on my Long Communications Course. The mature graduate is a common concept in the USA where it is quite normal for people in their twenties to give up three years of their working life to take a university degree.

The other argument we put forward was the inevitable one that the loss of three years' valuable fleet experience as a young officer would put the university graduate at a severe disadvantage with his peers when he eventually came to sea as a lieutenant of three years' seniority. There was also the question of whether the Services should have their own university. The favoured site was the Army College at Shrivenham. We were against this. Not having been to university myself, I have always understood that one of the main training experiences comes from the breadth of interest of the student body and the ability to mix, meet and debate. A joint services' university would be too introspective and three years of academic training in a service environment would be the worst of all possible worlds.

In the end the idea of a joint services university was dropped and instead a special course was organised at City University to which officers were nominated after a period at sea as acting and then confirmed sub-lieutenant. In effect it was a form of compromise but the academics insisted on the three-year course. Some years later my eldest son James was nominated for this course which he found both interesting and valuable, but later, when he was called forward early to do his Principal Warfare Officer's course, he had the misfortune to fail the course due to insufficient fleet experience.

My appointment as *Blake* Junior Divisional Officer was one of the most formative appointments in my naval career. For the first time I had effectively a 'command' in that with my team of assistant divisional officers and working in conjunction with those members of the academic staff who were attached to the division, I was directly responsible for the initial training and welfare of some 150 future naval officers. It was my task to train them to be smart, quick thinking, disciplined, well mannered and well rounded leaders of men. Whether I achieved this objective I do not know, but I certainly learned an enormous amount myself in the art of projecting myself to an audience and in thinking quickly on my feet. I am sure that any skills I may have acquired for public speaking, of which I was to do my share in the future, owe much to my experience on the staff at Dartmouth.

I met my first bunch of new entries on a cold May morning clustered gloomily under the arches alongside the parade ground. They had joined the college a week before the term was due to start and were receiving their first taste of the gunnery instructor's tongue at the outset of what would be the seven most arduous weeks of their lives. I was to see them later that morning so I confined myself to hovering in the shadows reflecting on my own memories of undergoing the same experience in the same place but some two years younger. There was the thrill of being at last part of the Royal Navy balanced by irritation at the apparently childish way in which we were treated. Used to the freedom of Eton, I was appalled by what seemed to me to be the petty restrictions imposed on us. In my day, of course, Dartmouth was more of a school than a naval college and many of those irritations were historic and unnecessary. The central theme of discipline, however, remains fundamental to any initial service training and this was what the first seven intensive weeks of new entry training was supposed to inculcate. It also gave us an opportunity to see how each cadet responded under pressure, and if necessary to identify those who were unlikely to complete the course at an early stage. It may have been something of a blunt weapon but it was an effective one, not least because it forged friendships between strangers through the sharing of common adversity.

Blake new entry cadets were the usual mixed bunch of young men from a range of social and educational backgrounds. The Winchester educated son of an ambassador stood shoulder to shoulder with the son of an east London docker; a young man whose name was a household word in naval history stood next to a greengrocer's son from High Wycombe. I spoke to them in the *Blake* senior gunroom after breakfast on their first morning at college. I took what I hope was a positive line by welcoming them to the college and congratulating them on their success at the interview board. I then told them that their first seven weeks would be a severe test. They would be stretched mentally and physically and some of them might not make it. I explained the twofold purpose of this endurance test they were about to undergo which was to instil a strong sense of discipline on the one hand and to weed out the non-performers early on so that they did not hold anyone else back. I strongly advised them that they should go with the system and not resist it. If they had problems they were welcome to share them with me or one of my colleagues who would be available at almost any time. I am a great believer in the 'open door' principle by which officers make themselves readily available to see their men at anytime if they have a serious problem which is concerning them.

The new entries then repaired to the gigantic cadets' mess hall and the tender mercies of Miss Bulla, a lady of remarkable presence and voice who had been the college caterer for countless years. Once a Wren, she had become a college institution. They were then subjected to a relentless programme of parade training, both theoretical and practical seamanship, with, for many, their first experience of boat work. Dress lectures and knife and fork lectures were interspersed with rigorous workouts in the gym and cross-country running. Many a cold morning hour was spent on the hill opposite the college reading Morse and semaphore signals. Overlying this activity were a series of practical exercises on the river and on Dartmoor, which increased in complexity as the weeks passed, designed to give each new cadet an opportunity to exercise his leadership qualities in some responsible role. In effect the new entry training reflected much of the pattern of normal college life except that it was carried out at double speed.

As was to be expected, the new entry training programme sorted out the sheep from the goats with a large grey area in between. As divisional officers we had come to know our new entry cadets, and identified those who would need help to pass out. Just occasionally there would be one or two cadets who were clearly unsuitable, but it was rare to remove them at this stage. I had one cadet from a naval family whose one ambition was to become a doctor. His father, a retired naval captain with something of a reputation, would not hear of it and insisted that he go to Dartmouth. It rapidly became clear that this lad was not suited to a naval career and I reported as much to the Captain of the College. The father was informed and descended on the college like a dragon breathing fire and brimstone and threatening all sorts of dire retribution. The bluster was of no avail however and the son left quietly at the end of his first term to commence his medical training.

It was our job as divisional officers to dream up practical exercises which would provide opportunities for each cadet to display and develop his leadership qualities. For this purpose we had available to us the river Dart with the huge fleet of college boats, and Dartmoor where the college had the use of an exceedingly basic dwelling in the middle of nowhere called Ditsworthy Warren. I came to know them both well.

On my first 'Divex' I took one of our spaniels, a black bitch who made up for her uselessness as a gun dog by the assiduity with which she pursued her abiding interest in food. After a hard day tramping the moor in the depth of winter we all turned in in our sleeping bags on the somewhat shaky first floor of this building. I had fond hopes of my canine hot water bottle but just as I had finally managed to fall asleep in the cold and discomfort, she developed an itch and proceeded to sit on the floor and scratch with an intensity that set the floor vibrating. She then embarked on a thorough search of the rows of prone bodies in the hope of finding a biscuit. When she had finally succeeded in waking the entire party she then treated us to an aria, the meaning of which was only too clear. She had explored the catering possibilities of this strange place, found them wanting and wished to be taken home. As we were something like an hour's walk from the road, this was out of the question. I managed to smother her in my sleeping bag but it was not a success and she never came again on one of those character-building exercises.

Back at the college, the professional side of the cadets' training was handled by the specialist departments. As their divisional officer, my concern was with broadening their minds, and preparing them for the strange situations they might find themselves in as the nation's ambassadors abroad. To this end I had three or four 'divisional' periods a week at which I had a free hand to organise lectures, discussions, debates and so on. It was as much of a test for me as it was for my staff and cadets to keep these periods interesting, relevant and original.

Out of hours there were of course endless games, each with their membership body or association which the keen participants joined. I believe there was also an amateur dramatic society, a naval history society and one or two others of that ilk. One glaring omission was music, where the absolutely splendid Music Master, Gerry King, was having a hard time gaining support for his ambitious musical projects. The fine arts was another area which received little attention. I went to see the Commander, Wid Graham, and with his approval we founded the Britannia Society of Music and the Arts, known as BSMA. Gerry King was a tremendous enthusiast. He had been at Dartmouth when I was cadet and had me playing Chopin preludes on the piano. He tried to teach me to sing and I once sang a bass solo in one of his musical evenings, but never again. Returning as a DO, I was entrapped as was anyone – staff, their wives and children, as well as the students, who had the faintest interest in playing or singing. Always the optimist, Gerry struggled in my case to make a silk purse out of a sow's ear but he never gave up hope.

His real love was choral work, and he had a great gift of being able to impart his infectious enthusiasm to a pretty average bunch of singers who thoroughly enjoyed themselves: what it sounded like to an audience I never knew. We sang our way through Dvorak's great *Stabat Mater*, and Bach's *St Matthew Passion*; we recorded and broadcast Faure's *Requiem*. It was a wonderful way to learn great works and I believe that the BSMA is now an established feature of the Dartmouth cultural scene, though Gerry himself has passed on.

While I was thoroughly enjoying my work at the college, Georgina was not quite so happy. An independent spirit, she felt the institutional life of the college somewhat oppressive and slightly resented being expected to be a part of it. A particular gripe was college chapel which for some reason wives were expected to attend. As time went on and she came to know the other wives and to make many friends, she enjoyed it rather more. For my part I sometimes found it difficult to adjust to being at one moment the smart, on the ball, divisional officer chasing cadets around the place, demanding an impossibly high standard of dress and tidiness, and then going home up the road to find toys littered all over the place and wet nappies steaming on the fireguard. Georgina, who saw little of me during the day, was less than enthusiastic about my new found craze for tidiness.

The river and its activities were for me an added bonus. I have always been fascinated by small boats and I greatly enjoyed instructing cadets in boat handling. Each Division had its own yacht; ours was called *Martlett*. These were specially-built sail training craft, designed by Laurent Giles in one of his less inspired moments. They were very long, narrow and wet, but they could accommodate eight or nine crew in modest discomfort. I took *Martlett* across the Channel on two occasions and it was as much an experience for me as it was for the young officers.

1967, my last year at Dartmouth was notable for two things. First, I was stricken by jaundice while on a cruise to Brittany. Second, I was sent for to see my uncle Michael at Sort, his holiday cottage in Dorset. The first spoilt my last summer term at Dartmouth but my frustration at being unable to take part in the college activities was mitigated by the arrival of my next appointment to relieve my friend Hugh Balfour as Staff Officer Operations and Flag Lieutenant to the Senior Naval Officer, West Indies. It must be one of, if not the best lieutenant-commander's job in the Navy after command, and I had trained my sights on it after our visit to the West Indies in *Rocket*. Not only was it likely to be fascinating from the professional angle, but Bermuda would be a lovely place for the family to live, and I would be following in my father's footsteps as Flag Lieutenant to the Commander-in-

Chief West Indies, my grandfather, Sir Michael Culme-Seymour (4th Bart), in the 1920s.

The second event which took place in early 1967 was the occasion related in Chapter 1 which resulted in my uncle giving me Rockingham.

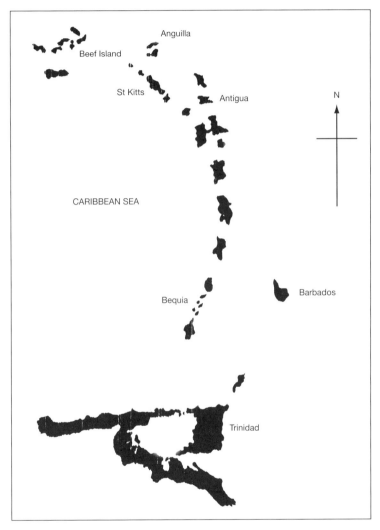

Anguilla – read on!

CHAPTER 4

'Don't stop the carnival' – the West Indies

After a week of intensive briefing I flew out to Bermuda on 4th September, 1967. As the BOAC VC10 came down out of the clouds, the brilliant azure sea came into view and I was reminded of that moment fourteen years earlier when as a cadet in the training cruiser, HMS *Devonshire*, we steamed out of a week of dark Atlantic gales into this brilliant paradise. It seemed a very long time ago, and so much had happened in the intervening years. The cadet struggling to make sense of life, insecure and unsure of himself or where he was going was now a lieutenant-commander, responsible for operations on the West Indies Station, married to a wonderful girl with two children, and in the background somewhere, Rockingham Castle estate.

The aircraft landed at the USAF base Kindley, which doubled as a civilian airport and there was the smiling face of Hugh Balfour standing on the tarmac to greet me. Hugh's meticulous turnover had included a reading list to prepare me for the West Indies. At the top of the list was the novel *Don't Stop the Carnival* by Herman Wouk, which, so aptly describes the special charm, frustration and volatility of the West Indian islands and their people that I have used the title to head up this chapter.

Hugh and Sheila had cleverly rented a delightful old plantation house in the middle of Somerset Island known as Cedar Hill. One of the older houses on the island it could well have dated from the 18th century. Set in two acres of coarse Bermuda grass, the house formed three sides of a square with the buttery, a small conical building very typical of Bermuda houses, and the entrance, the fourth. It was painted pink with the windows light blue, and a white roof stepped to catch the rainwater. Inside the furniture was a strange mixture with some rather good if battered pieces while the armchairs were covered in a sort of pale blue plastic material.

Within an hour of arrival we were swimming, and as I lay on my back in the clear sea, looking back at the glistening beaches, I thought once again how lucky I was to be working out here for the next two years. That evening there was a party, one of many given for Hugh and Sheila by their large circle of friends.

The following morning we set to work. Commodore John Townley, the Senior Naval Officer, West Indies – who was known to all by his short title, SNOWI – was away, which as it turned out made things much simpler. Our offices were housed in HMS *Malabar*, an imposing white colonial style building standing on an eminence looking down onto the part of the old naval dockyard which was still in use to berth HM ships when required. There was a secretarial staff under the Commodore's secretary, John Williams, a small base maintenance staff run by an engineer officer, Bill Hicks, and a communications team who operated the landline which we received as a tail off the US base in Norfolk, Virginia.

On the operational side, the army staff officer, Lieutenant Colonel Tony Way of the Grenadiers, doubled as defence attaché to the High Commissioner, Jamaica, and was responsible to the Commodore for liaising with the military units in the area. These ranged from local territorials such as the Bermuda Regiment, to troops on active service in Belize. He was supported by an intelligence officer, Major Peter Ferguson, Royal Marines. As Staff Officer Operations, I was responsible for all ship movements, and operations on the station together with the Commodore's personal arrangements and programme. It was a small compact staff which worked well together – an excellent example of the adage 'small is beautiful'.

SNOWI wore three military hats, each with a separate title. As the Senior Naval Officer West Indies, he was the single service commander responsible to the Commander in Chief Western Fleet for all maritime operations on the station. At the same time he was the Commander British Forces Caribbean, CBFC, a dormant appointment which came into effect whenever there were joint operations in the area, in which case he became responsible to what was known as the Commander-in-Chief's Committee West of Suez (CICCW). Finally he had the NATO appointment of Island Commander Bermuda (ISCOMBDA) in which capacity he reported to the Supreme Allied Commander, Atlantic (SACLANT) who was based at Norfolk, Virginia. It sounded complicated but it was really quite simple and had the great advantage of granting direct and immediate access to the three major players in the area.

The West Indies station itself, or at least SNOWI's sphere of interest, could roughly be described as a square bordered by Bermuda in the north east, and Guyana in the south east, with the western boundaries being Panama in the south and Mexico in the north. It included all the countries which were contained within or bordered the Caribbean basin. Altogether we had a close interest in 32 different countries, some foreign, some members of the Commonwealth, some in associated status with Britain, a sort of half-way house to independence, and some still colonies. It was a huge area, and with our base in Bermuda the distances involved were comparable to running the Mediterranean station from London.

The naval presence in the Caribbean had recently been reviewed and the two frigates permanently on station had been reduced to one. As is invariably the case with these reviews it is the financial side which is the driving force rather than the task, which generally remains unchanged. The West Indies station at this time was no exception. Apart from the routine tasks of showing the flag and exercising our responsibilities for the external defence and general security of the associated states and colonies, we had a specific operational task to prevent illegal immigrants from Dr Castro's Cuba arriving in the Bahamas. Then there were British troops stationed in British Honduras keeping Guatemala at bay. It was a highly volatile area, and trouble requiring a British military presence could and did break out at any time.

I met the Commodore for the first time on the tarmac of Bogotá airport in Colombia. He had been on a series of visits in Central America and I had flown down from Bermuda to join him. John Townley was very far from being a conventional naval officer. Possessed of a brilliant mind, he was not one to tolerate people he thought were fools, and he had fallen out with one or two senior officers as a result. Convinced that he would never make flag rank and that he had therefore nothing to lose, he was determined to enjoy himself to the hilt. In naval terms he had 'let the end go.'

He wore his hair long, and affected a totally laid-back attitude in which water skis and partying took a priority over almost anything else. His mind was however razor sharp and he knew better than anyone what was going on in the many corners of the Caribbean.

He hated any form of pomp and his particular bêtes noires were those members of the diplomatic service who took themselves and their position representing Her Majesty's Government rather too seriously. He enjoyed shocking them. His sentiments were reciprocated and a note was circulated among the embassies and high commissions in the region seeking support for his dismissal. It did not succeed, largely because his grasp of the overall political situation throughout the whole area of his command made him too valuable to be replaced.

After an initial exchange over the telephone between Bermuda and Mexico during which he hurled invective at me for, in all innocence, informing the Commander-in-Chief of his whereabouts which he preferred to keep secret, we got on well. He left me to do my job, trusting me to keep him informed, while he amused himself. But he was always available if I needed a decision.

We travelled a lot together. Our normal pattern would be to spend a fortnight or so in Bermuda followed by a similar period away. There were various areas of particular concern and people with whom we kept closely in touch. On the military side, these included the Resident Naval Officer, Bahamas, who came under SNOWI, the Chief of British Naval Staff in Washington, who was our nearest British senior officer, and our NATO Commander, the Supreme Allied Commander Atlantic, whose deputy was a British admiral. On the diplomatic front the key figures were the British Government Representative in St Lucia who was the diplomat responsible for the six groups of islands known as the Associated States – Antigua and Barbuda, St Kitts Nevis and Anguilla, Dominica, St Lucia, St Vincent and Grenada – and the High Commissioner in Barbados who was the senior diplomat in the area. We kept in constant touch by telephone with these people and tried to visit them at least once a quarter.

Then there were the islands which were still colonies such as Bermuda, the Bahamas, the British Virgin Islands, Montserrat and the Cayman Islands with their respective governors or administrators, the other Commonwealth countries, Jamaica, Trinidad and Guyana with their High Commissioners, and finally the foreign countries of Central and South America which bordered the Caribbean sea, with their ambassadors. Our target was to visit these every six months either personally or in a ship.

This constant coverage of the area gave the Commodore a unique bird's eye view which he used to summarise in monthly situation reports to the Commander-in-Chief who passed them on to the Foreign Office, where I gather they were gratefully received. The Foreign Office had only recently absorbed the Commonwealth and the Colonial Offices with their respective staffs. Responsibility for the area at desk level was therefore split on administrative lines which meant that while each desk officer knew what was going on in their particular area, they were less well informed about the others.

As far as the ships on the station were concerned, I used to work out a programme with the Captain based round the routine ship's maintenance periods which were generally spent in Bermuda, and taking in visits to places we felt needed to see the flag, or which the Commodore wished to visit officially. Every opportunity was taken to exercise with the US Navy at

San Juan or one of the foreign navies in the area, not forgetting to add on a visit to the eastern US seaboard to give the sailors a good run ashore. We had various commitments we tried to respect. One was the Bahamas patrol mentioned previously; another could be hurricane guardship. We endeavoured to keep a ship within a day's steaming of the Windward and Leeward Islands during the hurricane season, and of course we had to be ready to respond to cries of help when, from time to time, the internal security situation broke down in one of the islands for which we had responsibility.

A typical programme might be that of the frigate HMS *Leopard*, whose Captain, Norman King, had been for a short time my 'snotties' nurse in *Ceylon*. She arrived in Bermuda shortly after me. The Commodore was anxious to visit Acapulco where he had been offered a suite in some swell hotel. Norman and I therefore planned a programme which would take him to the Bahamas for a fortnight on patrol, then on to Panama where the Commodore and I would fly to join them for an official visit to Panama City. We would then sail up the east coast to Acapulco. This would be followed by a visit to Costa Rica from which the Commodore and I would fly back to Bermuda, while *Leopard* returned in her own time.

On this occasion the visit to Panama proved more than usually interesting. As we often found to be the case in the countries of Central and South America, the politicians are military men, some of whom may have been trained in England. They seem to feel more at home talking to other military men than civilian diplomats, and from time to time we picked up pieces of information of which the British ambassador was unaware. At Panama we were able to warn the ambassador of an imminent coup in his country about which we learned over lunch with the Chief of Police.

Our defence attaché in that part of the world was a great enthusiast, Commander Chipps Selby Bennett. He talked loudly and volubly in Spanish and the South Americans thought the world of him. His wife Dodo was also a great character. Very tall, dark and distinguished looking, she served with the French Resistance during the war and frequently found herself behind enemy lines. She spoke fluent French with a marked Dorset accent and it was a miracle that she was not recognised by the Germans. Together, Chipps and Dodo did wonderful things for Britain in the four countries to which Chipps was accredited – Venezuela, Colombia, Panama, and The Dominican Republic and we had a lot of fun with them.

Back in Bermuda, Georgina joined me soon after Hugh left, bringing with her our two children, James and Fiona, and expecting a third. We took on the Balfours lease, their car, their cleaning lady, and their friends. I had a personal servant, Leading Steward Leslie, who looked after me and my things impeccably. He also helped with the cleaning of the house and served at meals when we entertained. Then when Number Three arrived on 1st April our household was augmented by Sylvia, a farmer's daughter from Herefordshire, who took to Bermuda life like a duck to water.

Everyone was very welcoming and we soon made friends on a much wider scale than we ever did when we were at Dartmouth, where our circle was dominated by the college and its staff. I also had some vague task as a sort of supernumerary ADC to the Governor which involved turning up at Government House in uniform and aiguillettes on ceremonial occasions. It meant nothing but gave us a certain status within Bermuda society.

My first year passed in a whirl of activity which became increasingly frenetic as the date for John Townley's departure came nearer. A flying visit from the Commander-in-Chief, Admiral Sir John 'Burning' Bush, confirmed his fears that he was not to be promoted, and in the summer of 1968 he was replaced by Commodore Martin Lucey who, so he said, had been sent out to 'clean the place up'.

Martin Lucey was essentially a nice, kind man, but his mind did not have the sharp edge of his predecessor and he concealed what I believe was a fundamental sense of insecurity by focussing on detail. Where John Townley saw only the woods, Martin was concerned more with the trees. Furthermore, since I was associated with the old regime, my advice was suspect. Our first few weeks together were therefore not the easiest; but events soon took charge, and operationally the station suddenly came to life.

The Windward and Leeward Islands may look like a group of similar islands on a small-scale map of the Caribbean, but individually they are very different. Of volcanic origin, their physical characteristics vary depending on the height of the volcanic rock above or below the sea. The latter situation produces the coral atoll with white sand, a flat aspect, and relatively dry climate while the former gives rise to steep wooded hills with lush vegetation and black sand. Antigua is an example of the latter while Dominica is the archetypal example of the former.

The islanders themselves also differ in ethnic origin, depending upon a number of factors. Mostly they were originally imported as slaves to work the plantations. Some plantation owners were more particular than others and only took slaves from certain parts of Africa. The only indigenous people are the Caribs, some of whom still live in a reserve in Dominica. Then, as time went on, various islands changed hands between the French, the Dutch and the English. St Lucia changed hands between the English and the French fourteen times.

Some of the islands are more fertile than others but the traditional crops of sugar and bananas are no longer economic and they are mainly dependent on tourism as their principal source of employment. Almost every island has more population than it can support and while education is relatively good up to a certain age, the job opportunities are limited and the result is a large number of semi-educated young people with nothing to do and nowhere to go.

For some years Britain had been trying to find some viable means of granting the islands independence. The West Indies Federation was set up in 1958, the launch of which I attended in HMS *Messina*, but it was not a success. The larger islands like Trinidad, Barbados and Jamaica then became fully independent within the Commonwealth, and where possible the others were grouped according to their geographical proximity into what were known as Associated States who enjoyed a sort of semi-independence with responsibility for internal security and finance while Britain retained responsibility for their external affairs. Today most of these states have achieved formal independence within the Commonwealth.

Every so often there would be relatively minor flare ups of violence on one of the islands. These were generally part of a power struggle between one individual and another but it was no help to the tourist trade to have riots reported in the press. Antigua was one of the worst offenders. The Governor, Sir Wilfred Jacobs, was a fine man, but some of his ministers were not so scrupulous and from time to time he would call on us to send a ship which would lie off St John's, the capital, but do nothing because there was nothing it could do. In those days however the mere presence of a British warship was enough to give the rioters second thoughts and things generally calmed down.

On the broader front there was a subversive movement known as 'Black Power' led by a mysterious figure called Malcolm 'X', the object of which was to stir up trouble between whites and blacks. One day he arrived in Bermuda and it was as if an electric shock had struck the island. There were riots in the capital, Hamilton, and a number of department stores were burned. When I rode to work the next morning on my mobylette, instead of my usual cheerful greeting from the blacks sitting on the wall outside our local store, I was given the sign of the fist. I dropped in to see my old friend, Rocky Baseden, who had been a shipwright in the dockyard. He built me a boat and we used to have long talks about astronomy on which he was very knowledgeable. He told me to leave at once or they would burn his house down. The whole atmosphere had suddenly become highly charged and very unpleasant.

At an emergency meeting with the Governor that morning, the Bermuda Regiment was mobilised, and we decided to send for troops from UK. Curfews were ordered; all the service families were brought into the naval base and an armed guard posted. This was made up of my signalmen and the various cooks and stewards who were the only ratings on the island. The sight of my dear Leading Steward Leslie clutching an ancient .303 rifle peering down the road in his short sighted way, made me feel that we might have been safer to have stayed at home.

Anyway nothing happened; a company of the 5th Royal Inniskilling Dragoon Guards (The Skins) arrived the next morning, stayed for about ten days and left. After a week or two the mess was cleaned up and life resumed its usual peaceful pattern.

One morning I was awoken by the telephone ringing beside my bed. It was the radio operator on watch in the Main Signal Office.

'Good morning, sir' he said. 'I am sorry to ring you so early but I have something here that may interest you.'

My mind slowly climbed into gear as I wondered what crisis was about to break about my head.

'What is it?'

'It's the half-yearly promotions, sir'

'Oh, is that all? Well it can wait until I come into the office.'

'But your name is on it, sir.'

'What? I don't believe it.'

He was right. There it was at the bottom of the list, the most junior lieutenant-commander to be promoted to commander. It was another of those moments, like Michael's gift of Rockingham, which came as a bolt from the blue. I was barely in the zone and fully expected that I had at least a year or more before I even gave it thought. To be selected early like that is the first step onto the fast track. At once, it opens up the possibility of ultimate flag rank, though there are many things which could go wrong on the way. At the very least I could expect that my next appointment would be a command.

I was rapidly brought down to earth when I reported to the Commodore with his signals later that morning. His previous appointment had been the Director of Seaman Officer Appointments so he knew the background.

'I suppose I should congratulate you', he said rather grudgingly. 'It was a very weak batch' – implying that the competition was not strong.

For some time we had been concerned about the island of Anguilla. As its name implies it is shaped like an eel and is one of the northernmost islands in the Leeward group. Colonised by the British in the 17th century, its settlers had strong Irish connections.

Traditionally linked for administrative purposes with St Kitts, 70 miles away, it had somehow missed out in financial aid and still had neither metalled roads nor a proper airstrip. The Anguillans accepted these arrangements while St Kitts was administered directly from UK but when, in 1967, they found themselves permanently linked to St Kitts in the new associated state, they were less than happy. The Premier of St Kitts at this time was one Robert Bradshaw, a strange intense man whose great hero was Fidel Castro. He hated the Anguillans and they hated him so the relationship was doomed from the start.

Three months into associated status the Anguillans pulled out, declared independence, and set about looking at ways of making money. There was very little communication and rumours were rife. One was that the island had been taken over by the Mafia. Another was that a visiting yacht had been fired upon. As far as we were concerned it was a no go area.

On Monday 3rd March, 1969 the Commodore and I were having breakfast on board HMS *Rhyll* at the Colombian port of Cartagena, when a signal was received from the Foreign Office requiring us to report immediately to the residence of the High Commissioner in Barbados for a ministerial meeting that very evening to discuss Anguilla.

The nearest international airport was seventy miles away. The telephones in Colombia are not the most efficient and there were no direct flights from Colombia to Barbados. Somehow Chipps Selby Bennet, the indefatigable defence attaché, managed to find two Mercedes taxis to take us and our gear to the airport where we were assured we would be able to find seats on an aircraft but we had to leave immediately. My steward who was accompanying us on this occasion managed to throw our things into their suitcases and pile them into the first car while the Commodore and I piled into the second. Off we sped down the unsurfaced coast road. It soon became apparent that all was not well with our car and the driver pulled into the roadside. We had a puncture. The car ahead roared on, leaving a vivid picture which has been etched on my mind ever since, of Leading Steward Leslie's pebble spectacles looking anxiously out of the rear window of the Mercedes as it disappeared over the horizon in a cloud of dust with all our gear on board. I wondered whether we should ever see them again. Colombia was no safer then than it is today.

In the event, after a series of adventures, we made it to Barbados and reached the residence of the High Commissioner, John Bennett, just as the party were having their after dinner coffee on the terrace under the stars with the sea lapping the sand a few yards away. An idyllic Caribbean setting for a strange meeting leading to an even stranger series of events.

In addition to the High Commissioner the party included William Whitlock, the minister responsible for the Caribbean, two senior Foreign Office officials, and, I think, the Deputy British Government Representative, St Lucia, Desmond Kerr, who had responsibility for the Associated States.

It transpired that agreement had been reached with Robert Bradshaw, Premier of St Kitts, for Anguilla to revert to colonial status. The issue was how should this news be broken to the Anguillans, who by now had enjoyed almost two years of independence under their self-styled President, Ronald Webster. At that time we had three frigates on station, *Minerva*, *Rothesay*, and *Rhyll* and knowing the respect with which HM ships were held, the best course seemed to be to pay a formal visit to the island with the minister embarked, throw a cocktail party, organise a cricket match, and at some suitable moment, having cleared the way in advance with Mr Webster and his colleagues, announce the new arrangements to the islanders. This suggestion was rejected by the men from the FCO on the grounds that it would be seen as 'force' which was to be avoided at all costs.

It was finally decided that the minister would be flown in by private light aeroplane with a frigate standing by below the horizon in case of trouble. Accordingly on 11th March, Mr Whitlock accompanied by a Foreign Office official, Mr Tony Lee, the Commissioner designate, and a wireless operator from the Diplomatic Wireless Service flew into Anguilla. The Commodore was committed to an official visit to Guyana and I embarked in HMS *Minerva* with instructions to maintain contact with the wireless operator but remain out of sight below the horizon.

Things seemed to go wrong from the start. There was apparently quite a crowd at the airstrip as 'President' Webster waited to greet the man he thought was to be his guest. On landing however, the minister, on the advice of the Foreign Office one must assume, ignored the illegal reception party and proceeded to issue pamphlets to the bystanders. He then climbed into a waiting taxi with Mr Lee and the man from the FCO and disappeared. This much we learned from the diplomatic wireless operator who found himself stranded and surrounded by an increasingly unpleasant mob who locked him up in a building. At this point the communications failed.

David Armytage, Captain of *Minerva*, and I were becoming increasingly concerned as this drama unfolded. We knew that the minister planned to lunch with a previous Governor of St Kitts, one of the few white men living on the island, and it would appear that this was where he had gone, pursued, no doubt, by an angry mob infuriated by the snubbing of their leader. We were at that point some thirty miles offshore. We decided that the minister's safety was at risk and we should intervene. We rang on full speed and closed the island. *Minerva* was equipped with a Wasp helicopter designed to deliver an anti-submarine torpedo but which could carry three passengers. Our plan was to close the shore to a range of five miles so that the ship was clearly visible and send in the helicopter with three armed men, who would, we hoped, be able to extract the minister and escort him and his two colleagues to the waiting helicopter.

It was a most unsatisfactory plan. There were no rules of engagement, other than the rubric that under no circumstances should force be used. We had no idea whether Webster and his men were armed or what sort of opposition our tiny guard might face. However something had to be done. I signalled our intentions to the Commander in Chief at Northwood and the FCO. This was before the days of satellite communications and we had to rely on the vagaries of high frequency radio waves bouncing off the ionospheric layer for long range communications. There was no question therefore of waiting for a response from Whitehall.

About twenty minutes before we were within range to launch the helicopter, the radio crackled into life. Our diplomatic wireless friend had been reunited with a chastened minister and his party who had been drummed out of the island at gun point. They had landed in some strange island which turned out to be the Dutch island of St Martin. It was a colossal humiliation for a minister of the crown to be treated in this way, and insult was added to injury by his unannounced arrival on foreign territory.

Mr Whitlock returned to London to report to the Prime Minister, Harold Wilson, and I to Bermuda where I was reunited with the Commodore. It was clear that there could be no more messing around. We had to take the island back with such a show of force that hopefully the opposition would collapse and no one would be hurt. It was therefore decided that we should have a company of paratroopers from 2 Para, the battalion on standby, known as 'Spearhead'.

Two frigates would be involved, *Minerva* wearing SNOWI's broad pennant, his title now changed to Commander British Forces Caribbean (CBFC) for the duration of the operation, and HMS *Rothesay* commanded by Commander Dan Bradbury.

So much for the military force, but as we were to take back the island and administer it in the name of Her Majesty we had to be able to provide the full panoply of civil power. We had the Commissioner Designate, Tony Lee fresh from administering the prisons in Aden. We needed a magistrate, and a police force. It was at this point that elements of farce began to creep into what started as a serious operation. A magistrate was found in Guyana and volunteers were sought from among the Metropolitan police. There had recently been a series of anti-Vietnam riots in Grosvenor Square which had been successfully controlled by the Metropolitan police. The hero of the hour was Assistant Commissioner Andrew Way, a man of monumental proportions. He was to take charge of the temporary police force. The Met is a leaky old barrel and it was not long before the tabloids were full of the sight of London bobbies being prepared for a spell of duty in the West

Indies. Any question of surprise was therefore blown.

The Commodore and I flew out of Bermuda to join *Minerva* at Antigua on 13th March. We were offered copies of the local *Times of Bermuda* in the aircraft and I found myself idly scanning the astrology column. My eyes lighted on my sign which is Libra. It predicted that I should be in the eye of a storm over the next few days and my role would be to act as a calming influence and bring order out of chaos. It was a remarkably accurate forecast.

For the first time the two frigates were able to lie alongside in the new deep water harbour at St John's, Antigua. Shortly after we arrived we were joined by Colonel Tony Way, our Army Staff Officer, and Colonel Richard Dawnay, who commanded the landing force under the overall command of Commodore Lucey. Richard had been head boy of my prep school in my first term – a terrifying figure to a new boy. He had not changed much over the years. He exuded military competence and spoke very quickly in a staccato voice. Then suddenly the Captain's day cabin in which we were seated darkened as in an eclipse of the sun, and the vast figure of Assistant Commissioner Andrew Way eased itself into the space, followed by Tony Rushforth from the Foreign Office, who had been present at the Barbados meeting, and Tony Lee. With the arrival of the magistrate, the place was becoming somewhat crowded. We repaired to the wardroom to discuss the plan.

Hard intelligence was practically non-existent but it was known that Webster had a so-called Defence Force which could number up to 250, some of whom might be armed. There were rumours of a gun or two but we discounted them. The element of surprise had been lost in that the islanders knew they were to be invaded at some point, but the actual timing was still secret. We hoped that they would see sense and not attempt to oppose the landing but the West Indians are notoriously volatile and unpredictable. We therefore thought it wise to prepare for an opposed landing.

The landing plan was a simple one. The troops and the police were to fly out to Antigua on 18th March and embark under the cover of darkness in the two ships. After a short overnight passage *Minerva* would anchor in Road Bay, and *Rothesay* in Crown Bay a mile or two to the north east. The landing would take place by boat and helicopter at first light on 19th March. Once ashore, the objective would be to neutralise and disarm the defence force, if there was one, and to secure the airstrip and administration offices in the centre of the island. It would then be a question of handing over to the civil authority as soon as possible.

I asked the Assistant Commissioner what he proposed to do when he met Mr Webster, who would be bound to continue to regard himself as

President.

'I shall ask him for his driving licence,' was the confident reply. 'He won't have one so that will limit his activities.'

A feature of the operation which I had not foreseen was the amount of signal traffic that would be generated. The re-establishment of the Queen's writ in a country which has declared independence for some reason seemed to require page upon page of orders-in-council and other documentation, much of which had to be decrypted off-line. The Foreign Office, never noted for brevity in their telegrams, excelled themselves. The small wireless office staff in *Minerva* struggled manfully with all this paperwork but they nearly cracked when one of the senior officials found his way down there and insisted that he should be allowed to send his mother a telegram telling her that he had arrived safely.

Everything went according to plan. In all, over three hundred paratroops with the London policemen, embarked quietly and on schedule. The two frigates slipped and sailed out into the night. No one knew quite what to expect the following day and there was an air of tension between decks as the paratroops checked their gear and blackened their faces.

As we approached the island, the ships went to action stations; *Rothesay* was detached and each ship proceeded to its allotted anchorage. We expected that the islanders would be keeping a lookout on the cliffs and we were anxious to conceal our presence as long as possible. Silence was the order of the day and everyone spoke in whispers. *Minerva* anchored as quietly as possible; the jumping ladders were lowered over the side followed by the Gemini rubber dinghies and the paratroopers were invited to board them. Standing on the wing of the bridge I was aware of a certain hesitation among the dark groups on the upper deck. Could it be that the paras, used to leaping out of aircraft thousands of feet above the ground, were balking at the unfamiliar task of climbing down the ship's side fully equipped into the as yet invisible rubber dinghies bobbing about below?

Whatever the problem, it was soon overcome and the soldiers embarked. Then I heard a familiar sound; that of an outboard motor refusing to start. On the bridge the countdown to landing had started and it was time the boats were away. Nothing happened.

'What's the delay?' enquired the Commodore.

'The outboard motors won't start,' came the response.

'Were they tested?'

'Yes, sir, at four o'clock this morning.'

Eventually the ship's motor-boat had to be lowered and the small procession with the motor-boat towing the rubber dinghies loaded with paras in full battle kit disappeared into the gloaming rather behind schedule.

Inevitably all this activity against a lightening sky attracted the attention of the watchers on the cliffs who started flashing the headlights of their cars which we assumed was to alert the defence force. Then the headlights could be seen coming down towards the beach. We warned the landing force to stand by for opposition. The tension mounted on the bridge as the minutes ticked by to zero hour. Suddenly there was a flash on the beach, then another, and another. We counted six altogether. Such was the tension that we were all convinced that what we were seeing were shots fired in anger. The Commodore turned to me and said:

'Make a signal. Personal for Prime Minister. The landing has taken place, six shots have been fired'.

I suggested that we obtain a situation report first to see whether there were any casualties. By this time we were beginning to realise that something very strange was happening. What we had assumed was an opposed landing was taking place in total silence. Then a rather surprised voice came up on the radio.

'The landing force is now ashore and so far we have found no opposition apart from the world's press.'

The world's press indeed it was; some twenty or more journalists risked their lives to face a company of paratroopers landing on a beach who seriously thought they might be in for a gun battle. It must be the only time in history that an armed amphibious landing has been opposed solely by newspaper hacks.

As this message was received on the bridge of HMS *Minerva*, the tension audibly collapsed. It was now daylight and a thorough search of the area had confirmed that there was no islander to be seen. Meanwhile with the aid of the helicopter, the landing force were consolidating their beachhead before linking up with their colleagues from *Rothesay* and proceeding inland to secure the airstrip and administration buildings. RAF Hercules transport aircraft flew overhead dropping supplies and equipment.

On board *Minerva* the Commodore held a meeting to decide on the next step. The Foreign Office officials were adamant that no more force should be used than absolutely necessary. I was concerned that while there had been no opposition on the beach, we had no reason yet to assume that we were welcome. Should we not use the initiative which we now held to proceed with the objectives of disarming the defence force, and securing the key areas as had originally been agreed.

I was overruled and the Commodore ordered the landing force not to proceed inland but to remain in the area of the beachhead until further notice. He took the view that because there had been no opposition, it was now a matter for the civil authority to take over the reins, and for the military to keep a low profile.

The next task, therefore, was to land and establish the civil authority. The motor whaler was lowered and the Commissioner designate, Tony Lee, the Foreign Office Adviser, the Assistant Commissioner of Police, the Magistrate, and Desmond Kerr, the Deputy BGR St Lucia, who had been standing with me on the bridge throughout the early morning drama embarked. In addition the boat carried a notice board containing the Order-in-Council announcing Her Majesty's intention of taking the island of Anguilla under direct rule. Formally drafted along the lines of 'I, Elizabeth Regina, Imperatrix etc etc', it seemed somewhat incongruous in the circumstances but apparently its establishment on the island was a necessary part of the process.

The heavily loaded boat thus proceeded towards the beach where someone erected the notice, and the party moved off with a police escort in the direction of the administration buildings. Meanwhile the troops remained where they were.

The media, briefed by their editors to find evidence to support their contention that Britain was using a sledgehammer to crack a nut, and frustrated by the lack of action, were desperate for copy. In one case they tried to set up a scene with a soldier interrogating a youth rather violently, but the soldier would not play. We were not geared to handle the media and had made no special arrangements for press briefings, which was a mistake. We were still operating in the period when the chief qualification for the press liaison officer was an ability to drink journalists under the table. The Northern Ireland crisis has changed all that and brought relations with the press into forefront of all service operations. Nevertheless we should have known better.

About midday a somewhat crestfallen party returned to *Minerva*. The Commissioner designate and his party had been unable to enter the administration offices. A crowd of locals had occupied the grounds of the buildings and refused to allow them access. The London policemen had linked arms and tried to force a way through the crowd but they were no match for the West Indian mob, which does not observe the Marquess of Queensberry's rules and kneed them between the legs. Unprotected in this vital place, the policemen had had to retire hurt. Furthermore someone had removed the notice board which they had erected so carefully on the shore.

The Commodore called an instant meeting at which the Assistant Commissioner of Police reported that he was unable to install the Commissioner designate and needed the help of the army. Colonel Richard Dawnay said that he would be happy to help but it must be understood that if there was trouble his men might have to use their weapons and if they did so they would shoot to kill. This threw the cat among the pigeons.

'You can't do that,' exclaimed the man from the Foreign Office.

Stalemate then ensued. The military remained in their camp at Road Bay, while the civil authorities tried to find a way round the impasse and the policemen stripped off their blues and cooled themselves in the sea. It was becoming increasingly clear that someone was going to have to talk to Ronald Webster. An approach was made, and immediately rebuffed. He was not prepared to negotiate with the Commissioner designate, Tony Lee, or anyone else.

This situation continued for over a week. Meanwhile *Rothesay* and *Minerva* were replaced by *Rhyll*, whose Captain, Commander Geoff Duffy, had been my immediate boss as Training Commander at Dartmouth. The First Lieutenant was another old friend, Christopher Chamberlen.

Finally Ronald Webster agreed to meet Lord Caradon, the British Representative at the United Nations, who arrived on the morning of 28th March, nine days after the initial landing. A crowd of around 400 including Ronald Webster had gathered at the airstrip where he was met by Tony Lee who followed the aircraft down the runway in a police car. After touring the island, he met Webster and they exchanged views but no progress was made. At a subsequent debriefing meeting in HMS *Rhyll* Lord Caradon gave it as his view that there were two options. Either to restore the colonial administration by force or attempt a political settlement which might involve making some concessions. He was clearly in favour of the latter.

The negotiations proceeded for the next few days and finally agreement was reached; the soldiers flew home and life returned to normal. By way of an epilogue to this extraordinary operation, the Commodore received a signal from the Joint Forces Commander-in-Chief, General Sir John Mogg asking for his recommendations for honours and award. He replied that he did not propose to recommend any awards for an operation in which no shot had been fired. Sir John then responded, 'I should have thought this was a situation where an award might be due because no shot was fired.' The army commander, Richard Dawnay, was awarded the OBE but there was nothing for the Commodore. He was not best pleased.

Looking back on the Anguilla affair with the benefit of hindsight, three things struck me.

The first was that it was unnecessary and that our original suggestion of bringing the minister in by ship might have worked and would certainly have been more dignified than the method chosen. Second, I believe that when we had the initiative just after landing we should have proceeded with the plan to secure the administrative buildings. We were right on the other hand not to search the island for weapons. This would have definitely upset people and given the media some good copy. My third and most important point concerns the media for which we were quite unprepared. Today with the experience of Northern Ireland, the Falklands War and other more recent conflagrations behind us, these lessons will have been well learned.

Back in Bermuda I found waiting in my mail an appointment to command HMS *Jaguar*, a diesel frigate. To have a command is every naval officer's dream. *Jaguar* might be an old ship, but she would be mine, and I was thrilled. She was about to embark on a six month refit, which suited me down to the ground as it gave me a chance to get myself up to date in a whole range of areas. It was four years since I last served in a ship and I felt pretty rusty. We said goodbye to Bermuda and flew home on 24th August after a really wonderful two years.

CHAPTER 5

Swallowing the Anchor

(An old naval expression – leaving the Royal Navy)

We had not been home a week when I was sent for to call on my appointing officer, Geoff Duffy, lately Captain of HMS *Rhyll*. He greeted me with the news that HMS *Jaguar* would not be recommissioning and would I therefore pack my bags and proceed at once to Gibraltar where I was to take the old destroyer, HMS *Cavalier* out of reserve and bring her back to UK.

Not only was I deeply disappointed to lose *Jaguar*, I had only just started my five weeks foreign service leave and I had a whole week of meetings planned on Rockingham business coming up. Uncle Michael would be furious if I missed them. I asked Geoff if I could have a little more time to sort out my affairs. He knew perfectly well what I was talking about, but he pretended not to.

'Here I am offering you command of a destroyer for which most people would give their eye teeth, and you ask for more time. Why?'

'Well, as you know, I have only just returned from two years abroad. I am due at least another four weeks leave and I have a number of personal problems to sort out.'

'Such as?' he said pressing me beyond where I wanted to go. I had no alternative but to tell the truth.

'I have this castle and estate in Northamptonshire which requires my attention for about a week then I shall be able to go wherever you want.'

'Are you going to stay in the Navy?'

'I really cannot say at this stage'

'There are so many people out there dying for a command who are going to give their lives to the Navy. It would be most unfair to go off, command *Cavalier*, and then leave. It would take you two years to leave anyhow. I think the best solution would be for me to send you to the Ministry of Defence (MOD) for a spell while you sort yourself out.'

Fool, Saunders, I said to myself. Now you have blown it – and I had. There was no possibility of retraction, and not even a friendly word from the Chief of Staff to the Commander-in-Chief Western Fleet had any effect.

I was sent to the Directorate of Naval Administrative Planning to relieve a splendid man who had clearly been making Geof Duffys life a misery. He went off grinning from ear to ear to command what should have been my ship, and I settled down to serve out my time in the MOD.

I was naturally sickened at losing my ship, but I knew that there was no question of staying on in the Navy. I had promised Michael that I should leave and make Rockingham my home five years after the handover in March 1972. When I made that promise, I did not of course know that I should be promoted and appointed to command, but while it made leaving the Navy harder, it was certainly not grounds for reneging on my promise. Michael himself was unsympathetic.

'Your place is here,' he said, 'not fooling around the ocean in a destroyer.'

Looking back on that difficult time I have often wondered whether I could have played my cards differently; taken my command and left the Navy within the time scale promised. Given a more sympathetic appointing officer the answer is probably 'yes' but I should have had to offer my resignation after a year, halfway through the commission, and even then there might have been problems of timing. I doubt whether I should have been able to hold to the timescale I had promised Michael. Having now been through the process of handing over myself, I know how difficult it is to stay on in what used to be your own house after it has been handed over.

In practice everything worked out very well. After an interesting year in administrative planning during which my responsibilities included planning the logistic support ships of the future, I finally decided to retire two weeks after my 37th birthday by which time with two years seniority in the rank, I should be entitled to a commander's pension. Having made that decision I was then taken out of naval planning and given various jobs more appropriate to my sub specialisation of Signal Communications. These included chairing the committee responsible for drafting the new Allied Naval Signal Book. Later I chaired a rather different committee drafting a set of signal codes for SEATO in Bangkok.

Finally I was sent to the Central Staff as Signals Operations Officer (1) where I was responsible among other things for all communications into and out of the MOD. Since for reasons of state security (in other words to prevent a military coup) the practical business of handling the signals was all carried out by civilians in the defence communications centre, there was little for me to do, and I had plenty of time to swot up on farming.

Working in the MOD was a most interesting experience and I learned much which was of great benefit in my later life. In particular, working at close quarters with the civil service helped me to understand their culture, their language, and appreciate their motivation. Little did I realise when I left, that within four years I should be back in Whitehall working with other civil servants about other matters where my experience in the Ministry of Defence would be put to good use in a very different context.

Thus in October 1971 I retired from the Royal Navy and went with Georgina and our three children to live at Rockingham Castle.

There was a brief overlap during which we 'camped' in a farmhouse in the village. Then one day Michael and Faith gave a big party for all their friends. The next day they left for Dorset and did not return for over a year. They left behind the castle fully furnished apart from two rooms in the private quarters, the walls covered in pictures including many of the more valuable items in their own contemporary art collection, and the shelves full of books. It was difficult to feel they had actually left.

My aunt Faith was a minimalist in that she hated being surrounded by too many possessions and she had a particular dislike for anything Victorian. She threw out all the clutter which filled the passages of our childhood and much of the Victorian furniture would have shared the same fate if uncle Michael had not intercepted it and stashed it away in a secret store. Nevertheless she made the private wing of the castle very comfortable with a heating system which was the envy of all, and relieved the heavy Victorian stone of the Square Tower with brightly coloured wallpapers in the style of a King's Road coffee house. They are now arguably 'heritage' items.

First impressions of living in the castle were dominated by its size, and the distances one had to travel to carry out a comparatively simple chore like changing a light bulb. While I knew the building from childhood, I found myself dreaming of discovering yet more parts of the castle which did not exist. Then, during the daytime, there were people, seemingly everywhere. I could not go to the lavatory from my office without meeting at least two people, many more if the house was open. But the atmosphere was a happy one and while there was anxiety about the changes we might be going to make there, was also a tremendous fund of goodwill.

My uncle had taken pains to ensure that everything on the estate was in very good order. Nearly all the 45 cottages and farmhouses in the village had been modernised in the 1950s. The tenant farms were properly equipped with good modern buildings, and a major programme had recently been completed on the castle roof. There was, however, one rather important problem to be faced. My uncle was a great financial strategist and he possessed an understanding of the complex taxation situation facing landowners which was second to none, but the process of actually making money bored him. In common with many landowners of his generation he had no budgetary system or cash control arrangements. When I asked him how he managed, he replied rather vaguely:

'The money comes and the money goes.'

The balances book told the story month by month as the level of overdraft increased until in the margin appeared the words 'injected £xxxx' and for a short period order was restored. The figures were small by today's inflated standards but they were very significant in the context of 1971. The fact was that the estate was running at a substantial deficit on its trading account which was made up by injections of capital arising mainly from compulsory sales of land to the new town of Corby. This source of funding was now coming to an end and I had no other. There was therefore an urgent need to close this large and increasing gap between income and expenditure as quickly as possible.

My immediate task at Rockingham was now clear. It was to put the estate on a financial footing so that it could generate sufficient income from within its own resources to cover maintenance, repair and development costs. In addition, since my naval pension was but a tiny fraction of my pay, it had also to look after my family.

Looking further ahead I set myself the target of passing on the estate to the next generation in as good a condition as I received it, if not better, but certainly as a going concern. Achievement of the first part of this target became the subject of a political challenge which dominated much of my time at Rockingham but right now the priority was to staunch the haemorrhage of cash.

There were three businesses within the estate, each with its own account: the Farm, the House and Gardens, and the Estate. The first two were run directly by my uncle through his secretary, Bobby Gill, while the Estate was administered by Rob Gardiner, head of the Grantham office of Messrs Strutt and Parker, the agents.

Rob and I had been working together since the original handover. He was an agent of the old school, very much a countryman, but as shrewd as anyone. His role was essentially to deal with tenants and outside authorities and to advise on strategic matters. Together we examined the Estate account to see what could be done to reduce the deficit.

The Estate account was concerned principally with tenanted property, farms and cottages in Rockingham and neighbouring villages. Its income took the form of rents which were strictly controlled, and the tenancies were generally for life. There was therefore little immediate prospect of increasing income but costs could be better controlled. As always the biggest of these was labour. Traditionally agricultural estates paid relatively low wages but in return the employees enjoyed a degree of job security and free housing. The direct labour force had grown over the years and was now much bigger than we could usefully employ. I had been well advised that if staff had to go it were best done quickly during the first six months. There were vacancies locally and all redundant staff found alternative employment. No one had to move out of his house but within three months the estate wage bill was reduced by one third. Any repairs which were not essential were put on hold and a balanced budget which included maintenance of the castle became a realistic proposition.

The house and gardens account covered both the house opening and a so called market garden. The latter was a farce. Traditionally in the days when there were fourteen gardeners before the war, the head gardener, Mr Gildon used to sell produce not required for the house through local retailers. He was a particular expert on orchids and these too would be sold. But these sales were not so much a business as a means of disposing of surplus stock. When we arrived in 1971, Gildon had retired and his replacement had been employed on the strength of his sales abilities with a view to building up the market garden. The garden staff had been reduced to three plus an apprentice. Much of their time seemed to be spent in the kitchen garden and potting shed at the expense of the pleasure gardens. It was a source of constant irritation to see hardly anyone during the day and then at five o'clock when overtime started, so did the mowers.

It soon became clear that the market garden was costing far more than it made so we closed it down and concentrated on improving the pleasure gardens as an important background to the house opening. It was a decision we never regretted but the gardens at Rockingham are not easy to run being at once extensive in that they cover a large area, and intensive in that, for example, there are seven miles of edging. It was some time before we found the people, organisation, and equipment to manage them effectively.

The castle had been open to the public since the 1930s. My grandmother particularly enjoyed showing people round and telling them stories which were most entertaining even if they had little basis in truth. When Uncle Michael came back after the war to live at Rockingham she handed him a small embroidered purse containing £2500 in cash, her takings from admission fees lovingly preserved.

Michael and Faith continued to run the House Showing on a low key, opening on Thursday afternoons from Easter till the end of September and Sundays in August. They installed lavatories in one of the drum towers but there was no tearoom and no gift shop. The only souvenirs on offer were a few black-and-white photographs and a small but remarkably informative guidebook written by a member of the family before the war. It was known as 'The Little Red Book' and written in a fine rather dated prose. The following extract gives the flavour:

> '...the old high road winds down the hill and up ... under the great Norman towers... here a portcullis once blocked the way to the traveller but that has now gone and the way is open to all... The drive sweeps in a great circle up to the ancient nail-studded oak door. After plying the rusty knocker, you arrive in the Entrance Hall...'

Georgina and I came to Rockingham fully committed to building up the opening which we saw as the price for the privilege of living at Rockingham. Of course we needed the cash but there was another factor which weighed strongly with us. While we might 'own' Rockingham in every sense of the word, it was nevertheless part of the national heritage and should be shared with the public albeit on our terms and as our home.

In the months before our arrival we visited a number of people living in historic houses open to the public to learn from their experience. We found that there were two distinct approaches to opening a historic house. It is either run as a fully commercial tourist attraction in which the owner and his family might or might not live, or it is first and foremost a family home which is open to the public. In the former case the operation must observe proper commercial disciplines and be run by professionals. It should be profitable and it should fund all the costs of maintaining the historic house. In the case of the latter the opening operation will be lower key and probably run by the owner and his wife. It is unlikely that the margins will be sufficient to cover the full maintenance costs but they should make a substantial contribution and, most important, enable the opening operation to be classified by the revenue as a business for tax purposes[*].

Anything in between could be a route to financial disaster.

In fact Rockingham made the decision for us. It was neither big enough nor was it in the right area to attract and handle the numbers of visitors that would be required to run the operation on a fully commercial basis. We settled for the hands-on approach with Georgina running the tearooms, the gardens and the shop, while I looked after the publicity and administration, aided and abetted by the estate secretary, Bobby Gill. We calculated that, provided we kept our expenses down, we could cover the cost of

---

[*] Tax was a vital issue and there were a number of different tax rules which applied to agricultural estates. For the cognoscenti this passage refers to the need for open houses to be taxed as businesses under Case 1 of Schedule D. To achieve this with its valuable if not essential offsets, the 'business' had to be capable of showing a profit once every five years. See p.108.

maintaining the gardens and make provision for internal decoration and conservation, leaving the structural side of the castle to be covered as in the past by the estate account where some tax relief was already available under an arrangement known as the one estate election.*

Michael and Faith invited us to spend August bank holiday with them so that we could see at first hand what it was like. It was a salutary experience. Unlike the great Georgian palaces which were virtually designed to be shown off with each room flowing into the next, Rockingham's layout followed no such logical pattern and there was no way for visitors to tour the principal rooms without constantly retracing their footsteps. A free flow through the house was thus virtually impossible and visitors were taken round in parties of thirty to forty.

The visitors entered by the front door which is in the middle of the house facing the forecourt, and assembled in the great hall where they were formed into a party. The front door was then shut and everyone kept waiting outside until the party had left the great hall and the next party could be formed. As a result, even on days with relatively few visitors, queues would form outside the front door of people waiting to get in. Furthermore the visitors saw nothing of the Street and Kitchen area which was full of interest. Clearly something had to be done to improve the route, to allow a free flow, and to show more of the domestic area but – what and how?

Michael used as his office a small room known as the End Room, presumably because it was at the end of the gallery wing. His secretary, Bobby Gill, sat in the estate office across the front courtyard in a building known as Walker's house. They communicated by means of a field telephone.

I was not keen on this arrangement and, within a week of moving in, I had established my office in a bigger and much nicer room looking out onto the forecourt known as the Justice Room, and Bobby Gill with the estate office moved from Walker's house across the forecourt into Uncle Michael's old office.

One day I was sitting at my desk in my new office with my mind in a vacuum, when I realised that we had barely six months to sort out the route problems and organise a tearoom before the next season opened at Easter 1972. While I was pondering these seemingly intractable matters, I noticed

---

* The one estate election was a transitional income tax relief brought in when the old Schedule A property tax was repealed. It allowed the taxpayer to offset the maintenance costs of the mansion house against rental income provided that he included a notional rent for the mansion house in the overall Schedule A income. It has now been repealed.

across the courtyard the outline of an old Norman doorway which had been blocked up at some stage and a window inserted in its place. If this doorway was reopened, visitors could then walk through the old servants' hall, see the street and the old kitchen before arriving at the great hall. The servants' hall could act as a reception area and hopefully resolve the problem of queuing outside.

While this fairly simple modification would enable the building to absorb more visitors and greatly improve the quality of the tour by including the domestic area of the castle, it did not solve the problem of routing visitors logically through the rest of the house without going back on their tracks. A temporary solution was found by taking them out through my office which had its own door opening onto the front court. My office, like Nelson's Great Cabin, had to be cleared for action every time we opened to the public, and if I wanted to sit at my desk I became an exhibit.

We finally solved this problem by opening up another door leading from the billiard room onto the front court. At the same time, the billiard room was converted into a shop, and Salvin's tower which also led out of the billiard room was opened up.

We still had to find somewhere to site the tea room for which the obvious place was Walker's house. The building had been built above an earlier Tudor undercroft as part of the post Civil War reconstruction and housed the family while the main house was being repaired. Subsequently it became the agent's house after whom it was named, and when we arrived, one room was still in use as the estate office while the remaining rooms contained archives, trunks, boxes and furniture piled high to the ceiling.

Access from the forecourt led up a small flight of rather steep steps to a door which opened into a hallway with a fine old carved oak staircase on either side of which were two rooms capable of seating about 36 people in each. Space for a kitchen lay beyond up another flight of steps. Ergonomically it was far from ideal but it was the best we could do. We could have experimented with one room only and gradually dipped our toe in the water but we felt that this was something we had to do properly and after some discussion we made the bold decision to go ahead and convert the principal rooms of the building into a tea room.

The splendid Elizabethan staircase had to be retained at all costs which meant that we should have to keep the two room layout, but the removal of the wall separating the old estate office from the hallway gave us increased space for more tables, the price for which was exposure to the prevailing wind every time the door was opened. It did mean that on cold days with few visitors we could shut the outer room off and concentrate on building a cosy atmosphere in the near room.

With the aid of our architect, Keith Allsop, and with the full co-operation of the local authority and the representative of the Historic Buildings Council for England, these comparatively minor but essential alterations were achieved with the minimum of fuss. How different it is today when attempts to alter a historic feature to update the domestic area or to improve the public facilities can expect to be met with a negative reaction from conservation officials afraid to step out of line, preferring what they see as the 'safe' route of no change..

Much of the charm and interest in the 'lived in' historic house derives from the way it has been modified and adapted to meet the changing requirements of successive owners over time. This process carried out sensitively does not have to destroy what has gone before but if the rigid attitudes of some of those in authority prevail then this dynamic element will be lost and those remaining 'lived in' historic houses, if they are capable of being lived in, will be frozen in aspic.

We replanned the route to allow free flow and purchased a trolley from which to sell souvenirs (a plan to use the old hearse for this purpose was firmly turned down by the PCC). I prepared an advertising programme, and we drafted a press release. Guides were recruited by word of mouth; we waited with bated breath for our first Easter weekend.

Georgina, impressed with the simplicity of the cream teas on offer at Athelhampton in Dorset, decided to adopt the same approach. Fortunately there was a splendid body of village ladies, organised by Mrs Smith, the widow of the estate foreman, Jack Smith, who did teas in the village hall on Sundays in August when the castle was open, the proceeds going to the church. Georgina approached Mrs Smith, to see whether she and her team would move up to the castle where they would of course be paid. Some concern was expressed for the church but Mammon soon took over and the prospect of being paid outweighed any guilty conscience about the church.

Thus began an institution which lasted very nearly 25 years; Mrs Smith in firm charge dispensing scones and cakes and cream from a high table in the kitchen, supported by a team of older stalwarts operating the sink and urns, while the girls from the village and round about served as waitresses. It was a very happy team and certainly the fount of all village gossip. As a postscript, the church, opened with the castle on Sundays and holidays, took more in the safe from voluntary gifts than they ever made with the village hall teas.

While these developments were in train on the house showing front I was wrestling with the farm. The farm was one area of the estate which, properly run on a serious scale, could put the estate on its feet. On the other hand it could sink it altogether – and nearly did! It was a profession about which I knew nothing and in an attempt to correct this I did a series of correspondence courses in farming and agriculture while I was serving my time in the MOD. It may sound a strange way to learn such a practical subject but I found it extremely helpful. It taught me the language that farmers talked and it also taught me the complexity of the business with its many different product lines each one of which depended for success or otherwise on a range of factors some of which could be controlled and some of which could not.

By far the most valuable course I attended was a one week course on management accounting. This was a comparatively new idea which had come over from America and the course was laid on by the Country Landowners Association under the auspices of its far-seeing President, George Howard, who I came to know well in later years. The course was run by farm consultants, Lugg and Gould, and the subject covered budgeting, discounted cash flows, network analysis and a range of other management techniques – some of which on man management sounded distinctly American to my naval trained ears imbued with Nelsonic leadership.

The training in cash control was just what I needed, however. None such appeared to exist at Rockingham. Within weeks of arriving I had put together a budgeting system for each cash account which was then broken down month by month for comparison with actual cash flows. In the pre-computer, pre-word processor age I produced these tables in long hand, and they gained in accuracy of forecasting as time went on. If they did not always enable me to control the cash flow they at least gave me some idea of where the money had gone.

To give a practical edge to my theoretical training I enrolled at the Northamptonshire Agricultural College at Moulton where they very kindly arranged a special course for me covering the areas in which I was interested on a two day per week basis for my first year at Rockingham. Finally to cap this intensive course of instruction, my uncle retained a farm consultant from a local firm of land agents who marched me round the farm once a week. Clive Dixon was just the sort of man I liked; no mucking about; straight to the point, and with a range of farsighted ideas. He taught me an enormous amount and my cocker spaniel, Seumas, and I used to look forward to our long walks together.

The farm itself was a mess. In his generosity my uncle had ensured that the best land on the estate went to the tenants and he was left farming the heavy clay of the park, some of which had unwisely been ploughed up at the end of the war. Knowing little about farming he was at the mercy of any adviser who came along. There was a dairy herd initially of Red Poles which were subsequently changed to Friesians. By the time we arrived they were milking about fifty cows, most of which suffered from brucellosis which, again on advice, my uncle was attempting expensively to breed out. The dairy was in the old Home Farm and the slurry was accumulated in a tank alongside the back drive. Every so often it was pumped out onto the grass opposite where we hoped to park our visitors' cars.

A miscellaneous collection of animals occupied the indifferent grazing in the park. They included the remains of a single suckling herd, some Friesian heifers, a few steers of the small black variety better suited to the Highlands of Scotland and a bunch of mainly three-legged sheep. There did not seem to be any system. When a beast was ready it was taken to the market. Nobody seemed to know how long it had taken to finish or what it had cost.

Finally there were 500 acres of heavy wet arable land which my uncle had endeavoured to drain. Unfortunately the scheme went against the force of gravity, the contractor having failed to recognise that while the surface sloped to the north the impervious layer of blue clay below fell to the south.

1969 had been a disastrous year with unprecedented rainfall and it had been necessary to winch the combine through the field, axle deep in mud. The effect of this on an already weak soil structure need hardly be imagined. Yields were around the 25 cwt level and the fields were riddled with wild oats and black grass.

It was not surprising therefore that the farm was making a considerable contribution to the annual estate deficit. Two things became clear as Clive and I walked the farm together week after week. The farm in its present form could never be a viable prospect. There was not enough land of reasonable quality and the management was not up to the job.

My uncle was well aware that things were not as they should be but he had battled with it long enough not to want to change anything. What he had arranged however with his usual strategic farsightedness was for the son of a tenant farming 900 of the best acres on the estate to take on the tenancy of a 450 acre farm, and for the son-in-law to take on another smaller farm. These arrangements were conditional on the old tenant's farm reverting to the estate when he chose to retire.

In an effort to expedite this we offered the tenant, Charles Champion, a prime site on which to build his retirement bungalow which he accepted and in return agreed to give up the tenancy of his farm after harvest the following year. The Champion family were indeed the backbone of the estate. Charles's brother, Comer, farmed in the vicinity of Rockingham village and Charles's son-in-law, David Holloway had another small farm in Caldecott. The principle adopted by my uncle in the best traditions of landownership was to establish an estate farming tree by which tenants' sons could cut their teeth on a smaller farm before progressing to a larger unit. Sadly this admirable arrangement fell foul of the tax environment of the 1970s which made it very unattractive for landowners to let land. Farm rents were treated as if they were investment income and taxed up to 98 pence in the pound. No relief was available for estate duty and other taxes on capital. Furthermore the tenancies themselves were for the life of the tenant and ultimately for his chosen successor, giving the landowner no chance of repossession.

For these reasons therefore, coupled with the need to increase the income flow, and a strong feeling that if one owns land one should be closely involved with it, I was determined to take in hand as much land as I could and farm it directly. Looking back with the benefit of hindsight I am sure this policy has stood the test of time as far as Rockingham is concerned. With flexible tenancies and a more sympathetic tax regime, the picture today is very different.

Having made this decision, we had to put in place the appropriate management. Clive Dixon knew of a young man who was farming the farm at the Royal Agricultural Society showground, Stoneleigh. He was ambitious, able and with plenty of stretch. He would not get on with everybody but Clive thought that he and I might just hit if off. Clive was right, and for me it was the best thing that ever happened.

Ray Dalton, aged 28, came from farming stock in Lancashire where his grandfather had ruled the roost. Then the M6 was driven through the farm the remains of which were sold, and Ray felt that his birthright had gone. He was fired with ambition to make up for this loss. Highly intelligent and bursting with energy. I found him a most engaging character. As we walked the farm together on that first day of our meeting I was conscious firstly of a sense of relief that I should not have to wrestle with the day to day worries of the farm, because by then I knew I was no farmer. More importantly I was excited and stimulated by Ray's confidence, enthusiasm, and ideas. He was a man I felt I could trust absolutely. Ray must have wondered what he was in for with a retired naval commander and a castle. By the end of that day however I think we both knew that we could work together and what I like to call a partnership was formed between us which by and large, through thick and thin, served Rockingham pretty well for the next 27 years.

My all too brief introduction to farming was soon put to the test when I found myself in charge during the interregnum of three months between the departure of the old farm manager and Ray's arrival. A phone call from Ray a few days after his appointment announced that the next morning 350 sheep were arriving from the borders. Where were they to go? Our fencing might be good enough for the couple of dozen old ewes but would it hold these active young expensive Scottish half-breeds? I spent the next fortnight counting these wretched sheep every morning. Then they developed some disease of the feet and had to be driven down to the farmyard to be put through the dip. My spaniel might be of some use in the shooting field but as a sheep dog he was a disaster. Somehow, the sheep and I survived more or less intact.

I tried my hand at ploughing and made the beginner's mistake of ploughing at right angles to the road so that everyone could observe the ever-increasing curves of my furrows. Then we were into the harvest and I found myself on a combine harvester. In those days there was no such thing as an air-conditioned cab with radio, cigar lighter and computerised hydraulic controls – just a face mask, loads of dust and a clutch which kicked like a mule. It was all good experience but I was mighty glad when Ray eventually arrived and took over.

With the farm now poised to go forward, a repairs freeze and revised budget on the estate, coupled with the preparations we had made for the house showing, I hoped we were as ready as we ever would be to move towards paying our way.

Our first Easter Sunday opening was chaotic. We had received some publicity in the local and national press, including a fine photograph spread in the *Daily Telegraph* of the whole family standing below the drum towers, but we were totally unprepared for the invasion that was about to be unleashed upon us.

The opening hours of the castle were from 2pm to 6pm and the tickets were sold by Mr Willis the caretaker who sat at the gate in the back of the estate van. The cars started piling up from 12.30 and by opening time the queue extended well beyond the gate into the main road. Clearly we were going to have to reorganise the access arrangements. Mr Willis did his best and the cars began to pour into the grounds. The queue was transferred to the public entrance and then into the house itself. The visitors squeezed their way down the back passage but, once in the great hall where there was plenty of room to roam, they were reluctant to leave their place in the queue and they went through the house like toothpaste out of a tube.

On the Sunday we had 1,200 visitors and on the Monday 1,800. It was to set an almost unbeatable record for a weekend unsupported by any other attraction in the grounds. As Monday came to a close and the last visitor left, I walked through the house in the quiet of the evening and apologised to it for subjecting it to such pressure. I felt it smile reassuringly. 'Do not worry. I love people,' it seemed to say.

Such is the magic quality of Rockingham that even in that press of people, few visitors fail to be moved by its friendly atmosphere and human dimension.

One visitor that first weekend was less impressed. I was sent for by one of the guides who was having difficulty answering a visitor's questions. I found a small man with a moustache in a raincoat with the collar turned up. He wanted to know the identity of a crest on an iron-bound chest in the hall. I had to confess that I had no idea.

'You would get a great deal more from this house if you knew more about it,' came the uncompromising response. He looked like Sexton Blake, the detective in *Beano*. He was in fact Enoch Powell.

During the course of the first year we tried a number of different activities to see what suited us best. We held concerts and a fashion show in the long gallery. The long gallery, in spite of its rather shabby decoration, was a popular venue but the floor was weak and, while the space could take a comfortable 180 people or more, if the numbers exceeded 90, our architect insisted that the floor be supported by jacks in the two rooms underneath. It was thus not something we did every week and the profit margin after advertising was not encouraging.

The great hall was much easier to organise and equally atmospheric in a different way to the long gallery, but it could only take a hundred people theatre style. Acoustically it was excellent, and we had some really wonderful concerts with leading quartets sponsored by Corby Borough Council Arts Festival in the days when local authorities had money to spare for that sort of thing.

We looked at the possibility of holding private parties in the house. This was a potentially fruitful area of development but I was not comfortable with the idea of another person acting as host to his or her guests in my house. There was no serious logic behind this and I have no doubt I turned down a lot of good business, but I saw it as a point of principle which I maintained throughout my time at Rockingham.

I had no such problems with parties hosted by an institution or charitable body. They were more impersonal and we tried a number of these. The most notable was a soiree organised by the local British Medical Association to entertain some Danish guests. They were to have supper in the great hall and panel room and there was to be musical entertainment in the long gallery. Assuming that this was to be background music and in order to avoid jacking up the floor I suggested that we went without chairs and if people wanted to sit down they could sit on the floor.

It turned out that the music was far from background. We were given a superb performance of baroque music by an ensemble of the English Sinfonia orchestra led by Neville Dilkes, the erstwhile head of music at Corby Grammar School. The unexpected upshot of this highly successful evening was that Neville and I became great friends and, a few years later, when the English Sinfonia became an independent players orchestra, he asked me to become one of the non-playing directors. Thus began a highly enjoyable association with the orchestra which lasted over twenty years.

We were often asked how we could put up with having the public visiting our home. The fact was that we needed the money and the tax treatment that came with running the business of opening. Equally, we should not have been happy to live in a building so obviously part of the national heritage without sharing it in some way with the public. There is no doubt it was hard work and a major commitment in the summer season, particularly at bank holiday weekends, when we felt we had to be present. Looking back on it, while glad to be no longer involved, the house opening was an experience at once rewarding and on the whole enjoyable. Of course there were moments of worry, frustration, disappointment and hurt but they were well outweighed by the amount of pleasure so many people clearly experienced in their visits to Rockingham.

We regarded the visitors as our guests and expected them to behave likewise. If they appeared on a day when we were not open, I would descend on them with the ominous welcome 'Can I help you?' which was less an offer of actual assistance than the preliminary to a firm but polite request to leave the premises.

On one memorable occasion I was sitting in my office overlooking the forecourt when I observed six or seven men in dog collars walking up though the towers. It was a Monday morning and there was no question of the castle being open. This did not apparently concern these men of God who strode without hesitation up to the front door, opened it, and walked in. They did not even ring the bell.

I found them in the great hall. 'Good morning gentlemen, can I help you?'

'Er, no thank you,' said one of them. 'We are just looking round.'

'I thought it was a precondition of your profession that you should be able to read. You have just passed by no less than three notices saying that this is a private house and not open to the public today. Would you please now leave and come back when we are open. '

Somewhat put out and without any apology, they left.

Without question our least successful function was the Territorial Ball. The organisers really went to town and planned a party worthy of the castle. There was to be dancing in the panel room with a buffet in the great hall and sitting out on the stairs and in the long gallery. The place looked marvellous and the free champagne flowed. In pride of place at the centre of the buffet was an enormous boar's head made out of aspic.

The principal problem was that there were far too many people for the space available. This coupled with the abundant supply of champagne and an over ambitious buffet all contributed to what was for me a disastrous evening over which I had soon lost control. At an early stage the boar's head collapsed in the heat and became a pool of fatty liquid on the stone floor of the hall, the marks of which remain today. Then a gentleman in red military evening dress lurched up to me with a plate of bacon and eggs which he proceeded to pour all over the 16th century Dutch marquetry table by which we were standing. 'How do you like your house being used for this sort of thing?' he slurped.

I fled to the long gallery where things were quieter and found Earl Spencer, Princess Diana's grandfather, sitting on a sofa. I sat with him as he regaled me with stories about his visits to the Duke of Bedford's home, Woburn Abbey, where he amused himself by guessing who had paid for their dinner with a real duke and a real earl.

With the exception of our own family party to celebrate our silver wedding, James's twenty first, and Fiona's eighteenth birthday, we never had another ball at Rockingham.

After a year of experimenting we came to the conclusion that what we did best was opening the house to the public on two to three days per week with special parties and schools on non-open days, and we concentrated on this. Georgina's brother-in-law, Charles Forgan, who had some time on his hands, helped us with our public relations and also with the organisation of the tearoom kitchens. We built a shop in what used to be the billiard room; opened up Salvin's tower, and created a new exit from the shop to the forecourt in another old blocked-up doorway which allowed visitors to leave the castle without passing through my office. This pattern of opening supplemented with the odd conference or craft fair in the grounds served us well over the years peaking in 1985 with our major television series *By the Sword Divided* which boosted visitors by 60% – of which more later..

Financially, moving from a very low base, the returns began to mount. We adopted a policy of putting the price up a little every year. There was no prize to be gained from holding it for a year or two and then giving it a great hike. Right from the start we established with the Inland Revenue that we were running a serious business and were taxed accordingly, enabling us to offset the maintenance costs of the house after deducting a percentage for private use against income from other sources such as the farm.

Within the space of a year or two the surplus in the house and gardens account was sufficient to carry the costs of running the gardens and to enable us to set aside an annual sum for conservation and internal decoration. It was never going to be sufficient to cover the costs of maintaining and heating the castle, which were borne by the estate account where they could be relieved against rental income under an important and complex tax relief, now repealed, known as the one estate election. These reliefs against tax on income were vital to us if we were going to be able to keep Rockingham in good repair without drawing on capital, but of course we had to generate the income.*

The business to which we looked for income flow was the farm. Here Ray Dalton was achieving marvels. He gathered round him a team of young men and set about the desperately needed task of cleaning up the fields, and restoring the soil structure which in many cases had never recovered from being ploughed too deep during the war.

Within a year, as my uncle had planned, the estate's largest tenant, Charles Champion, retired, and his 900 acre farm at Wilbarston came in hand with some of the best land on the estate, bringing our total arable land to 1100 acres. For the first time, we had the basis of a really viable farming unit. We calculated that the equipment and manpower needed to farm this additional acreage would give us the capacity to farm 2,000 acres and the search was on to find more land.

At this time the estate had a number of outlying cottages and farmhouses in the surrounding villages, mostly in a poor state of repair. Rents were minimal and taxed at 98 pence in the pound by the then Labour government. There seemed to be no future in doing up property to rent, even if the money was available which it was not. I decided therefore that the best policy was to sell off the outlying cottages when they became available and roll the proceeds into buying more land.

By this means we were able to buy 200 acres of excellent land in the valley at Wilbarston which marched with our own. Then two further tenants retired bringing our total land in hand well in excess of our original target of 2,000 acres. All that was now required was the capital to farm it.

As I struggled with my budgets and cashflows I became aware that I was going to need to borrow a very substantial amount of money, in the order of £100,000, which in 1973 was a huge sum. I had never had an overdraft before and tended to regard the idea as a slippery slope to the debtor's court. I was not to know it at the time but we were about to experience a surge in grain prices, and I spent a number of sleepless nights wondering if I had done my sums correctly.

The bank manager said he could not deal with an overdraft of that level and arranged for me to have an interview with Regional Head Office in Peterborough. With some apprehension, clutching my cash flows, I arrived in the office and was shown upstairs to a reception room where I was greeted by the Regional Director, a senior man in the banking world whom

---

* Notes on pp77 and 108

I had met socially from time to time, and we sat down to an excellent lunch. The conversation ranged from salmon fishing to shooting and continued in this vein till coffee was served. Finally in desperation I said:

'This is a lovely lunch and I am thoroughly enjoying it but I thought I had come here to discuss my request for an overdraft.'

'Oh that, well there's no problem there.'

'But £100,000 is an awful lot of money. Have I done my sums right? Don't you want to see my business plan? '

'Oh no. Your credit is good.'

I was amazed and rather disappointed that my carefully worked out figures were not to be subjected to careful scrutiny. I had hoped at least for an endorsement of my plan but clearly all the bank was interested in was my credit rating. Another lesson learned.

Those early years were difficult and at times worrying as we clawed our way back into the black. There were moments when I looked into the abyss and wondered whether we should survive. These moments generally occurred at about three in the morning and I would get up, go down to the office and work through the budgets once more to see if I could find an expense to be cut out, or some extra money to be made. I sometimes wondered what people thought when they drove up the village street and past the great castle standing solidly on its hilltop. Could they possibly imagine how precariously poised it was financially?

After two years in the saddle, things began to ease up. Russia's clandestine purchase of almost the entire stock of American wheat sent the prices soaring to unknown levels. At last we could afford to pay a decent wage and young men in the village who had deserted the land for the factory floor came back into farming. For the first time in their lives, some village people bought a new car.

But there were other clouds on the horizon, the implications of which were far more dire for the future of the estate than a couple of years in the red.

CHAPTER 6

The Darkening Clouds

As the excitement and euphoria of that spring morning in 1967 when Michael offered me Rockingham became a reality, two thoughts lingered at the back of my mind. They were not second thoughts and I never doubted the decision I took that morning; they were more a realisation that the path I had chosen was not as secure as it might have at first appeared. I had achieved a modest start in my chosen profession, the Royal Navy; my career pattern was beginning to develop in an interesting way, and I was gaining confidence all the time. While nothing in service life is certain, it was going to be a wrench to put all this aside for the possibly even greater uncertainty of life at Rockingham.

Then there was Rockingham itself. Was it a viable proposition? While the castle stood on its hill, solid and strong, the economics were less clear and depended on agriculture, a subject about which I knew little and, I have to say, thought I liked less.

Possibly more important though was the political uncertainty surrounding the future of great houses and privately owned estates. While, through a combination of luck and superhuman effort, many had survived the war more or less intact, the traditional 'privileged' lifestyle that these large concentrations of private wealth represented in the public mind, was now out of date and the houses themselves were in danger of being swept away on a tide of social reform – unless they could prove their relevance to post-war contemporary society.

The more I thought these thoughts, however, the more I began to see them as an exciting challenge which would make the whole project of taking on Rockingham really worth while. I felt sure that Rockingham had an important role to play in contemporary society, both economically and culturally, and it would be for me to demonstrate this. There were of course moments when, having foregone my command as a newly promoted young commander, I found myself sidelined into what I thought was a backwater in the Ministry of Defence, where all I had to do was twiddle my thumbs and study the alimentary canal of a pig, that I wondered whether I had done the right thing. These moments of depression did not last and when the darkness of that particular period emerged into light, the challenge that lay ahead proved more fulfilling than I had ever imagined,

In 1973, after two years in the saddle, with the economics of the estate more or less under control, and the farm poised on a programme of expansion in the capable hands of Ray Dalton, my concerns about the political situation began to be put to the test. At the Labour Party Conference that autumn, Denis Healey, the Shadow Chancellor, made his famous speech in which he referred to 'Howls of anguish from... the rich....'[*] which became traduced into 'squeezing the rich until the pips squeak'. It was all good rabble rousing stuff, but underlying it was a determination on the part of the Labour party when it achieved power to use the tax system to redress the inequalities of wealth in society. While it may have been justified socially such a policy must inevitably spell problems for owners of historic houses whose wealth was locked up in illiquid assets devouring income rather than producing it.

These forebodings were confirmed when Labour won the snap election in February 1974 with a tiny majority, and proceeded to implement a manifesto committed to a redistribution of wealth. This was to be achieved in particular by two new capital taxes: an annual tax on wealth, and a tax on gifts and bequests. Proposals for the wealth tax were published in a Green Paper which was referred to a Select Committee and the principles of the capital transfer tax (short title CTT) were set out in the Finance Act 1974.

My immediate concern was with the wealth tax. I calculated that on the basis of the figures quoted in the Green Paper, a wealth tax on Rockingham could cost in the region of £75,000 per year – a staggering sum in those days. Where on earth would we find it? I recalled my uncle's wise advice: if pressed, let the house go but hold onto the land at all costs. Certainly, to sell off the land on which the house depended for its maintenance would have been madness.

This annual sum would therefore have to be met from the sales of works of art in the first instance, and ultimately from the sale of the house. On this basis I calculated that if the family was to continue in the castle, we could probably hold on for about five years by which time 450 years of Rockingham heritage would effectively have been dispersed. If the estate

---

[*] *The Time of My Life* by Denis Healey, Penguin Books 1989

managed to survive this slow strangulation by the wealth tax then capital transfer tax would deliver the *coup de grâce* by stripping it of its capital at least once every generation.

It was a gloomy prospect; but I had not given up my command and a promising career in the Navy for Rockingham just to give it to Denis Healey. This 'pip' was going to squeak, and loudly. I simply could not believe that this wholesale destruction of the heritage was what the government intended and I felt sure that if I could only communicate the problem to those in authority a compromise could be reached which would enable the heritage to remain intact for the benefit of the nation without breaching the fundamental principles of redistribution.

While I might be the legal and titular owner of Rockingham Castle, I regarded myself as no more than a steward for my generation, obliged to hand the castle and its estate on to my successor in as good a condition if not better than I received it. Substituting the national interest for this personal one held no problems for me, providing the conditions for doing so were reasonable.

I could envisage the basis of a deal. Historic houses and their estates, like Rockingham, were making an increasingly important contribution nationally as tourist attractions, and locally as sources of employment. They therefore had an economic value in addition to the unique cultural heritage which they represented. It was already clear from the experience of the National Trust and those few properties which were already in public ownership that historic houses were extremely expensive to maintain. If the majority of the nation's stock of historic houses which remain in private ownership were to be abandoned, the cost to the exchequer would be phenomenal and many historic properties would be lost. It must make better financial sense to leave them in private ownership. If, as a condition of exemption from capital taxes, the owner undertook to maintain his historic property and open it to the public then the nation would have a bargain.

It would be necessary to provide for the exemption of all the component parts which constitute the heritage entity – the historic house, the contents, the park and the gardens, together with an area of land surrounding the property required for its protection and, most important, a fund, which could be land or any income-producing asset to provide for its maintenance. Exemption would of course be conditional on observance of the undertakings. Failure to do so would necessitate payment of the tax foregone.

There was a precedent for this under estate duty, but the exemption only applied to outstanding works of art and not the buildings in which they were held. My proposal would go much further and if accepted in principle and established in law would secure the future of Britain's heritage in private hands for the foreseeable future.

It was all very well to have a solution. The question was how it was to be achieved. Three things had to happen: first people generally and ministers in particular needed to be made aware of the problem facing the heritage; then they had to be convinced of its value; and finally, they must be satisfied that continued private ownership offered the best way of achieving this need.

I soon found that I was not alone in recognising the threats to Britain's heritage of historic houses arising from the government's redistributive fiscal policy. Indeed the future for historic houses was pretty bleak even without the taxation overkill they were now facing and several initiatives were underway before the elections of 1974.

A prime mover in alerting everyone to the situation was Sir Alexander Glen, Chairman of the British Tourist Authority (BTA). Seeking to promote Britain abroad, Sandy Glen had identified three areas where Britain's attractions were unique – Harley Street, the bloodstock industry and historic houses. In 1966 the BTA formed a committee, known as the Historic Houses Committee, under Sir Hugh Wontner, a member of the BTA Board, to look into the situation. The committee soon realised that taxation in its many forms constituted the greatest threat to the survival of Britain's historic houses, most of which were still privately owned and a Taxation sub-committee was created under the chairmanship of George Howard to focus on this particular area.

Working closely with the Country Landowners Association, the Taxation sub-committee made representations to the Conservative government and went to see John Nott, then a junior minister at the Treasury. They were seeking exemption of historic buildings from estate duty and an amelioration of the rules for treating historic properties for income tax. The Minister responded courteously but without enthusiasm and nothing happened. The proposed new clauses to the Finance Bill were not called.

The Historic Houses Committee felt it was important for owners to meet each other and in 1971 they staged an event entitled 'The Standing Conference for Historic Houses' which met for the first time in November under the chairmanship of the Duke of Grafton. It was a grand affair held in the Mansion House. We drank champagne and ate smoked salmon sandwiches. People like Lord Kennet (better known then as the writer Wayland Young) and Tom Driberg spoke encouragingly about the heritage and the Duchess of Bedford informed us that she had met an American who never washed his hands again after shaking hers. It was all good fun but not very productive. By the time of the second Conference in 1972, however, it was becoming clear that some more formal arrangement for representing owners' interests was required and a working party was set up to examine the situation..

The working party recommended the formation of an association of owners of historic houses and at the third annual meeting of the Standing Conference in November 1973 Lord Montagu of Beaulieu proposed the formation of the Historic Houses Association with the Duke of Grafton as President, and an executive committee elected from the floor. Lord Montagu became Chairman and George Howard, Vice Chairman.[*]

Under these two able but very different men the HHA rapidly took shape. Edward Montagu had enormous energy, a fertile mind, and a tremendous flair for publicity – attributes well matched by George Howard's thoughtful wisdom and political acumen, sharpened by the experience gained as a former President of the Country Landowner's Association. David Coleman was seconded from the BTA as its first Secretary General and an office was found in the BTA building at 64 St James's Street. It was not a moment too soon. Formed in the first instance as a sort of trade association enabling owners to meet and share their experiences, the HHA almost immediately found itself thrown into a high profile political role in defence of the private owner. It was then, and would remain, a very small organisation heavily dependent on its officers rather than officials and I believe that this has been a great source of strength.

Among its first initiatives was to launch a petition seeking support for legislation to enable historic houses to survive. Cleverly worded so that it did not refer specifically to the private owner but rather to the historic property which was threatened, the petition was placed in members' houses throughout the 1975 season and attracted 1,116,253 signatures. One of the largest petitions on record it was presented to Parliament by Mr Ted Graham, Labour MP for Enfield and Chairman of the All Party Heritage Group in December 1975.

The various amenity societies were also very concerned at the threat to the heritage implicit in the government's fiscal policy. They formed a joint committee under the chairmanship of the Duke of Grafton which in turn spawned a tax committee under the chairmanship of the late Jeremy Benson. The hour produced the man; Jeremy was well known as a keen conservation architect, Vice President of the Georgian Society, and a pillar of the Society for the Protection of Ancient Buildings. His quick mind soon grasped the dire situation facing owners of historic houses, and the effect this would have on the heritage. He devoted the next decade of his life to becoming an expert in tax legislation, and a most determined and effective lobbyist for the heritage, deeply respected by politician and official alike.

---

[*]   These titles were soon changed to Patron, President and Deputy President respectively.

The plight of Britain's historic houses was first recognised officially by the Attlee Government after the war, and Hugh Dalton, the Chancellor of the Exchequer, set up a committee under Sir Ernest Gowers to look into the matter. The Gowers Report[*], beautifully written by the author of 'Plain Words', was a seminal work and formed the basis of conservation policy in Britain for the next twenty-five years. Its recommendations led to the creation of the Historic Buildings Councils of England, Wales and Scotland, with powers to recommend grant aid to assist in the repair of outstanding houses or groups of houses and their setting including property in private ownership. Among the recommendations not taken up, however, was one which recognised that not only was the conservation of the historic house important but that it could not be achieved without a fund dedicated to its maintenance[**]. This prescient point was to be at the centre of our subsequent efforts to achieve a package of tax relief to enable heritage property to pass from one generation to the next without being decimated by tax.

Stimulated by the happy coincidence of the twenty-fifth anniversary of the Gowers Report with the designation of 1975 as European Architectural Heritage Year, the Historic Houses Committee of the BTA commissioned a study (the cost of which was met by the owners themselves) by the late John Cornforth, one time architectural editor of *Country Life,* to examine the situation, look at what had happened over the past twenty-five years, and to make proposals as to what should be done to ensure the survival of historic houses in the future.[†] The timing of this publication was inspired. In his summary John Cornforth writes, 'The study was already in an advanced state at the time of the 1974 Finance Bill (which introduced Capital Transfer Tax (CTT)) and because the Green Paper (on A Wealth Tax) was not available, its scope was not significantly influenced by the proposed financial measures in the bill. On the other hand it is a statement about a situation that was already seen to be deteriorating in 1972 and 1973 and now appears to be developing into a major crisis that threatens not only our architectural and aesthetic heritage but makes nonsense of conservation policy.'

---

[*] Report of the Treasury Committee on Houses of Outstanding Historic or Architectural interest under Sir Ernest Gowers 1955.

[**] There will be a number of references to 'maintenance fund' as a crucial element in the heritage package. The concept was that it should comprise income yielding assets of which the income would be taxed at the settlor's rate and spent exclusively on the heritage property.

[†] *Country Houses in Britain: Can they Survive?* John Cornforth. Published for the BTA by *Country Life* 1974

A conversation between John Cornforth and Sir Roy Strong, Director of the Victoria and Albert Museum, led to a major exhibition entitled 'The Destruction of The Country House'. This was an amazing if depressing show. The visitor entered to the roar of falling masonry and was confronted with rows of houses, and associated artefacts, that had disappeared or been allowed to decay. In an introduction to the excellent book[*] which accompanied the exhibition, Roy Strong, addressing the dilemma of the country house, wrote, 'The country house as a work of art in its unity of building, contents, garden, and landscape can only survive with incentives to the owner from the Government. The wretchedness lies in the difficulty of any government giving tax concessions to what most regard as a very privileged section of the community. Death duties and capital gains tax, let alone the threatened forms of wealth and inheritance taxes, spell the final ruin of these most precious works of art. Created lovingly over the centuries, they will be slowly eroded to meet the demands of the Exchequer.'

Roy Strong may have taken a somewhat pessimistic view, but he had hit the nail on the head and there was a very real dilemma which had to be resolved if disaster was not to ensue. Owners of historic houses had to show convincingly that the heritage in their hands was important, both culturally and economically. Furthermore while they might appear wealthy and privileged, this was often not the case, especially where income was concerned, and such wealth as they possessed was consumed in maintaining the building.

The exhibition attracted a lot of attention and gave rise to a number of newspaper articles and television programmes. A leading light in the preparation of the exhibition and its subsequent promotion was the architectural historian, Marcus Binney, a man of great energy, enthusiasm and commitment to historic buildings. He founded the conservation pressure group, SAVE Britain's Heritage and with the capable help of Sophie Andreae as secretary, campaigned relentlessly for the retention and rehabilitation of historic buildings. With a gift for eye catching headlines, they ran a highly successful campaign. No one in the heritage world was immune from SAVE's thunder; owners who had let their property fall into disrepair, local authorities who had failed to exercise their powers under the listed building controls, ministers, Whitehall officials – all felt the scourge. SAVE, with no financial interest in the heritage, could say and do things that we could not in the HHA. They were in effect the shock troops of the heritage campaign,

---

[*] *The Destruction of the Country House* by Roy Strong and others, Thames and Hudson, London 1975

while the HHA and the amenity societies were the infantry.

Another articulate supporter was Simon Jenkins who used his increasingly high profile position as columnist and ultimately Editor of *The Times* to keep heritage issues in the forefront. In due course he became even more deeply involved as Deputy Chairman of the yet to be formed Historic Buildings and Monuments Commission, better known as English Heritage.

The autumn of 1974 saw the emergence of what was in effect the first draft of capital transfer tax in the Finance Bill 1975, and at the same time the select committee on a wealth tax was appointed under the chairmanship of Douglas Jay. Among its members was a Conservative MP Robert Cooke. Robin Cooke, as he was known, was the owner of Athelhampton Hall, and a very active supporter of the cause of private ownership of the heritage. It was a relief to see him appointed chairman of the sub committee set up to look in more detail at the implications of a wealth tax on the heritage.

John Cornforth came to see us in the summer of 1974 in the course of researching his book. In his quiet scholarly way John has written more than most about the heritage. His work was always carefully researched and if, at times, a little dry, it carried great authority and influence. I produced some figures on our costings for him and this inspired me to write a paper 'Is there a Future for the Privately Owned Estate' which I circulated to the various heritage committees, my MP, Sir Geoffrey de Freitas, and anyone else I could think of. The upshot of this was that Rockingham was selected by the BBC to take part in a TV programme entitled 'The Suffering Rich' to be shown under the auspices of the current affairs programme, Midweek.

I received a message that the producer, Clive Syddall, was coming to reconnoitre the site in early November. I was keen to demonstrate that Rockingham was a working estate and I made it my business to be found on a tractor ploughing in the valley. The poor chap had to struggle across two fields of heavy wet old Northamptonshire clay to meet me. How impressed he was by this, I never found out, but he was very friendly and assured me that it was not his intention to send me up. He was as good as his word and the programme was quite kind about Rockingham, but there were moments when we could have slipped if I had not been on my guard. For instance there was an episode when I was to be found doing something naturally, and they suggested that I might like to be filmed shooting a pheasant. While I do not think this was meant to be a trap, it could have given viewers quite the wrong impression and complicated the real issues we were discussing. I returned to my tractor.

However well disposed the producer and his team may feel towards the subject (and it is more generally the reverse) they tend to hear the Editor's voice ringing in their ears with preconceived ideas of the line they should take and what they expect to find and film. The programme, which was the first of a number in which we took part, focussed on the general effect of a wealth tax on the 'rich' rather than the heritage in particular but apart from a rather emotional scene involving father and son in the fireplace of the great hall the Rockingham part went quite well.

The programme did however underline for me the more general problem of establishing the validity of the heritage case in the eyes of the media. Even if they were broadly sympathetic, it was difficult to persuade them to take the historic houses issue seriously, and not to treat it as a faintly ridiculous item to be introduced by Noel Coward's ditty, 'The Stately Homes of England'.

Later in December 1974 with the Historic Houses Association now a year old, I felt it was time we became more organised on the local front. With the aid of the East Midlands Tourist Board and its director, Peter Chester, we convened a meeting of owners and administrators at Rockingham. Our guest of honour was Lord Sandford who had been Minister for the Environment with responsibility for the heritage under Edward Heath. An ex naval communicator who had taken holy orders, John Sandford was a great friend to the heritage, though he had no historic house himself. He later gave his name and time to administering the Sandford Award for historic properties achieving a standard of excellence in the provision of educational facilities. He impressed us all by arriving at the meeting with a copy of the Finance Bill 1975 hot off the press.

It was the first Bill I had seen, and the first time I had to wrestle with the language of the parliamentary draftsman. I managed to discover however that not only was the conditional exemption for works of art which applied under estate duty continued under CTT, but it was to be extended to outstanding land, buildings, and land and objects associated with such buildings. This was a huge step forward as it recognised the importance of historic buildings, their contents and environment as an entity to be protected from CTT, subject to proper maintenance and reasonable public access. There was however no mention of any fund for maintenance, without which exemption of the historic building alone would be virtually meaningless, and of course there was still the Wealth Tax monster hovering in the wings. It was nevertheless encouraging.

Also attending the Rockingham meeting was Sir Francis Dashwood, who had been charged by Edward Montagu with responsibility for recruiting new members to the HHA. He was in the process of setting up a regional organisation and he asked me if I would chair the East Midlands. I was very happy to do so and this meeting therefore became the inaugural meeting for the East Midlands Region of the HHA.

Shortly after this I received a note from Richard Miller, who had succeeded David Coleman as Secretary General of the HHA, asking me to lunch in January which resulted in an invitation to be co-opted onto the Executive Committee of the HHA. For some time I had been looking for an opportunity to contribute to the 'battle' at national level and here it was. I accepted with pleasure and attended my first meeting the following week, thus beginning a fifteen year relationship with the Association that brought me into contact with many people, not just in UK, but in Europe and the USA, and provided me with some of the most interesting years of my life.

As the national campaign to save the heritage gathered headway, I had a feeling that we should and could be doing more at local level to inform our political representatives about the problems facing the heritage. In the Navy, when we wanted to put a message across to politicians or other VIPs, we would invite them to come for a day at sea. Known as 'Exercise SHOPWINDOW', it was a means of showing off the ship and her capabilities – albeit in an artificial situation – but it seldom failed to impress our visitors. There was one splendid occasion in the Far East when I was serving in the *London* and we took the Prime Minister of Malaysia, The Tunku Abdul Rahman, and his cabinet to sea for a day's SHOPWINDOW. There was to be a demonstration of an anti-submarine operation. Two frigates hunted the submarine down while the Tunku watched it all in the Operations Room, then when it came to the kill he was invited up to the bridge to witness the live firing of the mortars from the participating frigate which was by that time steaming alongside us. 'Standby Mortars' came the cry over the radio. 'Fire.' There was a loud bang but instead of three splashes ahead of the frigate, there were two on either bow and a mortar bomb sticking out of the forecastle! Somebody had used light exercise charges instead of live ones to fire the live bombs. Luckily they did not go off and the Tunku thought it all marvellous.

Perhaps we could do something similar but without the pyrotechnics for MPs at Rockingham. I discussed the idea with Sir Geoffrey de Freitas, our local Labour MP, who was strongly in favour and offered his support. A junior minister under Attlee, he had been Governor and High Commissioner in Kenya, and subsequently President of the Council of Europe. An enthusiastic European, he was not very happy in the contemporary Labour Party and his days of power were now over but he still carried weight in the smoking room and his support was invaluable in establishing my *bona fides* with Labour colleagues who were deeply suspicious of any invitation from a landowner.

Lesson one in the art of lobbying MPs, as advised by Geoffrey, was that if you want them to come out of London it has to be either a Friday or Monday. We chose Friday 16th May and invited every MP in the East Midland Region of which there were about sixty. We had a remarkable response and thirty accepted. As this was something we had never done before, we decided to have a dress rehearsal the previous Friday and invite our local Corby District Council to come and test the course. It proved more fruitful than I could possibly have imagined.

Corby District Council was a bastion of what today would be called 'old' Labour. Passionately concerned with the welfare of Corby and its people, they also had a strong sense of their heritage, and Rockingham was very much part of that. The town itself was created by Stewarts and Lloyds, the steel firm, when they moved their workforce down from the Clyde to the ore fields of Northamptonshire in the 1930s. After the war it was designated as a New Town and much development took place in the 1950s and 1960s diluting to some extent the original Scottish population. Despite this Corby is still a small piece of Scotland in the middle of rural England. They are a robust friendly people and I found myself very much at home with them.

The councillors duly arrived led by their chairman, an able young teacher called John Wallace. We gave them coffee on the terrace and briefed them on the programme for the day. This involved a tour of the village followed by the adjacent woods returning by a somewhat precipitous route along the escarpment on the edge of the opencast iron workings. There were various halts at which I would introduce a member of staff who would speak on his subject be it farm, woods, or estate maintenance. The transport consisted of farm trailers equipped with bales of straw; not a form of transport to which the councillors were accustomed but they gamely mounted the steps and set off into the unknown. As we passed under the towers I mentioned to my neighbour how grateful we were for a grant the Council had given us towards their repair, despite the objections of the one dissenting Tory member. He replied with a grin, 'We thought that if we were going to take this place on we might as well make sure it was in good order.'

The tour went off well; no one fell off the escarpment, and we returned to the castle for a buffet lunch to which I invited all the estate staff. Up to now I had said nothing about the impact of the Government's fiscal policy on the future of the estate as I was anxious that the councillors should see for themselves what the estate was doing and who was doing it. I hoped also that by letting the staff speak for themselves, our visitors would come to understand that Rockingham was not just a fine old castle on top of a hill but a serious employer of highly skilled men and women who depended on the estate for their livelihood.

After lunch I took the floor and spoke for about ten minutes explaining the nature of the 4000-acre estate and the problems that it faced. I gave them my estimated costings. They were clearly much moved. They had never seen the estate before and like so many not concerned with land, had little idea of the number of people employed and the costs and sacrifices involved in running a historic house. They very kindly invited me to join them at their May Day rally the following day at which Denis Healey, the Chancellor of the Exchequer, was to be the guest speaker. I might have an opportunity to put my problems to the Chancellor directly.

The possibility of a one to one interview with the Chancellor was beyond my wildest dreams and I accepted with alacrity. Next morning I was faced with a problem. What should I wear for a May Day rally? I had no experience of practical politics and I thought that I would be least conspicuous if I wore my working clothes. I went in my corduroys and a polo necked sweater. On arrival at the Civic Centre I found the chairman's chauffeur waiting for me. He took me up to the chairman's office where I was met by a phalanx of blue suits and red ties. Ruefully I recalled how I had lectured future naval officers on how to dress for different occasions. I could not have been more wrong on this one!

A familiar figure advanced and shook my hand.

'I am so pleased to meet you,' said Denis Healey. 'I have heard nothing but Rockingham and its problems all lunch. Write to me, and we shall see what we can do to help.'

Encouraged by his friendly approach, I responded at once with a letter setting out the case as I saw it for a maintenance fund to be included within the list of property qualifying for conditional exemption from CTT. In his reply, the Chancellor, sympathised with the arguments but took refuge in the Select Committee on a Wealth Tax which was currently taking evidence and was due to report in the autumn.

After this the MPs visit the following week came as something of an ant-climax. It was nevertheless a success and we made a number of friends in the House of Commons which was to prove valuable in the future.

The media interest in the future of the British heritage continued and about this time I was approached by CBS, the American TV network, who were looking for a suitable historic house to feature on their programme, '60 Minutes', a current affairs programme similar to BBC's Panorama, presented by Morley Safer. Apparently the U.S. public were becoming concerned that Britain was going down the drain and dragging the heritage with it. Morley Safer was here to discover the real situation. The HHA had pointed them in our direction and I readily agreed. Both Morley and his producer were strong anglophiles and genuinely concerned (they both drove 'R'-type Bentleys). I suggested that the film would be most effective if the estate staff were allowed to participate and the result was an excellent production which brought together the whole estate with the castle and showed clearly the interrelationship between them. It was also particularly moving to hear members of our estate staff like Brian Lewin, the head woodman, speaking with pride about his job and expressing his concerns about the future. Sadly it was only shown in the USA.

As 1975 drew to a close our attention was focussed with bated breath on the publication of the report of the Select Committee on a Wealth Tax. We had given evidence to Robin Cooke's sub committee in the summer. Edward Montagu led our delegation and spoke for the large houses; I spoke for the medium sized and Mrs Oddie, owner of Heath Hall, for the smaller houses. We were received kindly but Robin was of course impartial as chairman, and if anything his questioning was quite aggressive. I thought our case was pretty well argued, but it was difficult to tell how it had gone down.

Finally in November a publication emerged with not one but four draft reports. The Committee had simply been unable to agree. There was a report by the chairman, Douglas Jay, by John Pardoe of the Liberal party, by Dr Jeremy Bray, and by Maurice Macmillan. With the exception of the report by Dr Bray all the reports recommended special reliefs for heritage property. Most importantly, the chairman's draft report recommended specifically that assets required for the maintenance of the historic property should qualify for conditional exemption from wealth tax and CTT. Dr Bray uniquely took a different view. He would like to have seen the heritage owned and maintained by the nation for the benefit of its people. In theory it was good pure socialist philosophy but hardly practical since not only would the nation be faced with a colossal bill but most of the houses would be empty shells, their contents having been sold off to pay the tax.

In his report to the second annual meeting of the HHA in November, the President, Lord Montagu commented that while we had started the year with a potentially disastrous situation facing the heritage, there had been some substantial concessions, and while there was still much uncertainty, there was all to play for and much work lay ahead.

Certainly things were looking better and we now knew that we had many friends out there. By creating a situation of taxation overkill the Government had generated such sympathy for heritage owners that there was a very real opportunity to put together a package of tax reliefs for heritage property which would protect it for all time from the ravages of capital tax. If we could achieve this with all-party support that would be a prize indeed.

Early on in this chapter I identified three criteria which had to be met before a deal could be struck. The first two, public awareness of the importance of the heritage, and the need for special measures to preserve it, had been well aired and were enjoying considerable support. Furthermore there was now a general acceptance of the third, that the best way to preserve the heritage was to leave it in private hands.

With singling out of owners of heritage property for conditional exemption from CTT in the Finance Bill, it might seem that we had very nearly achieved our objective. The reliefs, while important in principle, as drafted in the bill were, however, too tightly drawn to be of much practical use. The task before us therefore was to persuade Government to build on these reliefs and extend them so that owners would be prepared to use them while at the same time not opening them to abuse. It was a fine balance.

CHAPTER 7

Lobbying for the Heritage

Towards the end of 1975, George Howard, who had recently been appointed chairman of the Meat and Livestock Commission, summoned me to a very grand office he had just acquired in Grosvenor Place. Entering the boardroom, I was at once aware of a large picture on the opposite wall which comprised a wedge shaped pile of bricks, apparently in a state of collapse. Underneath it sat the massive figure of George at the head of a large table.

It was easy to be frightened of George. At first sight his impressive appearance and gruff manner were rather off-putting, but underneath this carapace was a kind heart and a very sharp brain. The better I came to know him, the more I liked him. He told me that he was very much over stretched, and that he was finding it difficult to do justice to the HHA/BTA Taxation sub-committee. Would I be prepared to act as chairman designate of the committee with a view to assuming the chair in the New Year.

Surprised and flattered by this unexpected proposal, my immediate reaction was that I was quite unqualified for such a role, but that did not worry George.

'You will pick it up as you go along,' he said, 'and there are plenty of people around who will help.'

With George's encouragement I began to see it as an exciting challenge which would put me at the centre of the campaign and was indeed just the sort of job I had been hoping might turn up to get me out of Rockingham and back into the swim. I agreed subject to having time to read myself in. If it was the first time I had taken on something about which I knew little, it was certainly not to be the last.

Things happened rather quicker than I had anticipated and by the middle of January 1975 I found myself Chairman of what was then a taxation sub committee of both the BTA Historic Houses Committee and the HHA Executive comprising members of both organisations with Jeremy Benson representing the Joint Committee of the Amenity Societies attending as an 'observer'. In practice of course he was very much a participator but he quite rightly felt it was important to preserve his impartiality on a committee of owners and operators. I used to tease him that he too had an interest since he was owner of a fine listed building, albeit not open to the public!

Jeremy's name will feature much in this chapter since we both worked very closely together as chairmen of our respective tax committees for the next seven years. A man of enormous charm he had an extraordinary capacity for detail and a tenacity of purpose which was almost impossible to resist. He shared an architectural practice with his wife Patricia and their lovely home, Walpole House, Chiswick Mall, with its superb garden, was a constant source of refreshment during the long hot summer of 1976, in between hours spent in the committee room of the House of Commons during the passage of the Finance Bill.

While today the corridors of Westminster are full of professional lobbyists, in the 1970s they were a rarity and there was certainly no guide to the art of lobbying. We had to follow our instincts augmented by my naval staff training.

In lobbying, as in everything else, it is important to have clearly identified objectives which in our case reflected closely the criteria set out at the end of the last chapter. In general our aim was to create a climate in which it was accepted that the best and most economic way to preserve the heritage is to leave it in private hands. To achieve this, the challenges faced by the private owners needed to be understood and the owners supported in their task. There were many areas in which we were unhappy with the application of CTT. In particular, we wanted to see maintenance funds added to the list of items qualifying for conditional exemption. We were also concerned about the treatment of historic houses for income tax and VAT. All this would require legislation by amending the Finance Bill.

As we awaited publication of the Finance Bill 1976, we were uncertain whether it was better to wait and see what emerged in the bill, or to take the bull by the horns and write to the Chancellor in advance of publication. Jeremy was in no two minds about this – we should write straightaway, and he was absolutely right. The time for submissions is the autumn when the bill is being prepared. It is possible to amend the bill during its various stages through Parliament, but it is far better to put in one's bid reasonably early so that there is plenty of time for discussion with ministers and officials.

We were still learning in 1976, and did not know whom to go and see or where. I then recalled that when I was giving evidence to the Select Committee on a Wealth Tax, at the back of the room was a young man who handed me his card. His name was Robin McConnochie and he was an Assistant Secretary in the Policy Division of the Inland Revenue. In some trepidation I rang his number. He was kindness itself and invited me to come and see him in Somerset House.

When my uncle was handing over Rockingham his lawyer sent him a cartoon of a gentleman from the Inland Revenue attired in bowler hat and striped trousers, mounted on a horse, levelling a jousting pole at the castle gates. It now hangs in pride of place in the lavatory where it reflects the traditional view of officials in the Inland Revenue as a bunch of joyless men out to make our lives a misery. Of course this is absolute nonsense but it nevertheless came as a pleasant surprise to find them so agreeable and prepared to talk to us. Robin McConnochie introduced me to his colleague, Ian Spence, who was responsible for CTT, and to their boss, Leonard Beighton. All three became friends and brought their families to stay at Rockingham. As the years passed and Governments came and went, this relationship with the Revenue continued and was one I greatly valued. Naturally we disagreed on many issues, but I believe we both understood and appreciated each other's position, and this was an enormous help in finding a practical solution to the many problems that arose.

From time to time I became involved with other government departments, notably the Treasury, and the Department of the Environment, and I made a number of friends though sometimes I wondered how helpful this was to the career of the civil servants themselves. The Treasury in particular was quick to detect 'colonisation' and to discourage too much fraternisation with the outside world. Our home civil service contains some of the best brains in the country but so rarefied is the world which they inhabit that it sometimes appears to bear very little resemblance to that of ordinary mortals over which they exercise such power.

From my initial meeting with Robin McConnochie a regular pattern emerged. We would submit a shopping list of desiderata to the Chancellor for consideration which would be followed by a meeting with the Inland Revenue. Discussions with the Inland Revenue took place at two different levels. In the early days, before trust had been established at desk level, we used to meet at a more senior level, generally in the boardroom at Somerset House. This was an impressive room which faced out over the Thames bathed in the morning sun.* Supplicants would be ushered into the glare of

---

* It is a well-known technique of parade instructors, always to position your squad so that they face the sun while you have the sun behind you.

the morning sun to be confronted by a series of tall shadows with their backs to the windows.

The senior man would sit in the middle, flanked by his juniors, the officials who did the real work. We would be welcomed courteously, and offered refreshment. The meeting would then open with a *tour d'horizon* by our side outlining our general problem which was then dealt with point by point by the officials concerned. Their first attempt to kick for touch would always be to ask whether we had costed whatever concession we were seeking. Of course we could not cost it; we had no facilities with which to do so. Nevertheless we would trot out a figure and so the discussions proceeded.

I used to find these meetings profoundly depressing because almost invariably our carefully worked up arguments were met with an elegant but determined brick wall. I believe in retrospect that they were worthwhile in that they enabled both parties to understand their respective positions better, and certainly I found it useful to learn how their minds worked and where their problems lay. More importantly, however, these formal meetings sometimes opened the way to further informal meetings with the official on a one to one basis, which were generally more productive.

The Finance Bill 1976 was published in April and contained much detail concerning CTT but no reference to the provision of a maintenance fund for which we had been pressing. The debate on the second reading of the bill took place on 3rd May. Jeremy and I listened to it in the Strangers Gallery and to our delight heard Joel Barnett, Chief Secretary to the Treasury, announce that the government would be tabling amendments to the bill to exempt maintenance funds for historic property from CTT.

It was very exciting to realise that we had actually managed to persuade the Government to change its mind on this important issue, but in practice it was only the beginning of a long hard struggle to achieve a viable arrangement with which owners and their advisers could feel comfortable.

The bill now went into the Committee Stage in the House of Commons, and this was our opportunity to amend it. This meant drafting the necessary amendments in language, which while not perfect, would at least make the point in appropriate legal terms. In this, my first encounter with parliamentary procedure, I was enormously grateful to have the support of Oliver Stanley and his taxation department at the CLA who did much of the drafting in these early days.

Then we had to find a friendly MP on the committee, preferably of the government party, to table our amendments for us. Ted Graham, Labour member for Edmonton, who had presented our petition, had been made a whip and could not speak for us. I sought advice from my own Labour MP for Corby, Sir Geoffrey de Freitas, who suggested David Watkins, member for Consett, another steel town. I wrote to David and we arranged to meet in the corridor outside the committee room.

We were both pretty wary. David was sponsored by the Amalgamated Union of Engineering Workers, and was said to be fairly left wing in his views. I for my part had no experience of talking to trade unionists.

'Are you a landowner?' he asked.

'In a manner of speaking I suppose I am in that I own land, but my chief concern is as an owner of a historic house which the land in fact maintains.'

David expressed some relief at this. He held no brief for landowners, he explained, since the Marquis of Londonderry imported Irish labour to work his coal mines, but historic house owners were a different matter. He told me about a visit he made to Poland on a trade union mission and how they had been taken to lunch in a castle where at the head of the table sat the Count. He turned to the Commissar and said

'I thought you had got rid of these chaps in the revolution?'

'On the contrary,' replied the Commissar, 'we pay them to stay there.'

In fact the Count was employed as an administrator and had no family connection with the building, but it was good enough for David Watkins and he needed no convincing that it would be cheaper and altogether better to leave the owners of historic houses where they were provided they maintained their properties properly and allowed public access. He agreed to help and was as good as his word.

The more we looked at the detailed heritage provisions in the bill, the more problems arose. It was a very complex piece of new tax law. It was vitally important that we should get it right now as the opportunity for further amendment might not arise again. It was very much a case of sitting down with a wet towel round one's head and trying hard to see through the obscurity of the Parliamentary draftsman's language to the practical effect that the provisions would have on someone trying to run an historic house.

There were one or two major practical problems with CTT, such as the need to wind up a maintenance fund at the end of the perpetuities period when the residue would have to go to charity. The maintenance fund would thus be a sinking fund with a terminal date, and not the permanent bastion of support for the historic house which was our objective. Furthermore, if people were to commit precious income producing assets to a maintenance fund for their historic property then it must be possible for them to recover these assets, by revoking the fund and paying any exempted tax in the event that the requirement to maintain the property ceases for whatever reason. Then there were a whole range of technical problems which had to be solved before the provisions could generally be said to be fair and workable.

CTT was not our only problem. We were very concerned with the way historic houses were treated for income tax. Inevitably the costs of heating, lighting, and maintaining a historic house of any size are a hugely expensive business. Few could afford it without some form of tax relief. This would only be available (under Case 1 of Schedule D to give it its official title) if the house was open to the public to such an extent that the owner could be described as 'carrying on a trade' with a view to a realisation of profits. Only the larger houses at the centre of a major tourism operation could hope to show a profit on a regular basis. The majority of the smaller houses like Rockingham, with 30,000 visitors a year or less, had to live under the continuous threat of losing Case 1 status and having not only to find their running costs after tax but possibly to pay huge sums in back tax to the revenue.

Another anomalous area was VAT, which was chargeable on repairs and restoration but not on demolition and new building. Like so many tax measures designed to achieve a certain effect, in this case to encourage the building of new houses, it brought in its wake other less desirable features such as positive encouragement to demolish the heritage rather then restore it.

With Oliver Stanley's help I drafted a number of amendments and new clauses to the Finance Bill. Each had to be accompanied by a brief to which the tabling MP could speak if necessary. Jeremy prepared his own on this occasion as he wished to keep his distance from the owners' organisations. Later on as our credentials became more widely known and trusted Jeremy and I were able to combine our efforts under the same hat – which made things easier with less chance of duplication and muddle.

I showed my list of sixteen amendments to David Watkins. Wisely he was very concerned to preserve the all-party approach on the heritage and he suggested that he might take some of the amendments and give others to the Opposition front bench which he would then support. He introduced me to John Horam, a Labour colleague on the Standing Committee, who he felt might be better placed to handle the more complex tax issues. John was at this time a keen young Labour member for Gateshead who subsequently became a junior minister before defecting to the SDP and ultimately the Tory party in which he also became a junior minister.

We then met David Howells, Opposition front bench spokesman on financial affairs and his Conservative colleagues on the Finance Committee, John Nott, Peter Hordern, and Robin Cooke. They agreed to table all our amendments which were not being taken by the Labour members.

With the amendments tabled it was then a question of whether they would be selected for debate in committee. This decision rested with the chairman but in fact the key figure is the committee clerk. To be selected the amendment (or new clause) had to refer to an item already mentioned in the Bill; it had to be realistically if not precisely worded, and it had to be workable, and 'stand up'. If the amendment was not selected for debate then that was generally the end of the matter. It was technically possible to table an amendment at report stage but without government support it would be very unlikely to be selected for debate.

We were fortunate in 1976 in that quite a number of our amendments were debated. While none were accepted as read, the various points were aired and drawn to the government's attention in a very public way with all-party support and would be pursued in later discussions.

It all took time, however, and Jeremy and I spent many hours in the House. Luckily our mentor Robin Cooke had a fine office which he kindly put at our disposal. For some reason the heritage always seemed to come up for debate in the middle of the night. It became almost normal to have to hang around until after 2 a.m. before our amendments were called. On one occasion Jeremy and I were there until well after 3 a.m. The House after midnight reminded me of a ship in harbour during the middle watch. The lights went down, people slept in odd corners, and the heart of the building seemed to beat more slowly with the silence broken only occasionally by the ping from the closed circuit television as a new speaker rose to address the almost empty floor.

I came to know the House of Commons well during this period. It is a strange warren of a place but I can understand how people can become very attached to its gaunt Victorian splendour. Sitting on those uncomfortable green benches under the soaring fluted columns of the central lobby with its glittering chandeliers, you feel you are at the core of the British democratic system, the interface between government and the governed; where any constituent can meet his representative on the legislature without let or hindrance. Despite the magnificence of the surroundings, and the grandeur of the house servants in their black breeches and heavy gold badges, there is an air of informality about it all which is very British and strangely heart-warming.

With the 1976 Finance Bill now on the statute book, it was time to take stock, and at first sight we had made great progress. The threat of a wealth tax was receding; and the principle of exemption from capital transfer tax conditional on proper maintenance and reasonable public access for a range of heritage property, including a maintenance fund, was now enshrined in law. Thus the immediate threat posed by these two taxes to the future of our privately owned heritage had at least been reduced, if not removed.

The devil however was in the detail. The interpretation of the law and the arrangements for putting it into practice remained to be worked out, and there were particular difficulties with the maintenance fund, the legislation for which was framed in such a way as to make it virtually unworkable. To some extent this was because the maintenance fund broke new ground in trust law and was in fact a sort of hybrid, neither charitable, nor discretionary, nor a straight settlement – but somewhere in between. As the law was drafted it had all the disadvantages of a trust with few advantages. We had plenty of homework for 1977.

1977 was Jubilee Year. It was also, for a few cognoscenti, Heritage Education Year. Edward Montagu, whose mind was generally well ahead of any one else on these issues, felt that we had been making so much fuss about tax that it was time we showed the politicians that there was more to the heritage than a lot of owners worrying about their tax bills. He had recently set up an education centre at Beaulieu and had been much impressed with the enthusiasm and interest of the children. He suggested that we should encourage other owners to do likewise. In order to draw attention to the use of historic buildings as educational resources we decided to designate 1977 as Heritage Education Year (HEY). I found myself chairman of the Steering Committee, and John Hodgson, at that time curator of Sudbury Hall (Lord Vernon's old home, now owned by the National Trust) where he had established a model education centre, as director.

HEY in itself was no big deal but it did provide a launching pad for a number of new initiatives. It also gave me the opportunity of inviting Lady (Alma) Birk to stay prior to launching the Year at a seminar at Sudbury in May. Alma was a junior minister at the DOE with responsibility for the heritage. The story went round that Harold Wilson had offered her husband, Ellis Birk, a peerage which he refused saying, 'Give it to Alma she'd love it.' It was an inspired move. She worked tirelessly for the heritage as a minister and then in opposition she seemed to be the spokesman in the Lords for nearly every subject under the sun. However she achieved it, she certainly justified her peerage.

She was fascinated by Rockingham as I think she realised for the first time what living and running a historic house really meant. She brought with her an Assistant Secretary from the Department of the Environment, Lloyd Warburton, and together they spent most of the night re-writing her speech. She spoke well, making a brave acknowledgement of the paradox faced by a Labour government committed to redistribution of wealth having to accept that some of the most conspicuously wealthy people living in grand houses needed support in order to maintain the nation's heritage.

Lloyd Warburton was at that time the civil servant in the DOE with responsibility for the heritage. I came to know him very well and to enjoy his dry humour when, having retired somewhat unhappily from the civil service, he took the honorary post of Secretary of the Union of European Historic Houses Associations where we had many laughs together. By way of contrast I recall sitting next to a French official at lunch one day who, I imagined, was roughly equivalent in rank and position to Lloyd, and asking him how he got on with his owners. His answer was emphatic.

'Les propriétaires privés, – Moi, je les déteste!'

There were a number of other interesting developments during 1977, one of which was the Mentmore sale. Mentmore is a large Victorian house near Tring which belonged to Lord Rosebery. In order to raise funds to meet the capital transfer tax due on his death it was decided to offer Mentmore and its contents to the nation in satisfaction of tax under the Land Fund scheme.

The Land Fund was set up by Chancellor Hugh Dalton out of sales of Government surplus war stocks. He specified that the fund should be used to purchase land in memory of those who died during the Second World War. In practice it was used mainly to reimburse the Inland Revenue for tax foregone when an item was accepted by the nation in lieu of estate duty. Unfortunately it was not regarded as sacrosanct by successive Chancellors and their ministers. Enoch Powell in particular, as First Secretary of the Treasury, is said to have removed a hefty portion so that the fund which had been worth in excess of £50m when set up was now only worth about £15m.

Nevertheless, it was still a substantial fund dedicated to purchasing 'heritage property' for the nation. Unfortunately it was administered by the Treasury and classed as public expenditure. In 1977 various economic crises had forced the Chancellor, Denis Healey, to seek a substantial loan from the International Monetary Fund – one of the conditions of which was a strict control of public expenditure. Regardless of where the money was coming from, therefore, the purchase of Mentmore for the nation was not approved and, as a result, first the magnificent furniture and furnishings were sold in a highly publicised sale follwed by the house itself. There was of course the most almighty row, and the heritage lobby was up in arms. At the HHA we kept a low profile as it was none of our business, and in any case, if there had to be a sacrificial cow, Mentmore was rather a good one.

Sacrificial cow it was, and, moved by the unfavourable public reaction, the Government referred the question of the Land Fund to the Expenditure Committee of the House of Commons which set up a special environment sub-committee under the chairmanship of Arthur Jones, MP for Daventry. The sub-committee recommended and, amazingly, the Treasury agreed, that the Land Fund, or what was left of it, should be withdrawn from the Treasury and vested in trustees. It was initially to be called the National Heritage

Fund but subsequently, at the suggestion of Tam Dalyell MP, the word Memorial was added and the NHMF was born. Under the inspired chairmanship of Martin, Lord Charteris of Amisfield, the fund was instrumental in saving a huge range of heritage items including endowing a number of great houses for the National Trust. Its creation was an enlightened move at a time of considerable financial difficulty, and various politicians have claimed credit for setting it up. The concept was agreed under Labour, and finally enshrined in law under Mrs Thatcher's first administration in 1980.

The senior civil servant in the Treasury responsible *inter alia* (as the Treasury would say) for arts funding was my old friend from Dartmouth days, Peter (later Sir Peter) Kemp. He had the misfortune to catch rheumatic fever lining the route as a cadet at the coronation, and had to be invalided out of the Navy. He became an accountant, and in due course a civil servant in the Ministry of Transport. Somehow he managed a transfer to the Treasury where he moved gracefully up the ladder almost to the very top. One of the few if not the only senior Treasury man not to have attended university, Peter never lost his freedom of thought, and was inevitably regarded with some suspicion by colleagues who felt safer with the conventional approach. Things came to a head in the 1990s when he was charged with modernising the civil service. Some of his recommendations went too far for the traditional civil service mind and he found himself out on his ear. Peter always claimed that the NHMF was his baby, and even though it has now been pretty well swallowed up by the Heritage Lottery Fund, the work that it has already done and will continue to do is a fitting tribute to Peter's freshness of approach in that ivory tower of all ivory towers.

Another influential civil servant who became a great friend was John Guinness, a member of Ted Heath's 'think tank' charged with investigating the future of the Land Fund. He asked me to come and see him in the Cabinet Office where he worked. We got on well, and I invited him to Rockingham. On arrival he opened his briefcase and took out a bundle of photographs.

'I think I have photographs of almost all your pictures here but there are one or two gaps,' he said.

He was an expert iconographer with a particular interest in 17th century sitters. He provided a totally new angle on those rather boring Lely-type portraits, all of whose sitters look much the same. At one point I had to refer to our working catalogue and, as I opened it, out fell a letter to my uncle from School House, Rugby, raising some question about one of our portraits, signed John Guinness. I had expected to be briefing him on life in an historic house. In fact the boot was on the other foot and I learned far more from him about Rockingham than he from me.

A key player in the heritage scene and a staunch supporter was Jennifer Jenkins, chairman of the Historic Buildings Council for England. This was an influential body of lay people who advised the Secretary of State for the Environment on a number of matters concerning historic buildings, including the making of grants and loans for repair and maintenance. Their strength lay in their independence of view coupled with direct access to ministers and Jennifer used her privileged position to great effect. Her quick mind rapidly grasped the issues; she was decisive, articulate and passionately concerned. It was a sad day when her HBC was subsumed into the new Historic Buildings and Monuments Commission and effectively lost its individual identity. Jennifer went on to become chairman of the National Trust, author of a major report on the future of the royal parks, adviser to the Heritage Lottery Fund. Countless other areas of the heritage were subjected to her remorseless logic and forthright views.

She spent a night with us at Rockingham on her way north to the Labour party conference. It so happened that Tom Bradley, a neighbour of ours in Kettering, had been her husband Roy's Parliamentary Private Secretary and he and his wife Joy joined us for dinner. His background was in the railways where he rose to become president of the Transport Salaried Staffs Union and was, at this particular moment, chairman of the Labour party. He subsequently became a member of the SDP as of course did Jennifer with Roy, and their views on the backstage activities of the Labour party conference were instructive to say the least.

While the ideological split in the Labour party which gave rise to the formation of the SDP was still some years away, the political situation at the end of 1976 was in a state of flux. The tiny majority with which Harold Wilson won the election in 1974 had been steadily eroded over the years and to remain in power the Government now led by James Callaghan was forced to do a deal with the Liberal party, and the Lib/Lab pact was born. What this meant in practice was never very clear but it did give rise to one somewhat dramatic incident which could have had quite far reaching effects for our cause in the HHA.

Towards the end of 1976 we produced our shopping list of suggestions for the Chancellor to include in his 1977 budget. The prevailing official view however was that the heritage had had a good airing in 1976 and it was now someone else's turn. This meant that we should be unlikely to find Labour party proposers for many of our proposed amendments in the Standing Committee on the Finance Bill. We therefore turned to the opposition for help and Nicholas Ridley was nominated as our point of contact.

Nicholas was a highly intelligent, idiosyncratic, mercurial character who, as the younger brother of Lord Ridley, owner of Blagdon Hall in Northumberland, affected to have no love for inherited wealth. He was unenthusiastic about our proposals and I was not at all clear whether he was willing to put them forward. He was a terrible tease, however, and loved twisting people's tails, sometimes expressing such outrageous views that it was difficult to know whether or not to take him seriously. I was therefore delighted when John Pardoe, the Liberal economic spokesman, approached me to say that the Chancellor had promised him an amendment to the Finance Bill and that he would like to propose something for the heritage. The notice was short and a decision was required immediately. I saw this as a real possibility of achieving something and with Jeremy Benson's agreement, I gave John an important technical amendment dealing with the treatment of income tax from the maintenance fund. I was unable to find Nicholas to tell him that Pardoe was taking one of his amendments but I did find Robin Cooke, who promised to square things with Ridley. I then departed for Glyndebourne leaving Jeremy to stand by in the forthcoming debate that evening

Little did I realise the scale of the time bomb that I had left for him. Apparently Nicholas arrived in the committee room equipped with briefs and a speech to propose our amendments unaware that one of the most important was being tabled by John Pardoe. His fury at what he saw as a serious political slight knew no bounds and poor Jeremy received the full brunt of it. Pardoe's amendment was duly accepted by government but, useful though it proved to be, it was barely worth the bad blood that it created with someone who was to become one of Mrs Thatcher's most influential ministers.

It was by now clear that the Labour government having gone so far, and it was a long way towards protecting the heritage from taxation, was unlikely to go much further. At a public event in London , the Prime Minister, James Callaghan, went so far as to say categorically that the best people to look after historic buildings are those who own and live in them. For the Prime Minister to volunteer this view without any briefing was extremely heartening, but to expect any more government time on fine-tuning the heritage exemption rules for CTT was unrealistic until after the next election.

It was also becoming clear that the life of the government was limited and that its chance of a third term was minimal. It was therefore essential that we brief the Conservative party on what was required to finish the job and, drawing on the goodwill that still existed towards the heritage on both sides of the House, to complete the package of measures necessary to enable families to continue to maintain their historic properties from one generation to the next for the benefit of the nation.

It so happened that the chairman of the HHA Thames and Chilterns Region, Mrs Marjorie Mockler, was a friend and constituent of the late Airey Neave, one of Mrs Thatcher's closest advisers. Marjorie felt it important that we should meet and arranged a lunch party at her home, Milton Manor House near Abingdon. It was a great success; Airey and his wife Diana were delightful and he at once was seized with the problem. He felt sure that Mrs Thatcher would see us. Indeed she had already met some historic house owners though who they were or what they said was not immediately clear.

Meanwhile other strings were being pulled and a meeting was arranged with the Leader of the Opposition in her room at the House of Commons early in 1978. Our side was led by the Duke of Grafton, Patron of the HHA, supported by Lord Montagu, George Howard and myself, with Lord Cottesloe and Lord de Lisle and Dudley added to lend weight and validity to our cause. Mrs Thatcher was surrounded by members of her shadow cabinet and others: Sir Geoffrey Howe, shadow Chancellor, Michael Heseltine, shadow Environment Secretary, Norman St John Stevas, shadow Leader of the House and Minister for the Arts, Peter Rees QC, shadow Financial Secretary, and Robin Cooke.

Hugh Grafton introduced our team and we stated our case, the burden of which was that the Labour Government, in pursuit of its policy of redistribution of wealth, had substituted capital transfer tax for estate duty which, if applied without relief to historic houses, their contents and environment, would spell the end of private ownership within a generation. All that would be left would be a series of empty buildings to be maintained at great expense by the state.

The effect of these taxes would exacerbate the already problematic situation facing the private sector of the heritage, and there was now considerable public sympathy and all-party support for a package of measures to protect the heritage from taxation subject to certain conditions. The Labour government had taken a number of important steps in this direction, and conditional exemption from CTT was now available for a range of heritage property, subject to reasonable public access to the property and proper maintenance. While the principles were sound, and indeed went much further than the old estate duty, the details still left much to be desired. There were a number of points which needed to be addressed before the package was sufficiently attractive to persuade owners and their advisers to seek conditional exemption for their property, as opposed to selling up and paying the tax. We hoped that the new Conservative government would take this one on board at an early stage and complete the work started by Labour.

Mrs Thatcher turned to Geoffrey Howe for his reaction.

'Margaret, as you know, when we come to power we shall reduce taxes and people will have more money in their pocket and more choice over how they spend it. If they wish to live in a historic house and spend it on that, well and good, but there should be no need for special tax measures.'

She turned to Michael Heseltine. 'I concur with Geoffrey. We shall change society; people will be able to think and do what they want with their money. We want to simplify the tax system not complicate it with further special reliefs for people to live in their ancestral homes.'

She looked round the rest of her team. They all nodded agreement. She then turned to Geoffrey Howe. 'I think you are quite wrong; I think you are all wrong. There is no way you are going to be able to reduce taxes sufficiently to enable, for instance, George Howard' – looking at George – 'to maintain Castle Howard out of income after tax. Geoffrey, set up a working party, look into the problem and report back to me within the month.'

'Of course, Margaret.'

She then turned to us and, drawing herself up in her chair, addressed us in ringing tones: 'Be in no doubt that our first priority will be to draw the teeth of this socialist tax, capital transfer tax, and then to reduce the level of income tax so that you will all have more money to spend. Now let's have a drink.'

It was an impressive demonstration of Mrs Thatcher's authority and her ability to listen. An ability which she seemed to lose in her later years as Prime Minister.

Peter Rees, an old friend from CLA days, and a tax barrister, was deputed to form a working party of one. He met with Jeremy and me on a number of occasions as a result of which he wrote a paper, which we were not allowed to see, recommending a range of measures needed to make the maintenance fund a practical proposition and also to improve the income tax position. This was followed by silence, and we were not sure whether our ideas had been taken on board or not. In fact we need not have worried. The CTT proposals appeared in the 1980 Finance Bill and met nearly all our points. The income tax problem was not so easily solvable, but guidelines were agreed and these certainly helped clarify the position and enabled a number of smaller houses to be taxed under Schedule D Case 1 as proper businesses instead of under Case 6 where they were treated as hobbies.

Meanwhile we had a wider agenda to address. We needed to build on what had already been achieved; to spread the word and create a body of informed opinion who not only appreciated the value of the heritage but understood the economic aspects. As far as Westminster was concerned, the all party Heritage Group was a very good way of introducing MPs to the issues. Patrick Cormack, chairman of the group, has been a stalwart supporter of the heritage for as many years as I can remember. It was very largely due to him that the 'heritage' enjoyed all-party support.

Together we arranged a number of fact-finding trips for members of the group to HHA houses. The first was to Woburn where Robin Tavistock laid on an excellent tour of the house and estate, while at lunch we met his staff. After that the coaches went to Rockingham and for some reason arrived initially at Desborough aerodrome where we were having a problem with gypsies. To go from Robin's exquisitely organised estate to a gypsy encampment at Rockingham was definitely passing from the sublime to the ridiculous but at least it gave our guests some idea of the problems we faced.

It was also an opportunity for us to get to know a number of MPs who we would not normally meet. One such was Tam Dalyell whom I sat next to on the bus. An old Etonian, who still lived in his family home, The House of The Binns, outside Edinburgh, which now belonged to the National Trust for Scotland, Tam enjoyed the respect of MPs from both sides of the House. A fellow member described him to me as a 'latter-day Hampden'. Where many backbench MPs complain that they have no authority, and are merely voting fodder, Tam knew just how to use the House of Commons to achieve whatever his particular objective might be, and was a constant source of embarrassment to ministers, both Labour and Conservative. A man of strong principles, you could not move him in a direction he did not want to go; on the other hand if you were travelling in the same direction then, tank-like, he would mow down or roll over anything or anyone who was in his way. He will probably go down in history as one of the most effective members of Parliament this century.

He was a friend both to me personally and also to the heritage. I greatly valued his advice and support. Later when I was chairman of the Heritage Education Trust, I was able to persuade his wife, Kathleen, to become a trustee.

In general I found members of the Labour party more receptive to issues concerning the heritage than their opposite numbers in the Conservative party. I think there may be two reasons for this. The interest in heritage matters shown by the intellectual wing of the Labour party goes back to the late 19th century when members of the Fabian Society, like the Webbs, George Bernard Shaw, and William Morris founded the Society for the Protection of Ancient Buildings. Conversely the trade union wing of the party supports the heritage because they are keen that the artisans of today should be free to enjoy the craftsmanship of the artisans of yesterday. The Conservative party looks at the heritage rather differently. Firstly, they assume that its owners are members of their party and therefore their votes are in the bag. Secondly, they are not too keen on 'old' money and thirdly, they find the idea of supporting ostensibly rich aristocrats in historic houses rather embarrassing. This is a gross over simplification, however, and there are many members of the Conservative party who support the heritage but it was much easier for them to do so when it became clear that the heritage was an all-party issue.

The trade union movement was very influential at this time and, properly briefed, could, I felt sure, be a source of support for the heritage. I had already met one or two union sponsored MPs, such as Tom Bradley and David Watkins and had been greatly impressed by them. I also met John Cousins at that time British Airways staff representative on the TGWU, at a seminar hosted by the Countryside Commission of which he was a commissioner. He and his wife Pauline came to stay at Rockingham. He was very keen to shoot something but it was out of season so we had to make do with potting rabbits from the Landrover with a .22 rifle. He was somewhat dismissive of his colleagues.

'If I was to walk into a room full of trade unionists and mention Shostakovitch,' he once said, 'No one would know what I was talking about.'

I assured him that if I was to do likewise in a group of landowners, I should be very likely to receive the same negative response. Later, when he was standing for the post of Secretary General of the TGWU on Jack Jones's retirement, he told me that if he won I would not recognise some of the things he said because he would have to lead the union from the left. I reflected that if I became president of the HHA I might have to lead from the right of centre while my natural instincts veered towards the left.

Edward Montagu was also keen to develop links with the trade unions. He gave a lunch party at Beaulieu for Clive Jenkins, the influential General Secretary of the ASTMS, to which he asked Georgina and me. Clive was good value and kept us all amused with a fund of stories about life behind the scenes at Congress House. He promised to talk to Len Murray, the General Secretary of the TUC, to gain his support for the HHA. He was as good as his word and Len Murray apparently responded enthusiastically to the idea that he might address an HHA meeting, but for some reason the initiative seemed to die a natural death at that point, and would in any case have been inappropriate when the Conservatives came to power.

In the autumn of 1978, Edward Montagu completed his five-year term as president of the HHA and was succeeded by George Howard. Edward asked me if I would stand as deputy president which I was happy to do, provided I could continue to chair my committee now known as the Taxation and Parliamentary Committee. I felt that there was still an unfinished agenda which I very much hoped an incoming Conservative Government would complete and I did not want to leave until that had been resolved.

During the past three years I had worked closely with Edward Montagu. It was a stimulating and enjoyable experience. He was very easy to work with provided you could keep up with him. He had a restless energy and his quick fertile mind was constantly bubbling with new ideas. Detail bored him however and he needed a good chief of staff to pick up the best ones and take them forward. I have an abiding memory of an evening at Beaulieu with Edward sitting on the sofa, writing Christmas cards with one hand, zapping across the TV channels with the other, and in between developing his ideas for promoting historic houses as education resources.

His achievements at Beaulieu where he personally created a major and highly successful tourist attraction with minimum impact on the environment are quite remarkable.

He was also instrumental in founding the HHA, and similarly the European equivalent EUHHA. He went on to become the first chairman of the newly formed Historic Buildings and Monuments Commission (known as English Heritage) which combined the functions of the Ancient Monuments division of the DoE with the conservation responsibilities of Historic Buildings Council. Unfortunately the former brought with it a heavily embedded bureaucracy which caused considerable frustration among owners and their advisers. It would have been a superhuman job, given the material that he had to work with, for Edward to have overcome these attitudes. He was more successful with the properties in care, where he succeeded in transforming their presentation, and crowned a career which had contributed hugely to both the heritage and the tourist industry. He deserved a great deal more than he received when his ten year assignment came to an end.

CHAPTER 8

The Historic Houses Association

With Europe increasingly important in our lives, it was becoming clear that political organisations like the HHA needed to have a point of contact with the European authorities, and that the time was approaching when lobbying the European Commission and Parliament would be as important as lobbying national governments.

The Treaty of Rome did not specifically address the question of the European heritage, and hitherto all attempts to interest the European Commission in heritage matters had been referred to the Council of Europe, the body nominally responsible for safeguarding the European heritage but which was in fact only a talking shop with no actual powers. Times were changing and the Commission was showing increasing interest in support for the heritage.

Other national organisations similar to ours in Europe were thinking along the same lines. Lord Montagu accordingly arranged a conference at Beaulieu to which all European historic house owners' organisations were invited and the European Union of Historic Houses was born with Edward as its first president and Richard Miller, from the HHA, as its first director. The idea was to share each others experiences and provide a common front for discussions with the European Commission and Parliament.

The principal objective of the EUHHA was therefore to establish contact with the European Commission, impress upon them the importance of the European heritage and to persuade them to bring pressure to bear on their member countries to adopt favourable tax policies for privately owned historic buildings. This was not the easiest task as not only were there wide differences in the way in which the heritage was treated, and we in Britain were by no means the best, but relations between historic house owners and their respective governments varied greatly.

Some success was achieved and in 1978 the Commission invited Professor Claeys Bouuart of Ghent University to undertake a study into 'The Tax Problems of Historic Houses'. The professor went to work with commendable speed and produced his report later that year. It was generally helpful in that it supported the idea of tax relief in principle, but inevitably, as with so many such reports, after a brief moment of glory it found its way onto the Commission's shelves where it has remained ever since.

There were a number of other organisations concerned with the preservation of historic buildings active on the European scene, and it was not always clear where the interests of one ended and another's began. Europa Nostra was the brainchild of Lord Duncan-Sandys and was a sort of European equivalent of the Civic Trust which he had started so successfully in UK. It was concerned mainly with the urban heritage scene, but liked to think that it was the umbrella body for Europe's heritage as a whole.

Then there was IBI (the International Burgen Institute) under the redoubtable Marquis de Amodio OBE who drove a silver Rolls Royce. IBI was concerned principally with castles. It had a Scientific Council which was a highly respected academic body, and it also enjoyed consultative status at the Council of Europe and UNESCO. There was a loyal membership of a hundred or more who attended an annual meeting in some historic setting and everybody had a good time. Johnnie Amodio was a tremendous enthusiast and under his direction IBI became all embracing. He was quite likely to claim that he represented the private owner as well as everybody else. This of course did not go down very well with EUHHA, particularly since Johnnie, for all his goodwill, had very little idea of the issues facing owners.

Finally there was ICOMOS. The International Council on Monuments and Sites which was another offspring of UNESCO, run from Paris with national branches in member countries including Britain. They were concerned more with sites than buildings and World Heritage sites in particular. Our paths crossed usefully on the subject of gardens and designed landscape in which they took a particular interest.

The Europeans love conferences and when they want to make a point to higher authority they set up a large conference and table resolutions which are then passed on to ministers. How effective this procedure was as a form of lobbying I am not too sure, but then the relationship between government and governed varies from country to country. We spent a great deal of time drafting resolutions which did not seem to achieve very much. On the other hand we had one or two amusing moments.

One of my first duties as deputy president was to accompany George Howard, the new president, to Brussels to attend a meeting of EUHHA in preparation for a big conference to be held the following spring. We were to meet at Beloiel, the magnificent chateau of Prince Antoine de Ligne.

He and his family lived very comfortably in the converted stables but in order to accommodate the meeting he had to flash up the main building. I use the naval expression advisedly as it was dead of winter and the boiler could have powered an Atlantic liner. Continuously banging and clattering the radiators were too hot to touch but so cold was the building that they made little impression on the ambient temperature.

Antoine greeted us on arrival and after we had all assembled, he took us over to the chateau to find our rooms. We were led up a magnificent great staircase at the top of which Antoine threw open a pair of large double doors to reveal a splendid state bedroom.

'Louis XIV's chamber for you Edward, President of the European Union,' he declaimed. Edward Montagu looked duly impressed.

We processed through the room to another set of double doors which Antoine flung apart to display an even grander room.

'And for you, Johnnie, Marquis de Amodio, President of IBI, Louis XVI's chamber.'

There was only one other 'president' in the party and that was George. There could not be another room on such a scale after Louis XVI, and he began to look rather glum.

However there was yet another set of double doors which Antoine threw open with an even greater flourish to display a room not far short of 100 feet long with an enormous four poster bed shaped like a scallop shell in the middle facing a roaring fire.

'For you, George, Marie Antoinette's chamber!'

Honour satisfied, George's face burst into a happy smile The following morning we all met for breakfast in Antoine's private quarters. George appeared looking very cross.

'Ah George, how did you sleep?' cried Antoine.

'Bloody awful. The hot water bottle burst and I spent the night drying the bedclothes in front of the fire.'

'Oh George, I'm so sorry, but you weren't meant to sit on it you know.'

I spent the night before the Beloeil meeting with the Dutch representative, Heike Kamerlingh Onnes. He and his wife Agnes lived in the perfect little medieval Casteel Vosbergen, surrounded by no less than three moats. As a present I had taken him a Rockingham oak, a young sapling which I had personally dug up in the park. It was a bit twisted but, by our standard, a fair specimen. The customs man gave it an old fashioned look but let it through. When I arrived at Vosbergen, however, I found avenues of great tall oaks, each perfectly pruned and straight as ramrods, radiating from the house in all directions. My offering was a poor thing by comparison.

Heike was a great asset on the European scene. He had had a legal training before joining the Netherlands foreign service and combined an understanding of tax with fluency in four European languages. Pragmatic in a typically Dutch way, he liked to get things done while most of our colleagues preferred to talk about them.

EUHHA bumbled on happily for a few years. Then in 1982 there was a mini revolution arising from a reluctance of some members to pay their subscriptions and a general feeling that the Union had lost its way, which resulted in Heike Kamerlingh Onnes assuming the Presidency. He put his formidable energy behind EUHHA and it became for him a life's mission at which he slaved for the next nineteen years until his death in 2001. Meanwhile in the UK we were coming to terms with a political scene very different to the socialist environment to which we had become accustomed. We now had a reforming Conservative government and a lady Prime Minister

Michael Heseltine became Secretary of State for the Environment, and George and I made an early appointment to see him. It was an extraordinary meeting. He sat in his office with John Stanley and Hector Munro, his junior ministers, and three officials. George led off with a *tour d'horizon* of the general situation concluding with what we considered to be a major achievement – the conditional exemption for heritage property and maintenance funds. Of course we fully accepted the requirement to provide public access in return for tax relief.

Michael Heseltine's response was that public access to private property was an appalling idea. He could not disagree with it more. His officials who up till now had spent much of their time insisting on us offering public access looked glumly at the table.

We stressed that we were concerned to maintain the all party consensus towards the heritage, and there was no way that the socialists would countenance tax relief without access.

This was a red rag to a bull, and off he went in a tirade about a new society with new values and a new approach to old things.

'If you cannot afford to live in your historic house,' he said, 'sell it to someone who can.'

He had, as it happened, just bought Thenford, a delightful Georgian house in south Northamptonshire.

We left the meeting wondering where to go from there, but fortunately Michael Heseltine was not speaking for the Government as a whole, though there were many who shared his view, Nicholas Ridley being one. Peter Rees, Parliamentary Under-Secretary to the Treasury, certainly understood our position but his responsibility covered only income tax and capital tax came under Lord Cockfield.

Jeremy Benson and I arranged to go and see Lord Cockfield at the Treasury early in 1980 hoping to run through the points agreed in our meetings with Peter Rees. Arthur Cockfield was an Inland Revenue man who became chairman of Boots. He had a strange manner of addressing you in a toneless booming voice as if he was talking down a large tube. It did not make for an easy conversation and indeed the meeting felt more like an interview between two schoolboys and their headmaster. At one point Jeremy was reduced to addressing Lord Cockfield as 'sir'. The revenue official responsible for capital taxes at this time was Michael Elliott, a very pleasant individual with whom we had had several conversations in the past. I suspect he was as embarrassed by his minister's manner as we were.

Lord Cockfield's bark proved worse than his bite and, notwithstanding this unsatisfactory interview, the 1980 Finance Bill, contained a range of measures dealing with maintenance funds which with the odd amendment here and there sorted out the various problems arising from the initial legislation and made the maintenance fund a practical proposition. Thus we achieved what we set out to do six years earlier when we were faced with the threat of an annual wealth tax coupled with an unavoidable tax on gifts. There now existed on the statute book a package of measures which would protect historic houses, their contents and environment from capital transfer tax. Furthermore, the measures enjoyed the support of both sides of the House, and could in principle be applied to any future tax on gifts or death. Admittedly owners seeking exemption from tax would have to sacrifice some privacy and allow the Inland Revenue to poke its long nose even deeper into their affairs, but in the context of the political environment in which it was conceived, exemption from tax in exchange for public access and proper maintenance was a reasonable deal.

When, in the following year, capital transfer tax was replaced by inheritance tax, it became possible once again to make lifetime gifts free of tax (known as Provisionally Exempt Transfers or PETs), the arrangements for which we had fought so hard appeared restrictive by comparison if not redundant. While it is obviously attractive to hand on one's property, if one can, without restriction, and I have done so myself, it is good to know that if the donor dies within the seven years, then conditional exemption is available as an alternative to paying the tax. As for maintenance funds, they are a useful means of identifying the heritage property and putting the structure in place well before death actually occurs when there are so many other things to do. Finally while the political situation today is very different to that of the '70s, who is to say how long the principle of a PET will continue to be politically acceptable, as the gap between the rich and the poor grows ever wider.

Towards the end of the summer of 1980, George Howard was appointed Chairman of the Governors of the BBC. He was keen to continue as President of the HHA, not least because the BBC was technically a part-time job and it was helpful to be able to demonstrate another occupation. It did mean, however, that he would have less time for visits to the regions. I could see that as there were going to be more calls on my time, I should be thinking of handing on the chair of the Tax and Parliamentary Committee. While we had been relying heavily on the expert advice of people like Oliver Stanley it was important in my view that the chairman should be the owner of an historic house, preferably, though not necessarily, one open to the public. In the small world of historic house owners there are not many who have the time, the knowledge, and the aptitude to gain the confidence of officials in the Revenue and MPs and to be able to interpret to the membership some of the more complex tax issues with which they may be confronted.

Through Jeremy Benson I met Anthony Furse, an accountant trained merchant banker from Liverpool who, with his architect wife, had taken on and restored a beautiful 17th century house in North Wales. I asked him to join our committee and it soon became clear that his knowledge of the taxation issues was matched only by his enthusiasm.

Straightaway he recognised that our committee was too amateur, and dependent for its advice from outside. He introduced the lawyer, Charles King-Farlow, who also joined the committee, and over the years has been largely responsible for the high quality of the HHA's technical input. He was joined by Stephen Oliver, a tax silk, and Gerald Drew, a leading accountant, also became involved. The HHA gained enormously from the input of these highly priced experts, and I dread to think what it would have cost if they had charged for their time.

In the general context of taxation, the heritage occupies only a very small part but for those concerned it is of enormous significance and being at the sharp end, as it were, I found that over the years that I worked for the HHA, I became acquainted with many of the land agents of the bigger estates, and most of the leading lawyers and accountants whose clients were involved with heritage property. It was a two way exercise; I learned from their experience and in return I was able to brief them on the latest position. I greatly valued these links with the top professionals as it was through them that I was able to confirm that the measures we were seeking, which tended to be based on my own personal experience at Rockingham, were equally relevant to others.

Towards the end of 1980, Richard Miller, the Director General, indicated that he felt the time had come for a change. He had done a good job building up the organisation and the membership from scratch on a shoestring but he had property north of the border and was keen to move to Scotland where he had been offered a job with the National Trust for Scotland. George asked me to draft an advertisement and set in motion the interview procedure. I felt that we needed someone with political flair who would be equally at home with a dowager as with a trade unionist. He or she must be able to write clearly, take minutes and speak in public. The salary was minimal by current standards; he would have to work in a garret, make his own tea and probably type his own letters. I doubted that such a paragon existed.

But he did, and after sifting through seventy odd responses and interviewing six short-listed candidates in George's office in the BBC, we appointed Terry Empson. Terry had spent his working life in the foreign service but now wanted out of that particular rat race and a change of scenery. He certainly found that at the HHA. Brilliant on paper, an excellent speaker, an astute political operator, and a glutton for hard work, Terry possessed all the qualities we were seeking and more. He brought to the Association a professionalism which enabled it to punch well above its weight and earn the respect of officials and politicians alike for the balance and quality of its submissions.

The HHA at this point was occupying offices in Ebury Street on the fifth floor of a house owned by the Westminster Estate and let at a concessionary rent to various charities. For Terry Empson, a garret in Ebury Street was a far cry from the spacious office that he had occupied in the Foreign Office. He wasted no time however in acquiring suitable furniture and with the board room which we shared with our neighbours these modest offices served us well throughout my time with the HHA.

With George pretty well tied up in the BBC, I found myself being drawn more and more into the administration of the HHA and the challenges faced by the membership. Ownership of a historic house open to the public calls for expertise in a whole range of areas, in all of which the HHA had to be capable of sensible comment if not direct support. These included tax planning, publicity and promotion, education, retailing, catering, acting as a film location, conservation of historic buildings and their collections of paintings, furniture, furnishings, books and archives, each a speciality on its own, to say nothing of estate management, and agriculture.

At this point the office staff consisted of Terry Empson, Director General, his assistant, Sarah Greenwood, a secretary, and a part-time ex bank manager as accountant. In addition we were fortunate to retain the services of Norman Hudson on a part time basis as technical adviser. The output of this small staff was prodigious. In addition to keeping the steadily increasing membership happy, they produced a quarterly journal, *Historic House*, published by Michael McCartney, a range of advisory leaflets and organised seminars on almost every subject under the sun. Never was the saying 'small is beautiful' more apposite. If the HHA has been one of the more successful representative organisations in its field, I am quite sure it has been largely due not just to the quality of the staff, but to remaining small and specialised. We were also helped by various members who gave freely of their expertise. One such was Bill Cash – constitutional lawyer and owner of a lovely house in Cheshire. He wrote the first advisory manual for the HHA. Later he became an MP and made his name as an anti-European.

Towards the end of 1981 there were some interesting developments on the political front as the increasing influence of the left wing in the Labour party became too much for some of its more moderate members and a break-away group, led by the so-called 'Gang of Four' – Roy Jenkins, Shirley Williams, David Owen, and John Rogers – formed the Social Democratic party. It was an exciting moment for those who believed in social democracy but were unable to accept the outdated socialist dogma which plagued the Labour party. Not surprisingly these included a number of my friends such as Tom Bradley, and John Horam.

The Rockingham political heritage, if it could be called that, originated in the 18th century when its occupants were very much of the Whig persuasion. Lewis Monson-Watson, 1st Lord Sondes, married Grace Pelham daughter of the Rt Hon Henry Pelham, who succeeded Sir Robert Walpole as First Lord of the Treasury and was the brother of that ubiquitous 'fixer', the Duke of Newcastle. The Whig tradition was carried forward under the 2nd Marquis of Rockingham who led the party in the latter half of the eighteenth century. Then in the nineteenth century, Richard Watson was Liberal MP for Peterborough and very active in matters such as adult education. There was nothing particularly altruistic about the Whigs. They were wealthy, lived well, and wanted to keep things that way. They preferred trade to war, and they were concerned not to rock the boat. The 18th century Conservatives were mainly drawn from the squirearchy who were keen to better themselves and took every opportunity to do so, including going to war with America over the latter's independence.

My uncle, Michael Culme-Seymour, was ostensibly a Conservative and stood under that banner for the county council. For a Conservative his views were decidedly left of centre. I for my part have never belonged to a political party and am proud to have been asked by both the Conservative party and the Labour party to stand in their respective causes. I refused them both. I have always admired Labour's concern for the welfare of the individual, particularly for those at the less privileged end of the scale, but it is too centralised for my taste, and I find its bossiness irritating. I appreciate the freedom and opportunities under the Conservatives but abhor their arrogance. The SDP therefore interested me in that it might care for the individual while at the same time allowing him or her plenty of space to do their own thing.

It so happened that there was a strong SDP presence in Kettering and the candidate, Celia Goodheart, was an old friend and an excellent candidate. We gave them their first fund-raising party at Rockingham and I debated whether I should join. There were too many other things going on at the time, however, and I never took it any further. As things turned out, masterly inactivity was the best course.

With Mrs Thatcher's first administration now in its fourth year and an election over the horizon it was time to remind our political friends of the importance of the heritage in the hope that it might feature in their manifestos. We embarked on a flurry of political activity. On 16th January through the good offices of Andrew Faulds, Jeremy Benson and I met Robin Cook* and Jack Straw, both at that time up and coming young Labour MPs and front bench spokesmen on Finance. Robin Cook was clearly very intelligent but he was the more cautious of the two and I was conscious of some tension between us. In response to an invitation to visit Rockingham, he said that he never left the House of Commons except to visit his constituency, Jack Straw by contrast was relaxed, open and very sensible.

I then met Nicholas Ridley, the Chief Secretary of the Treasury. He brought with him Michael Elliott of the Inland Revenue. The object of the meeting was to talk about our recently published leaflet 'Incentives for Conservation' which argued the case for listed building repair allowances. It was, I fear, a lost cause almost before we started as Nick Ridley was of the firm view that owners of historic houses, or 'nouveau pauvres' as he subsequently called them, should not have any special relief. In fact he was against the idea of tax reliefs at all, preferring to keep income tax down. Unfortunately this was never a practical proposition on the scale needed to make any difference.

The following week we gave a dinner party for Giles Radice his wife Lisette, and our local MP Bill Homewood. They represented both wings of

---

* Not to be confused with Robin (later Sir Robert) Cooke, Tory MP for Bristol West

the Labour party, Giles, the intellectual, and Bill, the trade unionist. Sadly Giles never held office in Government but he was an influential thinker behind the scenes. Bill was a late entrant to Parliament. He represented Corby at a difficult time during the closure of the steelworks, and he did a good job as a constituency MP, even helping me on occasions with heritage amendments in the finance committee. He lost his seat in 1983 and died shortly after.

Then on 10th February Terry and I gave a dinner in my flat to senior members of the SDP. John Horam and John Roper who had crossed the floor of the House. Dick Taverne, a Treasury Minister under Harold Wilson, who had resigned from Labour earlier and failed to be re-elected; and David Cargill, a farmer and SDP Chairman for East Anglia. We were supposed to be talking about the SDP's policy for the heritage but the discussion soon went beyond that and broadened out into almost every area of future policy. It was a heady moment. The SDP were running at some 25% in the polls with a real chance of holding the balance of power, and here they were starting with a clean sheet.

Inevitably however as time went on it became apparent that the SDP consisted mainly of intellectuals with no real power base either in industry and commerce or the unions. This fact was brought home to me when I led a delegation representing the heritage before the SDP Environment Committee under the chairmanship of my friend Celia Goodheart. We met at around 7pm at their headquarters in Cowley Street. Apart from Celia and David Astor, I did not know any of the other SDP members. There were about a dozen of them, all very serious and academic. The meeting ground on to well past 11pm with some quite hostile questioning. It soon became clear that winning over the SDP for the private sector of the heritage would be no easy task. I reflected that we might have had a better reception at Congress House where at least the trade unionists would have understood the practical aspects of what we were trying to do and have had some idea of the economic issues.

In the event the election did not take place until 9th June 1983. It so happened that I had arranged for Sir William Rees Mogg, the new Chairman of the Arts Council to come to lunch at the flat accompanied by his Chief Executive designate, Luke Rittner,. We were of course meant to be talking about arts events in houses and how they might be encouraged, but needless to say the election took over and in particular how the SDP would do. Sir William was convinced that they could easily win seventy seats and hold the balance of power. This would indeed have been an interesting result but I am afraid the political mould remained intact and Mrs Thatcher won with a substantial if reduced majority. In the meantime we had other things to occupy our minds.

At the end of March 1982 George Howard convened a meeting in the boardroom of the BBC to discuss the possibility of staging a major exhibition in the brand-new east wing of the National Gallery of Art in Washington. Carter Brown, the energetic and ambitious director, had hit on the idea of exhibiting a British country house with all its features from kitchen to garden. He actually wanted to 'build' a historic house in the gallery. The curator of the exhibition was to be John Harris from the RIBA, assisted by Gervase Jackson-Stops, historic buildings adviser to the National Trust. It was a very exciting idea and a wonderful opportunity to promote British historic houses not just to the American public but also to our own ministers who would be able to bask in the glory of what would be one of the greatest exhibitions ever exported from Britain and appreciate the dollar earning potential of the British heritage.

The exhibition, which became known as 'Treasure Houses of Britain', and was due to open in Washington in 1985 had what could only be described as a bumpy start. The concept of actually building a country house posed immense difficulties. What period would it be? There is no such thing as a typical country house, and that is part of their charm. But, apart from the aesthetic problems, there was a more serious practical one; there was as yet no sponsor to finance this extremely expensive and grandiose concept.

John Harris had cold feet. He could see huge difficulties ahead and at a fairly early stage he resigned from the project and Gervase took his place. Gervase probably knew more about Britain's historic houses than anyone else, but he was an unknown quantity as an organiser at least of anything on this scale. In practice his quiet, hesitant, scholarly manner belied a steely determination. He did a wonderful job and with his deep knowledge, his personal charm and tactful handling of difficult owners, he achieved miracles in a way not always appreciated by his Washington colleagues.

Finally a sponsor was found and the Ford Motor Company agreed to pick up the tab for a figure said to be in the region of $8m, though in practice I believe it came to considerably more. Gervase and his American colleagues set about planning what was to be a unique exhibition not only in the value but the variety of objects loaned, the majority of which were still privately owned.

It soon became clear that the original concept of ' building' a historic house in the gallery was impractical and it was decided instead to design a series of rooms, some copies of originals and some imagined, ranging from a medieval great hall to the Waterloo chamber. These rooms would have on display appropriate objects loaned from the houses themselves. In theory these should have covered a broad range from the curious to the great work of art. In practice the exhibition concentrated on the latter end of the scale and the focus was on excellence at the expense of the eclecticism which is such an interesting feature of the historic house as a family home. 'Treasure Houses of Britain' was an exhibition of astonishing quality.

At this early stage my concern on behalf of the HHA was to use this heaven-sent opportunity to demonstrate to politicians the economic importance of Britain's historic houses. I felt sure that the uniquely prestigious nature of the exhibition could be turned to economic advantage by being linked with a major trade fair of British quality goods such as Wedgwood china, Purdey guns, and Rolls Royce. As soon as it was confirmed that the exhibition would take place, I arranged a meeting with the British Overseas Trade Board to discuss this possibility. The officials did not really want to know. They were adamant that their programmes were all arranged at least five years ahead and there was no question of altering them now. We could have an antiques fair if we liked.

'Certainly not!' I said. 'That is one thing we will not have. These items on display are not for sale.'

I went on to explain that this was probably the biggest thing to hit America from Britain since the war; it would achieve wide coverage across the USA; Prince Charles was expected to make it the occasion of his first official visit with his new wife; it was an unrepeatable opportunity to promote all that is best in Britain across the length and breadth of the USA.

I was wasting my breath; the officials were unmoved. It was a typical example of what I call the Noel Coward syndrome – 'The stately homes of England....etc'. Anything which involved stately homes was seen as faintly ridiculous and certainly not a matter for serious consideration. This lack of imagination and inflexibility of approach , though very disappointing, came as no surprise. I had had no previous dealings with the Trade Department, but I had met similar attitudes in the foreign office in my naval days. It has always seemed strange that we leave so much of our overseas sales promotion in the hands of people who have never had to sell anything for a living.

In the event Prince Charles is said to have enquired after a trade fair that he could open. Fortunately for the Embassy there was a small British promotion at J.C.Penny, a multiple store on the lines of Woolworth. A wonderful opportunity to promote British products had been well and truly missed.

Towards the end of 1982 the government published a National Heritage Bill with the object of establishing boards of trustees to assume responsibility for certain public bodies hitherto administered by government departments. By granting a measure of independence to these bodies it was hoped that they might become more efficient and 'user friendly', though the more cynical saw the measure as a response to the Prime Minister's call for a reduction in civil servants. The bodies concerned which thus swelled the ranks of what were known as QUANGOS (Quasi Autonomous Government Organisations) included a number of old friends such as the Victoria and Albert Museum, the Science Museum, the Armouries and Kew Gardens. Added to their number was a new body to be called the Commission for Ancient Monuments and Historic Buildings for England which would combine the functions of the Ancient Monuments Division of the Department of the Environment with the Historic Buildings Council for England.

This was not news to us as the Environment Secretary, Michael Heseltine, had used the occasion of our 1982 AGM to announce the establishment of this new body. The proposal had a mixed reception. Some were enthusiastic about the creation of a large powerful body to look after and lobby government on behalf of the heritage; others, myself included, were less enthusiastic. I could see every sense in hiving off the Ancient Monuments Division into a semi-independent quango where it would be able to pursue a more entrepreneurial role in the management and promotion of our ancient monuments. I was very dubious, however, of the value of combining it with the functions of the Historic Buildings Council. Firstly, there was a possible conflict of interests where the responsibility for maintaining and promoting state owned ancient monuments was combined within the same body whose function was also to make grants for conserving the private sector. It would be only natural for priority to be given to the former where the glory lay, at the expense of the latter. More importantly, the HBC, with its lay membership and small staff, was able to respond positively and quickly to emergency situations. I feared that it might become swallowed up in the bureaucracy of the new body.

Most important of all was the fact that the lay chairman of the Council had direct access to the Secretary of State, which the current chairman, Dame Jennifer Jenkins, used to remarkable effect. It was a far more influential position than simply being one of a number of committee chairmen on a body outside government. I am pretty certain that Jennifer shared my view but we were in the minority and in the general excitement about the new and powerful body representing the heritage these discordant notes were swept aside. The official argument was that the conservation officers who advised the HBC needed to have access to and work with the technical officers in the Ancient Monuments Division, though why this could not have been achieved by leaving the HBC where it was was not at all clear. Interestingly Scotland and Wales who were

Rockingham Castle by Tillemans dated 1721, One of the earliest pictures of the Castle.

erial photograph of Rockingham taken in about 1980. Note buildings outside curtain wall and
wers have been removed.

Richard Watson by Hayter.
Courtesy Photographic Research Library, Courtauld Institute.

Lieutenant (later Commander) Sir Michael Culme-Seymour 5th Bart (MSW's Uncle Michael).
Courtesy Courtauld Photographic Research Library, Courtauld Institute.

Liebe Saunders (MSW's mother) with Alasdair, Elizabeth, and Michael

Captain L.S. Saunders DSO
Royal Navy (MSW's father)

HMS *Trinidad* (Captain Saunders) sunk on Arctic convoy duty 1941

Britannia Royal Naval College, Dartmouth

HMS *Ceylon* escorting RMS *Gothic* acting as temporary Royal Yacht during HM The Queen's post Coronation Commonwealth Tour

Watercolour of the quarterdeck of HMS *Ceylon* in Colombo Harbour by Robert Chitham

Hoisting out an LCM (weighing 32 tons) from HMS *Messina* in the Pacific

The bomb

HMS *Eagle*, Fleet Aircraft Carrier © Crown Copyright/MOD

Georgina with her father, Admiral Sir William Davis GCB DSO

The Dell, Crafthole, Cornwall, our first home. *Watercolour by MSW*

'est Down Cottage, Soberton, Hampshire. Our home from 1960 to 1971. *Watercolour by Anne Vail*

HMS *Broadsword* at speed. © Crown Copyright/MOD

HMS *Rocket* approaching HMS *Hermes* for a jackstay transfer © Crown Copyright/MOD

HMS *Broadsword* entering Venice

The Aircraft Carrier Squadron manoeuvering
© Crown Copyright/MOD

HMS *London* in the Trinidad Channel, Chile © Crown Copyright/MOD

HMS *London* visits
Bangkok.
l to r: Sub
Lieutenant
Bridges, Crown
Prince of Thailand,
Captain Bartosik,
MSW

Cedar Hill, our home in Bermuda. *Watercolour by Elizabeth Davis*

MSW (newly promoted) with Commodore Martin Lucey, Senior Naval Officer, West Indies

Transport problems during the Governor, Bahamas tour of the Outer Islands.
l to r: Resident Naval Officer, Nassau, Lieut. Cdr Terry Butler, The Hon. Lyndon
Pindling, Chief Minister, MSW, HE Sir Francis Cumming-Bruce, Governor of the
Bahamas, Commodore Martin Lucey, Senior Naval Officer, West Indies

Three generations
of sailors. l to r:
Sub Lieutenant
James Saunders
Watson, son,
Captain Leslie
Saunders DSO,
father, Commander
Michael Saunders
Watson, CBE,
Admiral Sir William
Davis GCB DSO,
father in law.

Arrival at Rockingham Autumn 1971. l to r: Fiona, David, MSW,
Georgina, James. with Seumas seated in front

Lord Montagu of
Beaulieu and Ted
Graham MP (later
Lord Graham of
Edmonton) with a
petition
containing over
one and a quarter
million signatures
seeking
Government
support for the
heritage

George Howard (later, Lord Howard of Henderskelfe) at Castle Howard. Courtesy Mirrorpix

ltmore Asheville, North Carolina. Built by Cornelius nderbilt in 1890 and reputedly the largest private house in e world. Used with permission from The Biltmore Company, Asheville, rth Carolina

Casteel Vosbergen, a perfect little Dutch medieval castle with three moats. Home of Heike Kammerlingh Onnes

Collage of newspaper reports on HWG

MSW in the space which would be the Science Reading Room of the new British Library building. Courtesy of The British Library

The exterior of the new building under construction alongside the Midland Hotel at St Pancras. Courtesy of The British Library

Castle under siege. BBC TV Series *By The Sword Divided* filmed at Rockingham 1985/6

Family group circa 1985. l to r: Fiona, Georgina, MSW, David, Lizzie and James

offered the same arrangement chose not to incorporate their HBCs into the body running their monuments.

The bill being before Parliament, we now had to do the best we could to make it reasonably workable. Jeremy Benson threw himself into it with his usual dogged enthusiasm given added edge by his personal experience as a member of the HBC. Lord Montagu took charge in the House of Lords and formed an *ad hoc* committee to examine the details.

I was glad to see that the functions of the new Commission included a requirement to 'provide in England education and instruction to the public in relation to...buildings and areas of special architectural or historic interest'. I hoped that this might mean that the Commission would offer advice and assistance to houses wishing to set up education facilities. Unfortunately the Commission interpreted this provision as referring solely to their own property and, rather than assist the private sector, set themselves up in opposition – or so it seemed at the time.

Concentrating as we were on the aspects of the bill which affected the Historic Buildings and Monuments Commission (HBMC) I little thought that I should personally be involved in one of the other bodies concerned, and it came as a complete surprise when early in the new year I received a telephone call from Michael Jopling, the Secretary of State for Agriculture, asking me if I would be prepared to become one of the founder trustees of Kew Gardens. Various members of my family have strong botanical interests but I have never counted myself among them and my role in the garden is principally that of destruction. My appointment to Kew therefore caused something of a stir. It was the first but not the last time that a Government appointment was greeted by my loved ones with a chorus of 'Why You?'

The answer was fairly simple. Earlier in the year I had made a point of meeting all the principal officers of the various bodies which advised the government on aspects of heritage property. Included in these was the director of Kew, Professor Arthur Bell. He came to lunch with me in my flat and we had a long discussion about the importance of designed landscape in relation to historic buildings. Kew has a large number of listed buildings and Arthur clearly felt that it would be helpful to have on his new board someone acquainted with the issues, and his eye fell upon me. I had met Michael Jopling, the Secretary of State for Agriculture, Fisheries and Food, on a number of occasions and so when my name was put forward he recognised it.

I found myself sitting on a board of scientists and public figures administering a body with whose principal field of activity I was unfamiliar. I took heart however from my neighbour at our first meeting who had been chairman of the Scientific Advisory Council. A distinguished scientist and

Fellow of the Royal Society, I confessed to him that I knew very little about plants and barely understood the difference between a daisy and a chrysanthemum.

'That makes two of us,' he replied. 'My subject is seaweed.'

I then realised that we were all pretty well in the dark about what we were supposed to be doing and that we each had our own particular area of expertise on which to draw and contribute.

I served as a trustee of Kew for eight years and found it totally absorbing. With its satellite at Wakehurst Place, Kew's purpose is essentially scientific and the fine gardens in both places enjoyed by over three million people a year are there for scientific purposes. This point struck me forcibly in the aftermath of the great gale in 1987 which occurred while we were having a board meeting. The curator, John Simmons, reported on the loss of some particularly valuable specimen and the Chief Scientist rubbed his hands with glee.

'I have been dying to get at the roots of that tree for years.'

Touring the Jodrell laboratory one day I was introduced to a group of scientists working away with their test tubes and microscopes. On being asked what they were doing, they said that they were studying the properties of aloes. In my ignorance of matters of pure science, I then asked why they were studying aloes in particular and what the economic outcome of their studies might be. They replied that they were not sure whether aloes had an economic application. They thought that they might be used as some sort of emetic in the USA.

I was amazed that such effort should be being put into a study the economic outcome of which was apparently unimportant. But this is what pure scientific research is all about and later on in the tour we met a lady who thought she might have stumbled across an antidote to AIDS.

The Herbarium, where plant material collected over the years is preserved, identified and named, had a distinctly imperial flavour about it. The building itself resplendent in its fine wrought-iron balustrades epitomised Victorian imperial confidence and it was not difficult to imagine it at the hub of a network of proconsuls and traders sending in their specimens from far flung points of the earth.

As trustees we found ourselves taking over a scientific research establishment which had hitherto been part of the Department of Agriculture and it was staffed as such. There was no one on the complement qualified to run the very considerable public enterprise involving over three million visitors per year. The Treasury controlled the complement and pocketed the entrance fees. The catering was franchised and of a very low standard, and the shop was run by the Chief Scientist who really had other more important matters to attend to.

Wresting control from the sticky hands of the Treasury took a long time and much patient argument by our chairman, John Eccles. It must have been at least five years before the trustees really felt themselves in charge.

My particular duties were to chair the Buildings committee and be the board member with responsibility for Wakehurst Place, Kew's satellite in Sussex. There were 250 listed buildings at Kew and several major building projects which were proceeding under the supervision of the Property Services Agency (PSA). The latter included the restoration of the Temperate House which had just been completed, and was to be followed by the Palm House. Then there were two important new buildings, the very sophisticated Princess of Wales building, and a new Museum building. In the longer term there were plans for a proper visitor reception area, an extension to the Jodrell laboratory, and the restoration of the pagoda. There was plenty for my committee to do.

One of the trustees on the Buildings committee was the architect Sir Philip Dowson, who subsequently became President of the Royal Academy. He should have been chairman, but he refused, preferring for some reason to serve under me. I was very glad to have the benefit of his expertise.

Our first task was to appoint a consultant architect. We had a number of applications from heavyweights in the architectural world attracted by this prestigious post. Each candidate was given the task of designing a visitor centre for the main gate which opened on to Kew Green. It was a fascinating exercise and Sir Philip came into his own putting these experts through their paces. We were shown some remarkable schemes; one envisaged placing the Aroid House on stilts over the main gate.

Then there was the restoration of the Palm House. Designed by Decimus Burton and built in the middle of the 19th century, it is one of the great examples of Victorian technology, but it had various features which related to the age in which it was built and were no longer required. In particular the glazing bars were made of cast iron, a material no longer readily available. We planned to replace them with stainless steel which when painted white would look no different to cast iron. This was not good enough for the Victorian Society who objected to the plans and had to be convinced that there was no practical alternative. All this took time and time was of the essence.

First, a temporary house had to be built to accommodate the collections while the restoration work was underway, and then the collections had to be moved into the temporary palm house. The restoration work had to be completed before the winter so that the collections could be returned before the frosts came. If this programme was not adhered to there was a risk that the Giant Palm would burst out of its temporary home with disastrous results.

Early in October concern started to be expressed that there might be slippage in this tight programme. There did not seem to be a proper sense of urgency on the part of the contractors. The board had a crisis meeting. The chairman sent for the chairman of the contractors and informed him in no uncertain terms of the humiliation his firm would suffer if they failed to hold to schedule. The transformation was amazing. Where the site had been virtually empty, it was suddenly crawling with men. The work was completed on schedule and the Giant Palm returned to its home in good order. The same success story could not be said to apply to the new Museum building, where serious delays in completion were caused by difficulties in commissioning the heating system.

Quite apart from the pleasure of working with people of the calibre of Philip Dowson and David Attenborough, the experience I gained at Kew, particularly on the buildings sub-committee came in very useful when I found myself dealing with a much bigger building project, the British Library.

CHAPTER 9

President

It was becoming clear during the summer that riding out the Falklands crisis at the BBC had taken its toll on George Howard's health and he was finding his duties as chairman increasingly demanding. He indicated that he wished to step down as President of the HHA at the AGM after four years in the chair and as his deputy I was invited to stand as the next president. Needless to say I felt greatly honoured and was very happy to accept. The question then arose of who should be the deputy president. As the president's term of office was a maximum of five years it was not essential that the deputy should necessarily be seen as the next president – at least not in the early stages of the presidency. I had long admired the balanced and sensible views of Charles, Earl of March which were very similar to my own, and his commercial success at Goodwood was plain for all to see. Furthermore in an organisation such as the HHA it is no bad thing where the president is a commoner, for his deputy to be a member of the aristocracy. I was delighted therefore when Charles agreed to put his name forward.

Robin, Marquess of Tavistock had proved himself as a highly competent operator in the city, in addition to presiding over one of the largest and most efficient tourist operations at Woburn. Very much a realist, he was an ideal choice for treasurer to succeed Charles March. These appointments were duly confirmed at the annual general meeting on 26th October. With Terry Empson now firmly in the saddle, I felt that I had a pretty strong team.

Following George Howard as president of the HHA was nevertheless an awesome task. George, as founder deputy president, had set the Association up and put flesh on the bones of Edward Montagu's idea. Furthermore, he was experienced in the world of politics and a much respected public figure. I was unknown outside the small circle of those concerned with taxation and management of heritage property. As George's deputy for the past four years however I had been closely involved with the administration of the Association and had met quite a number of its members.

This was before the days when everyone has to have a business plan with objectives almost from the date of birth, but I did set myself some targets for my first year as president. My first priority was to go out and about and meet more people, particularly those connected with the heritage. Secondly, I needed to know more about the membership; what their needs were and what they expected of the Association. Finally, I felt our administrative arrangements were too cumbersome to deal with the many different issues that arose. The present Executive Committee numbered over thirty and included 'observer' representatives from other related bodies. I wanted one or two shoulders to lean on, one or two brains to pick and rather fancied the idea of a small Finance and Policy Committee meeting once a month with delegated powers from an expanded Executive Council with elected representatives of the regions sitting on it, which met once a quarter.

Terry Empson, the director general, agreed wholeheartedly and we decided to set up an away day for the officers of the Association to take these thoughts a stage further. My new colleagues, Charles March and Robin Tavistock, thought this an excellent idea, and Robin kindly agreed to act as host. We met in December at Woburn. Terry joined us and we covered much useful ground ranging from my proposed constitutional change to a policy for Friends of the Association, in surroundings of the greatest comfort and interest.

For some time I had been aware that all was not well in Scotland, and I determined at an early stage to pay an extensive visit to meet the members and to hear at first hand some of their problems. Scotland is a big country and with only one representative on the HHA Council it was not surprising that some of our Scottish members should feel rather out on a limb. Georgina and I planned this tour to take place in February, which may not have been altogether wise, but from our point of view it was a great success. We visited ten different houses and castles, and were received in great style. Without doubt the most memorable occasion was our visit to Robin Linzee Gordon and his late wife Sheena at Cluny Castle in Aberdeenshire.

Robin had warned me that Cluny in February was colder than a trench in Flanders. He was absolutely right. It is one of those immense granite piles beloved of Victorian grandees in the late 19th century which seem to go on for miles with tower upon tower. Robin and Sheena lived in one of the towers which was heated mainly by the Aga. As soon as you emerged into the main house you were hit by a wall of damp cold. Our bedroom had no less than three portable gas stoves but you would not have known. There was nothing cold about our welcome, however, and Sheena prepared a dinner for twenty-four for which the main course was a cauldron of pigeon breasts cooked in chocolate and calvados, while Robin lined up bottles of Famous Grouse on the capacious sideboard.

Aberdeenshire is unique in Great Britain in that it probably has more castles and large houses within its boundaries than anywhere else. Some owners were capitalising on the oil boom and going in for corporate entertainment in a big way, others were struggling to farm, others, notably Rothiemurchus, were running large outdoor pursuits centres, but the general message was that there was not enough business to go round and that these places were hugely expensive to maintain.

Our final day was spent with the National Trust of Scotland. The Director, Jamie Stormonth-Darling and his wife Mary were the kindest of hosts in their very modern house at Dirleton on the North Berwick coast. The first time we arrived we had with us two spaniels one of which, Chico, was a bit shy and loved diving under things, particularly beds. As we were greeted by Jamie and Mary, Chico shot out of the car into the house, very much a no dog area, and dived into the first room she came to. This turned out to be their bedroom and the next half hour was spent with our hosts on the floor trying to tempt her out from under their bed!

Jamie took me under his wing in Edinburgh and introduced me to everyone who was anyone in the Scottish heritage scene. In those days the National Trust of Scotland was run on a very personal basis by three Colonels: Jamie himself, John Davey, and Mickey Blacklock; the Chairman was John, Marquis of Bute, and the President, David, Earl of Wemyss, half-brother of Jeremy Benson. It was a very friendly party and very supportive of private owners, in contrast to the somewhat standoffish attitude of their larger counterpart in the south.

On my return to Ebury Street, it was evident that the Washington exhibition was beginning to take shape and the curator, Gervase Jackson-Stops, was busy drawing up his list of desiderata. It was a long one and included treasures of untold value. Some owners were going to be asked to loan more than twenty items including furniture, pictures and books. It was clearly going to be important if the owners were to co-operate that we reap maximum advantage out of the exhibition by way of promoting participating houses. I felt that an early visit to the USA might help things along in the right direction and enable me to brief myself on the situation.

The US system for encouraging preservation of historic buildings is very different to ours. There is no tax relief on income or capital tax, and they looked with envy on our arrangements for conditional exemption on death or transfer. Their rates of tax were lower than ours, but pretty swingeing all the same. Many of their historic houses comprise smallish terraced and semi-detached buildings in old towns such as Fredericksburg, and Annapolis. The local preservation society endeavours to buy from the individual owners the right to control the decoration and alteration of the front of the house, so that the integrity and homogeneity of the street can be maintained.

Undoubtedly the highlight of my USA trip was a visit to Biltmore, North Carolina, home of my opposite number, Bill Cecil, Chairman of the Historic Houses Association of America. Biltmore, built in 1895 by George Vanderbilt, youngest son of William Vanderbilt and grandson of the famous 'Commodore' Cornelius Vanderbilt, is probably one of the largest 'stately homes' in the world – if not the largest. Designed on the lines of a vast 16th century French chateau by Richard Morris Hunt, and standing in extensive grounds and park landscaped by Frederick Law Olmsted, it is a hugely impressive building.

Apart from the size, its principal fascination for me was that it was built at the leading edge of modern domestic technology and represents the apogee of what we would know in Britain as the great Edwardian country house. It had a sophisticated electrical system using the first of Edison's filament bulbs, central heating, plumbing, refrigeration and a complex elevator and dumbwaiter system serving the thirty-three guest bedrooms – each of which had its own ensuite bathroom with hot and cold water, a bath and a shower shaped like a gigantic sunflower with huge temperature controls to match.

The arrangements down below were no less impressive. There were thirteen pantries, two walk-in refrigerators driven by a central plant together with an ice making machine located in the basement, three kitchens, and a vast servants' dining room feeding the 80 servants required to look after the house and 40 stables. Finally in the basement were a fully equipped gymnasium, an indoor swimming pool, and a full-size bowling alley. All that was missing was the sauna! It was amazing to reflect that this house was designed in 1890.

Vanderbilt was equally concerned with the development of his estate, which at one time ran to 125,000 acres. He built a model village to house the estate workers, and developed a series of large dairy farms ostensibly to supply his guests with fresh dairy produce. Such was the demand locally however that before long Biltmore Dairy Farms Ltd was one of the largest dairies in the south. There was a huge forestry operation and recently the present owner, Bill Cecil, has just developed a major winery.

Biltmore may be larger than life, so too is Bill Cecil. A big man, bursting with energy and bubbling enthusiasm, it was fascinating to listen to him talking of all his schemes for the future. Biltmore was big business. The house and estate attracted five hundred thousand visitors per year paying $10 per head. Even my limited arithmetical skills could calculate a healthy turnover.

He took me to visit his publicity agents in Asheville who gave us a presentation. It is difficult for visitors to the USA to appreciate its enormous scale, and the fact that there is no national newspaper which is regularly read by readers across the States. Attracting potential visitors is something of a problem. A huge amount of money could be spent (Bill's budget was $1m) trying to draw people to visit Asheville, North Carolina which simply disappears into a black hole because few want to go all the way to Asheville to see a house, however magnificent. Bill's agent's approach was to follow the convention world. They would find a convention taking place, say, in Miami, advertise first in the convention material and then saturate all the towns whose routes to Miami passed within 500 miles of Biltmore with copy like:' ...and on your way to Miami, why not stop off at Asheville NC and visit the greatest etc etc....' It was a most interesting and instructive session.

Bill and his wife Mimi lived like any other business couple in an interesting largish house in the woods. Somewhat sparsely furnished in contrast to the grandeur of Biltmore it was nevertheless a comfortable if unconventional home. Bill's one extravagance was Air Force One, a Lear Jet which flew me to Atlanta for my homeward journey.

I returned home to find the country in the grip of an election campaign. The government under Mrs Thatcher was not particularly popular but she was still basking in the aftermath of her Falkland victory and the opposition were split and badly organised. The unknown factor was the Social Democratic party which at one point had been polling almost 25% of the votes. In fact Mrs Thatcher won with a substantial if reduced majority.

In the subsequent reshuffle, the post of Secretary of State for the Environment became something of a political football. Michael Heseltine went to Defence to be succeeded by Tom King for six months. Then Patrick Jenkin, managed to hold the post for two years before he in turn was succeeded by Kenneth Baker for a year, and finally Nicholas Ridley, who saw out my Presidency. Four Secretaries of State in six years! The Environment may not be the most important or exciting Department but it is a big one, and such a rapid turnover of senior ministers must make it very difficult for the incumbent to make informed decisions without relying heavily on the advice of his civil servants.

Michael Heseltine with four years in post knew what he was about and after the first blustery meeting showed a genuine concern for and interest in heritage matters. Patrick Jenkin came from a similar position on the political spectrum and as Chief Secretary in an earlier Heath administration, he had given a dusty answer to my uncle Michael, leading a CLA deputation on historic houses before the days of the HHA – but at least he was a friendly face.

Of the other ministers with whom we were concerned, Peter Rees was still in the Treasury, but as Chief Secretary he would be more concerned with public expenditure than matters of tax detail. Lord Cockfield had been moved to Trade, and subsequently to Europe, and we had a new Financial Secretary, John Moore. Considered something of a bright spark, I found him impressive and receptive and it was a sad moment for the Tory party when his health forced his retirement from politics a year or two later.

For some reason September always seems to be the month for conferences. I am not a great enthusiast for big conferences; they are expensive to mount; a great deal of hot air is released and you are unlikely to learn very much from them – but they do offer an opportunity to meet others in the business, and on occasions they can provide a platform for a minister to speak. This means that he and his officials are forced to address the issue which is no bad thing. Putting your side of it is another matter, as the minister very rarely attends long enough to hear anything you have to say. What they like to do is to arrive in a cloud of blue smoke minutes before they are due to speak, answer the odd question, tour the trade fair and away. Understandably they do not want to have their ears bent on a subject which does not happen to be one of their priorities.

The British Tourist Authority led off the season with a monster conference at Oxford in September on tourism and heritage. There was a long list of speakers, and we discussed everything from partnership to employment, taxation and market research. It was a marathon effort lasting three days. The minister concerned was Norman Lamont, who as a junior minister in the Department of Trade held the tourism portfolio. He was not a particularly striking person to meet but when, subsequently, he went to the Treasury as Financial Secretary, I found him concerned and keen to help.

The conference was chaired by Robin Cooke in his usual grandiose way but the mastermind behind it was the Director General of the BTA, Len Lickorish. Len was a quiet unassuming figure, with almost forty years experience in the travel business, the last sixteen as Director General of the BTA. He was one of those people, unusual in an industry given to generating much hot air, who knew what to do and did it with the minimum of fuss. With first Sir Alexander Glen, and then Sir Henry Marking as chairman, Len was instrumental in providing the positive support in the shape of staff and office space that set the HHA up in the first instance, and we owe him a great debt for that. At a later date I was privileged to be a guest at a luncheon given in Len's honour by Lord Forte. The impressive line up of celebrities who attended was a fitting tribute to Len's major contribution to the tourist industry.

The BTA conference was followed rapidly by the Museums' Association conference at the Brangwyn Hall in Swansea. Edward Montagu, the current chairman, had invited me to speak at one of the plenary sessions following Lord Parry of Neyland, chairman of the Welsh Tourist Board. The Brangwyn Hall is a huge place, and there must have been three hundred or more in the audience, some of whom might not be all that well disposed to owners of historic houses. I was therefore feeling somewhat apprehensive wondering how I could possibly match Lord Parry's fine Welsh oratory when the lights went out and we were plunged into total darkness. Lord Parry did not hesitate, but continued in full spate as if nothing had happened for the next quarter of an hour or so till the lights came on again. It was a virtuoso performance. When he eventually sat down, however, I was left with five minutes to give a talk which was scheduled for forty.

The previous evening I had the chance of a quiet word with Edward and he told me in confidence that he had just been invited to chair the new Historic Buildings and Monuments Commission. It was a great triumph for Edward who had worked so hard for the Bill in the House of Lords, and I was delighted that he had been offered the top job. While I should have preferred to retain the old Historic Buildings Council for reasons already expressed, the Commission was now a fact and it was very good that we had a friend in the chair.

As soon as the Swansea conference was over I drove to Sheerness to take the boat to Holland for the annual meeting of the European Union of Historic Houses Associations. Our host and President, Heike Kamerlingh Onnes, was determined to show us that, while Holland may be a small country, it has a fine heritage of historic houses. One of the first to suggest 'downgrading' the meetings and making them what he called 'wifeless', when it was Heike's turn to be host, he laid on one of the most lavish occasions.

The seemingly endless stream of conferences and regional meetings continued throughout 1983 into 1984. Of particular note was the occasion which we called rather flippantly 'Heirs and Graces', an overnight session at Goodwood for heirs to give them an opportunity for an input into the Association. It was interesting, if not rather horrifying, to discover that in a number of cases the parents had simply never mentioned to their heirs whether or not they were planning to hand over the estate, let alone take any part in running it. In an organisation such as the HHA where the central objective is to seek continuity of ownership the attitude of heirs and more particularly their spouses is of the greatest importance, and as a result of these discussions, a special committee was set up to focus on the interests of the next generation.

Another occasion which demonstrated the universal nature of the HHA was the gardens course at Wye College in Kent. One of a series run by Tom Wright of Wye College focussing on the practical issues of maintaining a large garden open to the public. Head gardeners sat down with their owners and studied together underlining the close relationship that should exist between keen gardening owners and their professional staff.

Then in June of 1984 I was invited to attend a conference at Leeds Castle on the future of the heritage. It was chaired by Jennifer Jenkins and comprised about thirty people including Brian Lang who had recently become the director of the newly created National Heritage Memorial Fund. I had met him once or twice before when he was Secretary to the Historic Buildings Council for Scotland. Leeds Castle provided an opportunity to know him better. There was something compelling about this highly intelligent, articulate Scot and I found him stimulating company. We used to meet regularly for lunch or dinner and on one occasion speculated on the possibility that we might do something together. A passing remark which remained in my mind and which I was able to put into effect some years later at the British Library.

After so much talking, it was good to go and see some practical results of all this activity, and the Scottish annual meting at Thirlestane Castle in the Borders provided just such an opportunity. Thirlestane is a fine example of the exuberance of some Scottish architecture. The Central structure is essentially a large fortress on which Sir William Bruce in 1672 superimposed a magnificent Renaissance front, which was itself extended by Bryce in the 19th century in true Scottish baronial style adding conical roofs to the towers and battlements all over the place. Home of the Maitland family, the Earls of Lauderdale, since the 13th century, by the time the present owner, Bunny Maitland-Carew, inherited in 1972, it was in a mess. Water poured through the roof; a survey revealed 48 outbreaks of dry rot; there was no estate to speak of, and resources were limited. It was a prospect to daunt the bravest heart and hardly encouraging for the new heir when he visited the 'Destruction of the Country House' exhibition at the V & A to find that, unbeknown to him, visitors were greeted with a large photograph of Thirlestane over which was placed an even larger red question mark.

As an act of faith, Bunny sank all he had into Thirlstane and, with the aid of a substantial grant from the HBC for Scotland, managed to restore it to its former splendour, but was now faced with the problem of how to keep it there. The National Heritage Memorial Fund (NHMF) then came to the rescue with a modest endowment. Thirlestane now stands with its future reasonably secure, a much loved family home open to the public, when. it could so easily have joined that pile of rubble exhibited at the V&A.

We came home to attend a large private function at Doddington Hall in Lincolnshire, another great house inherited in difficult circumstances with a heavy tax bill and major structural problems. But Doddington too, now stands secure, structurally sound, redecorated and a lively family home. Doddington was saved by a provision in the same Act which set up the National Heritage Memorial Fund and enabled the Government to accept objects in lieu of tax and allow them to remain *in situ*, subject to the usual conditions of access and maintenance. Doddington has a large portrait of the Delaval family by Joshua Reynolds which was painted for and hangs in the long gallery. This work was accepted under the in lieu provisions, freeing up the money for the badly needed repairs which would otherwise have gone in tax.

Thus through measures enacted in the recent past, two major houses had been saved for future enjoyment by the public and, I hope too, by their owners. While these successes might owe something to the activities of the HHA there were many others involved, not least the owners themselves without whose determination and commitment nothing might have happened. Writing in the Association journal *Historic House* that autumn, I warned that this justified glow of satisfaction would be short-lived and it would not be long before we faced the next crisis as owners grappled with the increasing costs of specialist maintenance, the vagaries of the tourist industry, and a tax system that still threatened those 'eccentrics' who choose to live in a historic house in the 20th century.

We did not have long to wait. By the turn of the year, three major houses were in crisis: Kedlstone, Nostell Priory and Weston Park. The situation in each was different but the common factor was that deaths in the family had given rise to tax bills which could not be paid without offering the house, its contents or both to the government in lieu of tax, and the Government was unwilling to take them on. In the past this would have been a matter for the National Trust but experience had shown that most of their houses were under-endowed and they were determined not to accept an historic property unless it came with an endowment on such a scale that it would cover every eventuality.

One cannot blame the Trust for this since their resources are finite and their responsibilities infinite. Nevertheless, private owners, struggling to run their houses and pay tax, sometimes look with envy at the National Trust which enjoys not only tax-free status but also, I sometimes suspect, the lion's share of grant aid. We have relatively few National Trust properties in the East Midlands but where they abound, as for instance in Dorset, with their huge membership enjoying 'free' access, the private owners used to feel that they were competing in the tourist market with their hands tied behind their back. These grumbles aside, the Trust has a difficult job to do and does it well.

In the case of the three houses mentioned above, the government came to the rescue by topping up the funds allocated to the National Heritage Memorial Fund and enabling appropriate endowments to be created. Once again it reminded everybody of the costs involved in maintaining the heritage when the owner can no longer play his part.

In October 1984 Kenneth Baker, Secretary of State for Education, accepted an invitation to open a Heritage Education Conference at Lamport Hall and a major Youth Resource building in Northampton for the Northamptonshire Association of Youth Clubs of which I was chairman. He and his wife, Anne, spent the previous night with us at Rockingham. They were fascinated by Rockingham and in particular with the garden where we were in the process of restoring the yew hedge round the rose garden. I mention this visit because it was to have ramifications later.

Then in December came the sad news of George Howard's death. He had been suffering from diabetes for some time and had lost an enormous amount of weight. Granted a peerage on retirement from the chair of the BBC he was just beginning to enjoy himself in the House of Lords where he was performing very effectively. He had been appointed chairman of the Museums and Galleries Commission, but more importantly for us, he was President of Honour for the Washington Exhibition due to take place in the autumn of 1985. It was of vital importance that we had a successor of at least equivalent status who understood what we were trying to do.

There was no shortage of candidates who fancied themselves for the job. There was however one man who, were he prepared to do it, would be superb. Lord Charteris of Amisfield, lately Private Secretary to the Queen, and at that time Provost of Eton and chairman of the recently set up National Heritage Memorial Fund. The question was how to engineer this before the powerful lobbies forced a decision behind closed doors. Speed was of the essence.

As it happened fortune played into our hand. By sheer coincidence I happened to be sitting in the Central Lobby of the House of Commons discussing this matter with Brian Lang, Secretary to NHMF, who was very enthusiastic about the idea, when Robin Cooke who was a trustee of NHMF appeared. Robin had recently been deselected as MP for Bristol West, and knighted for his services by Mrs Thatcher. Having lost his seat he was now very much involved in tourism as a member of the British Tourist Authority and was hoping for the job himself. On the spur of the moment I went up to him and said:

'Robin, you are just the man.' He beamed. 'You know Martin Charteris well. Would you ask him whether he would be prepared to be President of Honour for the Washington exhibition?'

'Of course,' he said at once, generously. 'What a brilliant idea.'

In the event, Martin agreed, and, as we all knew he would, did the job with great panache and charm.

Without doubt the Washington exhibition 'Treasure Houses of Britain' was the highlight of my time as president of the HHA. Subtitled 'Five Hundred Years of Private Patronage and Art Collecting', both in the quality and the quantity of objects loaned, it must have been one of the greatest exhibitions ever to be exported from the United Kingdom. The catalogue itself was a work of art with 680 pages weighing 6lbs. A substantial majority of the 185 lenders were private individuals, some lending up to thirty articles of untold value. As most of the lenders were members of the HHA, the gallery used us as a point of contact. A key figure in this was Cami Greer, the staff member of the National Gallery responsible for liaising with the lenders. Her charm and competence won the day and remarkably few problems arose.

The J Paul Getty Fund at Malibu offered a grant towards any restoration that was needed. This in itself was a major breakthrough as never before had such funds been made available for private owners. The British Council organised the packing and despatch with superb efficiency, British Airways carried them, and the whole operation was sponsored by the Ford Motor Company.

In his introduction to the catalogue[*], Carter Brown, the director of the National Gallery of Art in Washington, recognised the unique position of what he continued to call the 'English' country house (despite the fact that Scotland, Wales and Northern Ireland have their share) as deriving from the fact that it has always been the centre of a community, a background for politics, for agriculture, sport, and, he could have added, science, for the social round and family gatherings, and for art collecting. This coupled with peace since the Civil War of the 17th century, the rule of primogeniture, where the eldest son inherits the estate and the rest make do with what is left over, and a respect for evolution rather then revolution has lead to the survival of family art collections to a degree unequalled anywhere else in Europe. He mentioned the importance of the country house in the patronage of the arts and how it portrays the developing attitudes and changing tastes which form part of the common cultural heritage between

---

[*]   The Treasure Houses of Britain – 500 years of Private Patronage and Art Collecting. Catalogue of a loan exhibition held at the National Gallery. Copyright 1985 Board of Trustees National Gallery of Art, Washington

the two countries.

He went on to say: 'Knowing that the contents of British (at last!) country houses taken together, would outweigh the holdings of almost any museum in the world, it has long been a dream of mine to mount an exhibition which would show something of these riches for the first time to an international audience' – and he might have added, in one place.

I had hoped that the exhibition as originally conceived might have shown more of the economic role of the country house in its estate which, I believe, was the original idea. It was now very much art orientated, but Carter was determined not just to display a random selection of 'treasures' from country house collections but rather to 'try to separate the many layers of taste that they represent and to show in a broadly chronological way how they were formed'.

It was an ambitious scheme and it worked superbly. The highly flexible and architecturally exciting East Building, designed by I.M.Pei, lent itself to the creation of a number of spaces representing in some cases particular rooms in particular houses, but, in most cases, a typical room representing a particular period in the 500 years since the Tudor succession. The designers led by Gailliard Revenal worked with Gervaise Jackson-Stops, the curator, in choosing the objects and produced some remarkably convincing settings.

My only regret in this great display of private patronage and taste is that so little room was left for the latter half of the 20th century. We are perhaps unusual at Rockingham in having a substantial collection of modern art of museum quality; but there are others and I believe it is important to show that private patronage of the arts in historic houses, while not on the scale it has been in the past, is far from dead. I had hoped therefore that they might display our Stanley Spencer but he was not so well known in the USA as he is now and they settled for the safer John Piper and Henry Moore.

The exhibition was due to open on 3rd November 1985 but we should have to be there a few days before and after – which meant at least a week in Washington. Georgina and I decided to use this as an opportunity to see something of America and on 10th October we left on an epic journey which took us from the brilliant colours of New England in the fall to the raw grandeur of the 'Gardens of the Gods' in Arizona, to frontier life in a log cabin hunting deer in Utah, to provincial America in Rockingham County, North Carolina, and finally to the White House.

It was a trip full of contrasts, and we returned feeling we knew a little more about this great country and its people. Above all we were impressed with its sheer enormity which was only matched by the warmth of the welcome we received wherever we went.

We flew into Washington on 29th October in some style with Bill Cecil in his Lear Jet, having spent the past couple of days with him and his wife Mimi at their home in Asheville, North Carolina, recovering from a splendid but somewhat exhausting visit to Rockingham County as guests of honour for their bicentenary celebrations. We were met by that essentially American form of transport, the 'stretch limo', which whisked us to our hotel and then on to the National Gallery of Art.

The exhibition had had a tremendous build-up and I was a little apprehensive lest it failed to meet our expectations. We need not have worried; it was magnificent. To quote my diary, 'The exhibition is out of this world. It is clearly one of the greatest and fulfils all our hopes and more.'

We had barely time for a quick tour before the press interviews started and continued almost without cease whenever there was a spare minute or two in the crowded programme of the next few days.

Cami Greer, the gallery's liaison officer, had kindly arranged for me to have an area of the staff dining room cordoned off for private parties, and on our first day in Washington I was able to return some of Bill Cecil's hospitality by giving him lunch followed by a private tour of the exhibition. We were halfway through the tour when I received a message to go at once to the entrance desk. There I found the unmistakable figure of George Schultz, the Secretary of State, who had turned up unexpectedly to see the exhibition and as no one else was available, would I take him round?

Bill and Mimi were staunch Democrats and I am not sure that they were best pleased to find their exclusive tour upstaged in this way – however they did not show it. Schultz must have been a hard negotiator. His deadpan expression gave nothing away.

There was one chink of humour however when we paused in front of that magnificent picture known as The Rainbow Portrait of Queen Elizabeth I in which her robe is embroidered with eyes and ears.

'Gee,' said Schultz, 'I guess that must be the first bugged skirt in history.'

The second day in Washington was a repeat of the first with tours of the exhibition for friends and VIPs interspersed with press interviews, involving at one moment climbing into a dinner jacket in the middle of the morning. Another lunch party, this time including more friends and Henri de Breteuil, the President of Les Demeures Historiques, our French equivalent.

The pre-arranged programme for lenders started that evening with a press reception followed by another at the British embassy. The following morning we were formally welcomed at the gallery by Carter Brown before being despatched on a tour of Washington in three double-decker London buses, a form of transport which our hosts felt was appropriate for a bunch of British stately home owners!

We visited the Capitol which was unexpectedly small and rather beautiful. It is easy to forget that this huge most powerful country in the world was once a small group of colonies. Both the older public buildings in Washington, and the plantation houses of Virginia in their size and elegance stood in stark contrast to the pomp and grandeur of Whitehall which reflects an imperial might now lost to history.

The tour ended at the White House where we were regally received by Nancy Reagan in the President's absence. Again I was struck with how small and elegant the White House was in contrast to the plush vulgarity of Buckingham Palace. As the reception proceeded I became dimly aware of a mounting crisis. We were due at the gallery in a dinner jacket for the lenders dinner in under an hour and Washington's streets were jammed with rush hour traffic.

No problem. The Presidential motorcade was activated there and then, and the next thing we knew was that we were flying through Washington to the accompaniment of a motorcycle escort with blaring sirens and flashing lights. I shall never forget the expressions on the faces of the astonished motorists held up at the crossroads by what they thought was the President of the USA, only to find the motorcade consisted of three old London double-deckers full of grinning British aristocrats.

Dinner at the gallery was, as one might have expected, beautifully arranged. The East Building designed by I.M.Pei, who subsequently designed the controversial pyramid at the Louvre, is indeed a remarkable construction, with its sharply acute angles and low-key entrance giving way to a towering hall: it is a work of art in itself, but it combines this with a flexibility of use which we saw used to perfection that evening. When I subsequently became involved with the British Library building at St Pancras, I was to be reminded of this; there are indeed similarities between the two buildings though their design and purpose come from two different directions.

The following morning we staged a joint symposium with the National Trust for Historic Preservation, the US equivalent of our National Trust, on preserving historic houses in the US and the UK. I gave the opening talk before an audience of some 200 which included people like Kenneth Baker, at that time Secretary of State for the Environment. It is very rare to have the ear of a cabinet minister for a whole half-hour and I made good use of it, emphasising the importance of tax relief much more than I would otherwise have done to that audience. Ken took the point and was good enough to come up afterwards and congratulate me on my talk.

One of our concerns during the exhibition was to make the most of the potential for attracting US tourists to come to Britain and visit our historic houses. It seemed a heaven sent opportunity but all sorts of obstacles arose and it proved a very difficult task. Firstly we had the refusal of the British Overseas Trade Board to take any interest, and secondly the gallery's rules forbade it from displaying any promotional material that did not relate to the gallery itself – which at once ruled out any distribution point for leaflets. The British Tourist Authority (BTA), who were as helpful as they could be, managed to lease some space in a building known as the Old Post Office which was about half a mile down the street from the gallery. It was a fine building and a good display but, sadly, too far from the exhibition for the two to be linked in visitors' minds.

The BTA then laid on two workshops for owners and their representatives to meet the travel trade, one in Washington and one in New York. These were reasonably well attended but at once the problem of reaching across America became apparent. There is no national newspaper or TV system and despite its size and power, America is essentially the provincial country which we saw at first hand in Rockingham County.

Nevertheless we made some valuable contacts and were hopeful that at least one or two tours might be arranged. All hopes were dashed early next year, however, when President Reagan bombed Libya via British airfields and Britain came to be regarded across America as a war zone bringing US tourism virtually to a standstill.

Thus for us ended our immediate role in the great Washington exhibition into which so much time and effort had been put. The exhibition itself was a tremendous success and remains one of the greatest ever staged at the National Gallery of Art, or for that matter ever exported from Britain. So successful was it that it was extended an extra month.

Was it all worth while? Certainly the gallery's already high reputation had been enhanced. As far as we, the lenders, were concerned, we had had a good time being fêted in Washington. We had also had an unparalleled opportunity to promote those of our houses which were open to the American public. More importantly we had had a chance to show our own ministers how Britain's heritage is held in such high esteem in the USA, and that it is not some hangover from the past but a very real economic resource. It has to be said, however, that on both these counts we were less than totally successful.

On the tourism front, despite valiant efforts of the BTA, the restrictions imposed by the gallery coupled with the empty threats of Colonel Gaddaffi virtually put paid to any measurable impact on US visits to UK historic houses. On the political front, most ministers, I think, took the point. Certainly they were keen to visit the exhibition. It was a one-off exercise, never to be repeated in our lifetime, and very much more could have been done to link it to some major trade promotion if those concerned in the Foreign Office and Trade Departments had shown more imagination and flexibility.

After all the glamour of Washington and New York, returning to the UK and Ebury Street came as rather an anti climax. On the political front we were concentrating much effort on the issues raised by chattels of heritage value. The issue surfaced in a number of ways. Firstly, there was the procedure where objects of pre-eminent importance could be offered to the government in lieu of inheritance tax, with a 25% rebate on the tax due on the chattel itself, known as the 'douceur'. There was also provision in the legislation, where the object had strong historical connections with a building, that it could remain 'in situ'. A famous example of this was the vast painting of the Delaval family by Reynolds which dominated the long gallery at Doddington and was allowed to remain there after it had been accepted in lieu of tax.*

It was a good arrangement, in which everyone had their cake and were able to eat it. I wanted to see a similar arrangement apply to the allied procedure of 'private treaty' sale, whereby a pre-eminent object could be sold to a public institution at a mutually agreed price with the vendor enjoying the benefit of the 25% douceur. Such a scheme would enable owners faced with heavy repair bills to utilise some of the capital locked up in their works of art without having to break up the collection.

There were issues such as who or which institution should take responsibility for the object, its physical security, environmental condition, insurance and access. And of course the scheme was not widely popular with museum directors who preferred to have the object under their eye. We tried various angles such as sharing the douceur with the purchaser, or sharing the object, but despite its obvious merits, it never really gained ground.

Another potentially more serious issue concerning heritage objects was the unexpected arrival of the VAT man on the scene with a publication of a booklet entitled VAT and Works of Art. This stated that where a work of art that had been on display to the public was sold it should be regarded as an asset of the business and VAT should be charged on the sale price. The fact that the work of art had been inherited before the days of VAT meant nothing. Equally the fact that the value of the work of art, which could run into millions, bore little or no relation to the business, which possibly turned over hundreds or less, meant nothing.

It was typical of the way our administrators interpret regulations and, when it was pointed out to them, the Customs and Excise did agree that it

* See p. 145.

seemed rather unfair but regulations were regulations and it was not in their power to alter them. We managed to persuade them, however, that if the object was removed from public view for a period and then sold it might escape the VAT charge.

Leading our representations at this time was Tony Furze who had succeeded me as chairman of the Tax and Parliamentary Committee. He had done stalwart work in turning the somewhat amateur committee which he inherited from me into a thoroughly professional body with access to some of the greatest legal and accounting brains in the heritage field and highly respected by officials and other professionals alike. Chairing this group was a demanding task and I was not surprised when Tony intimated that he would like to step down. It is not easy to find a replacement who is an owner of an historic house, understands the tax system, and can both write and speak to revenue officials in their language. For some time I had my eye on William Proby, who lived at Elton Hall near Peterborough. He was accountant trained, had a first-class brain and an engaging manner. Having been a merchant banker, he now ran a company in the city which seemed to occupy him three days a week, so he had a little time to spare. He would make an ideal chairman of the Tax and Parliamentary Committee and possibly president in due course. The only problem was that he had political ambitions and was in the process of going through the various hoops necessary to become a Conservative candidate. I worked hard on him (and his wife Merry) to persuade him that he would have far more fun, and indeed satisfaction, in working for the HHA than he would as a politician and to my relief I found I was pushing at an open door. I do not think either William or Merry regretted his change of tack, and he made an excellent chairman and subsequently president. He went on to become Chairman of the National Trust, an office he still holds at the time of writing.

Meanwhile my own position was coming to the end of its statutory five years and I needed to identify my successor. I had always hoped that it might be my deputy president, Charles, Earl of March. The Association had often benefited from his wise advice both in the political and financial field where he was also a trained accountant. Sadly he felt that he could not take on the presidency as well as run Goodwood and his many other public activities but luckily there was in the wings an excellent candidate in the form of Charles, Earl of Shelburne. Charlie Shelburne, owner of Bowood House, had already made a name for himself as leader of his local district council by introducing an original scheme to solve a housing shortage by using private sector accommodation. Full of bright ideas, and energetic enthusiasm, with contacts in high places, he seemed just the man but he too had political ambitions. Furthermore he had only recently joined the

Finance and Policy Committee and was still relatively unknown to the membership at large. It was decided therefore that he should stand as deputy president in place of Charles March at the 1987 AGM, and that I should seek to have my term extended by a year.

As one who had been involved in the early stages of its creation, I greatly admired the work of the National Heritage Memorial Fund (NHMF) under its chairman, Lord Charteris. With a distinguished body of trustees appointed by the Prime Minister, and a very small staff ably headed up by my friend, Brian Lang, it was able to respond to calls for help in double quick time with the minimum of bureaucratic fuss. Sensibly the trustees never actually defined the 'heritage', preferring to take each case on its merits and rely on their collective subjective judgement. This enabled them to give grants to a wide range of projects from raising a World War Two bomber from Loch Ness to purchasing important works of art for museums. The fund kept a low profile and, apart from those directly involved, few people were aware of is existence. In my view it was the king of quangos so I was very honoured and thrilled to be invited to become a trustee in place of Robin Cooke who had sadly and rather suddenly died of motor neurone disease.

Robin was never an easy person to deal with. He had an arrogant manner and could be very rude to people whom he regarded as his inferiors. He was however of very great assistance to Jeremy Benson and I when we were working on successive Finance Bills, and the courage, dignity and stoicism with which he bore the progressive disablement of his fatal disease was an example to us all.

The NHMF had been in existence for seven years when I joined in 1987 and a number of the original trustees were still in office. They were a remarkable group of people; each had achieved distinction in their own particular field. They included Michael McCrum ex-headmaster of Eton, now Master of a Cambridge College, Sir Frederick Holliday, Vice Chancellor of Durham University, who appeared to have an intimate knowledge of virtually every site of Special Scientific Interest; Sir Norman (later Lord) Macfarlane from Scotland; Professor Brian Morris (later Lord Morris of Castle Morris), Principal of Lampeter St David's University College; the Marquess of Anglesey, cousin of the chairman; a trade unionist, Clive Jenkins; Sir Martin Jacomb, Chairman of the Pru; Sir Nicholas Goodison, Chairman of the Trustee Savings Bank and also of the National Arts Collections Fund – himself a very considerable scholar of the arts – and others of equal distinction. It was a pretty awe-inspiring bunch. Martin Charteris chaired the meetings with a light touch and a fine sense of humour. The debates sparkled, and to listen to Clive Jenkins and Henry Anglesey discussing the relative merits in heritage terms of a painting by Miro and a row of terraced houses in Bradford was an education in itself.

The NHMF enjoyed all the advantages of a small efficient organisation. With the exception of one or two special cases for which we were given additional funding (off the back of the lorry, as the expression went) we spent around £10-15 million a year on heritage projects. The trustees used their money well, and there were a number of occasions when the fertile mind of our legal adviser, Sir Matthew Farrer, was able to devise schemes in which a relatively small amount of money could achieve great things. It was all rather different when the trustees took on responsibility for distributing the Heritage Lottery and our £15 million became £350 million – but that is another story. I was glad and proud to have been a member of the original team.

As my time as president of the HHA drew to a close, I tried to visit as many of our members as possible, including a protracted visit to Scotland – which was no problem as we were building a house in Argyll at the time. All too soon, the year came to an end and for my final AGM the guest speaker was Nicholas Ridley, at that point Secretary of State for the Environment.

I had known Nick on and off for some time and our relations had been somewhat strained, particularly after the disastrous occasion when I gave one of his amendments to John Pardoe at the time of the Lib/Lab pact. He was himself a great tease, and I am sure that much of what he said could only have been with his tongue in his cheek, but I could have been wrong. Certainly his speech to the HHA in which he referred to historic house owners as the *ancien pauvres* did not go down well with his audience. Actually I thought it was rather a good speech. He told us all in so many words to get off our backsides and stop whingeing, a message that one or two of our members could well take to heart. A man of many talents and considerable ability, he would have carried more conviction if he had not allowed his bitterness at being the second son to show so clearly. His early death deprived the Conservative party of one of its better brains and sharper tongues.

So in November 1988 I stepped down as president after nearly 15 years working for the HHA and an immensely satisfying and exciting time it had been. I had become involved in the first instance driven by the need to find a solution to the continuing depredation of our heritage of historic houses caused by taxation at least once a generation. It was satisfying therefore to feel that there was now on the statute book a package of reliefs from inheritance tax which would enable an historic house, its contents and its estate to pass from one generation to the next .The legislation could be said to have been achieved with all party agreement and had a very good chance, all things being equal, of surviving yet another change in the structure of capital tax. Thus provided people played the game on public access and the arrangements were not abused, they offered a reasonably secure route for those families that wished to retain control and ownership of their historic properties. Many people and organisations had a hand in achieving this but the HHA certainly played a leading role throughout.

At the helm

CHAPTER 10

The History Working Group – Laying the Foundations

As my term of office as president of the HHA drew to a close in the autumn of 1988, I began to wonder what might take its place. For the past fifteen years a large part of my time and mental energy had been taken up with matters concerning the heritage and historic houses in particular. It was now time to move on. I already had two Government appointments as a trustee of the Royal Botanic Gardens, Kew, and also of the National Heritage Memorial Fund, together with a number of other commitments but I felt I still had time and spare capacity to take on something else.

Then, one morning in November during my last week at the HHA, I received a telephone call from the Department of Education and Science informing me that the Secretary of State, Kenneth Baker, would like a word with me later that morning, and would I be able to take his call at 11.30pm.

Filled with curiosity and some apprehension, I waited by my telephone and on the dot of 11.30, it rang.

'Hullo, Michael,' came a cheerful voice. 'How are you and how is your yew hedge?'

This was a reference to the hedge round the rose garden that we had been pruning back at the time of his visit in 1984.

'You know the national curriculum we are introducing?' I had heard something about it.... 'It involves setting up working groups to look at the individual subjects. I know that you share with me an interest in history, and I should like you to chair the History Working Group. You will have a secretariat provided by the DES and it will take about a year. Will you do it?'

'You must have got the wrong chap. I may have an interest in history and some practical experience of living in it, but I am certainly not an historian in the academic sense and I have not even been to university!'

'That is precisely why I am asking you to chair this group. History is a very controversial subject as you will find, if you do not know already. I want someone who can bring a fresh mind to bear on the subject and who has no axe to grind. You will have a group of experts in their field and to my mind it is important that the chairman is not an expert.'

I was intrigued. To become involved with the specialist input to the national curriculum was the last thing I expected, and it was certainly not the high profile administrative post I had been hoping for but it sounded a fascinating and challenging exercise, and after all I did need something to do to take the place of the HHA which had occupied so much of my time and thoughts.

'Would you like a little time to think about it?' said Kenneth. 'I do want to be able to make an appointment fairly soon.'

I have sometimes been accused of acting precipitately but I hate having decisions hanging over me. I had no idea what I was taking on or whether I was capable of doing the job but if Kenneth Baker thought I could (and I knew history was his pet subject), then that was good enough for me.

'OK,' I said, 'I'll give it a whirl.'

'That's splendid news,' he said. 'My office will be in touch with you directly.'

I went straightaway to tell Georgina. Her reaction 'Why You?' was shortly to be echoed across the common rooms and educational media as academics struggled to make sense of this strange appointment of an ex-naval officer to what I was shortly to discover was one of the most controversial posts in the academic world.

It was a question they were entitled to ask and I did not have the answer. On the face of it my qualifications were pretty meagre. In practice they were not so bad and, as ever, my varied experience in the Navy and later with the HHA came to my rescue. In particular I was well versed in chairing groups of all kinds and on a wide range of subjects. I had had some experience of teaching as Head of Communications and Blake Divisional Officer at the Royal Naval College at Dartmouth. I had served in the Ministry of Defence and knew at first hand how the civil service worked. I had an intimate knowledge of the parliamentary system, and was acquainted with a large number of politicians. As far as history was concerned, I lived in a building built by William the Conqueror which was a living example of 900 years of developing architectural and domestic living styles, and I was instrumental in setting up the Heritage Education Trust to encourage the use of historic houses as education resources. I hoped this would be sufficient.

I had met Kenneth Baker on a number of occasions when he was Environment Secretary; he had heard me speak at the Washington exhibition, and he had been to stay at Rockingham when he came to open a Heritage Education seminar at Lamport Hall which I was chairing. The media of course leapt on the latter and tried to run the fact that Kenneth and I were old cronies. It sounded good. Who was this unknown naval commander who lived in a castle? What could he possibly know about history or any other academic subject for that matter? The appointment could only have been made on the basis of cronyism. In developing this hypothesis they happily ignored the fact that the unpaid post of chairman of HWG which called for one, two and sometimes three days work per week for over a year was no gravy train, though I am sure that there were many professionals who would have died for the job.

It was Martyn Dyer, chief executive of the Heritage Education Trust which I then chaired, himself an ex-Head of History at St Mary's College, Strawberry Hill, who first warned me of the minefield I was entering. History is a highly political subject and people have strong opposing views on both how and what history should be taught. The traditionalists believe that history is made up of a series of facts mainly of a political nature linked to a date line, which should be learned, preferably by heart. The modernists see history as a broader subject, as much social as political, eschew learning anything by heart and seek to teach pupils by encouraging them to think their own way through the subject. An important feature of the latter is the opportunity to 'empathise' with historical characters. This is a gross over-simplification of a complex area, but both these views had influential, vocal and articulate protagonists backed by action groups drawn up ready for battle to promote their cause at every available opportunity.

As things stood, the modernists had made considerable gains since the teaching revolution of the 'swinging sixties' and the traditionalists looked to the National Curriculum to regain ground. The modernists were apprehensive that they might lose it.

Before taking up my appointment at the Royal Naval College, Dartmouth in the 1960s, I was sent on an instructional technique course. I found that the teaching process had gone through a metamorphosis since my own time at school. No longer did the teacher pronounce from the dais or instruct the class to read chapter so and so, and answer questions on it. Now the procedure was for the teacher to put questions to individual members of the class which would lead them through the subject. The idea was that the pupils would be more likely to absorb information they had thought through for themselves than if it had been handed down from on high requiring no great thought on their part.

This pupil-centred approach had clear benefits as a teaching process but it involved a good deal more work and careful preparation from the teacher and when applied to the teaching of history, was open to abuse. There was a tendency, especially at primary level, to allow the pupil's imagination to be given a free rein with little serious history being systematically taught or learned. Clearly this needed tightening up. Equally, it would be a mistake to revert to the old system based on a dry process which, as well as being incredibly boring, failed to address the breadth of the subject. I felt that there must be a middle road which built on the undoubted merits of both these points of view.

All this was in the future, however, and my problem right now was to understand precisely what my group and I were required to do. A meeting was arranged the following week with Miss Jenny Bacon, Head of Schools Branch 3, who was responsible for development of the national curriculum, in her room at Elizabeth House, the home of the Department of Education and Science as it then was known. Situated south of the river backing on to Waterloo station, Elizabeth House was one of the worst examples of post war office building. Long, rectangular, featureless and faceless with miles of lino separating rows of identical boxlike offices, it did not exactly lift the spirit. Its one saving grace was its site on the South Bank, and I used to look forward to my early morning walk through Parliament Square and over the river.

Jenny Bacon, as befitted her rank, had a double office to herself. I was shown in and immediately confronted with a bicycle and one of those rubber bouncing exercise balls. From behind the desk a cheerful figure emerged and my hand was almost pulled off its wrist. Jenny was the very antithesis of everyone's idea of a civil servant. As I recall she was dressed very informally in a sort of track suit, but that may have been my imagination, and radiated a form of kinetic energy which propelled her onward and upward through the civil service. Sadly for us, as she was a brilliant and much respected advocate in the Department, this meant that we lost her after a few months when she moved on to higher things.

Jenny Bacon introduced me to another Jenny, Jenny Worsfold, who was to be the secretary of our group and also to Roger Hennessey, Her Majesty's Inspector for History who was to be the group's mentor. These two were to be my close colleagues for the next fifteen months, and I could not have wished for more competent or agreeable companions with whom to share the roller coaster ride that lay ahead of us.

Jenny Worsfold's mild manner concealed a strong, logical, imaginative mind and a fierce determination. She possessed a shrewd political sense which was invaluable as she guided us through the labyrinthine corridors of the Department. Her arrangements ran like clockwork, and she had that rare gift of extracting order out of apparent chaos. I had read how ministers felt cosseted by their civil servants, and I came to understand exactly what that meant.

While Jenny guided us through the civil service, Roger somehow managed to lead us through the maze of education-speak and moving goalposts with which we were constantly being confronted. He had an intimate knowledge of history and, almost more important, the contemporary politics and personalities of history. His role was that of both minder and leader, which he combined with elegance and charm, and while his benign influence pervaded the work of the group, he never sought to impose his views on the group's thinking.

The discussion at this preliminary meeting was mainly about the group and its constitution. The teaching of history being such a controversial subject, both in method and content, it was important, if the group was to make progress, that the membership was reasonably compatible and did not include some of the more vociferous advocates of one view or another. The plan was to have ten members drawn from the whole spectrum of educational activity, with myself as chairman and Roger Hennessey as observer. We should be able to co-opt experts to help us in our work as required.

Roger was a major contributor in the process of submitting names for inclusion in the Group and his selection was masterly. They included a primary school teacher, Robert Guyver; a Head of History in a secondary school, Carol White; a Director of Education, Jim Hendy; an author who was also chairman of Somerset County Council, Henry Hobhouse; a history adviser, Peter Livesey; a lecturer in education from Bristol University, Mrs Ann Low-Beer; the secretary and librarian of the Institute of Historical Research, University of London, Dr Alice Prochaska; and an expert in world history, the Warden of Merton College, Oxford, Dr John Roberts. Dr Roberts was succeeded after six months by an eminent expert in imperial and commonwealth history, Professor Peter Marshall of King's College, London. Finally, we had Dr Gareth Elwyn Jones, Reader in Education, University College of Wales, Swansea, who was our link with the History Committee for Wales. In the latter stages of our work we had some assistance from Chris Culpin, a widely respected freelance writer on history education, and Tim Lomas, a Local Education Adviser from Lincolnshire. In addition to Jenny and Roger, Jenny's immediate boss, Michael Phipps, and later, his successor, Barney Baker, as head of the particular schools curriculum policy division which included history, attended our meetings on behalf of the Department.

It was an impressive list of educational experts. They were strong characters with views of their own, but despite the complexities with which we had to deal and the controversial matters we had to address, I think it is fair to say that although we may have argued long into the night on many occasions, we never failed to reach a consensus, and I like to think we all remained friends to the end. Individual politics was never an issue nor a factor in selection. Indeed I was unaware of members' personal political affiliations. I suspect that we were pretty evenly split; there was certainly no preponderance of overt Tory supporters, as was sometimes suggested in the media. There was some criticism of the fact that the group contained only two teachers, but both Carol White and Robert Guyver were well able to keep their end up, and as the work progressed we co-opted two more experts, both of whom had been history teachers, Dr Tim Lomas and Chris Culpin, to help us with the programmes of study.

The Welsh dimension is an interesting one. As a consequence of the Act of Union, Scotland is responsible for its own education and was therefore outside our remit. Wales also had its own education system under the aegis of the Welsh Office, but it had some close and pragmatic links with the English system and generally adopted the English national curriculum framework. Our recommendations had, therefore, to be framed in such a way that they could be adapted for use in Wales. This was no easy matter. Welsh history is emphatically not English history, even if the two have occasionally connected in important ways. Accordingly and wisely, the Welsh set up their own History Committee for Wales, charged with suggesting to the Welsh Office a Welsh history curriculum model, keeping in kilter with the History Working Group model as far as practicable.

I and my group had been tasked by both the Secretary of State for Education and the Secretary of State or Wales. It was a situation which could have led to problems and misunderstandings, but Gareth Jones, who sat on both committees and had the sometimes difficult task of keeping them both in line, managed magnificently. At an early opportunity I met my Welsh opposite number, Professor Rees Davies, and we at once established a warm relationship which enabled us to resolve any differences before they assumed crisis proportions.

The group's task, as expressed in the draft terms of reference, was deceptively brief. We were to advise on a statutory 'framework' for history within which teachers could 'use their professional talents and skills to develop their own schemes of work' and to report by Christmas 1989.

We were asked to submit an interim report by 30th June which would outline our views on 'the contribution which history should make to the overall school curriculum... our provisional thinking about the knowledge, skills and understanding pupils of different abilities and maturities should have attained ...at key ages, and our thinking about the programmes of study....'

These phrases all seemed fairly straightforward, as I have set them out in sanitised form. In fact they were larded with a strange language which needed a wet towel and very careful concentration to understand. Having mastered the education-speak, a closer study revealed that the first part of our task was governed by a progressive assessment system devised by the Task Group on Assessment and Testing (TGAT) chaired by an eminent mathematician[*]. We were to recommend a range of attainment targets, group them into 'profile components' and to devise 'statements ' to support ten levels of attainment within each target. Pupils would then be assessed on the basis of the statements at various key stages during their school career and given a level within each attainment target.

It was an ingenious, essentially logical but also very complex scheme and it made sense when applied to naturally progressive subjects such as mathematics, or science, or even English language, but it was inappropriate for a humanities subject such as history to be confined in so rigid a structure. Indeed this was to cause us endless problems in the future and lead to much misunderstanding of our recommendations.

The second part of our remit was more comprehensible. We were to recommend programmes of study consistent with the attainment targets and the key elements within them that we considered were 'essential' at each key stage. We were also to take account of a number of factors including the assessment arrangements, the contribution history can make to other subjects and cross-curricular themes, best practice, and the results of any research and development.

The terms of reference were expanded in a supplementary guidance to the chairman which, amongst other things, told us that we should assume that 'in England normally the equivalent of some 3–4 periods of a 40 period weekly timetable...will be available for history during primary schooling and for years 1–3 in secondary school'. We were then to assume for pupils in year 4–5 an average of 4 periods a week for those taking GCSE history (or its equivalent) and an average of 2 periods a week for those who were not. Sadly these figures were to prove hopelessly unrealistic in practice.

I was sent home from the preliminary meeting with a suitcase of paper to read, including reports of previous working parties, HMI papers and, most interesting of all, their survey reports on the teaching of history in schools. It was pretty clear from these that the teaching of history, particularly at

---

[*] Task Group on Assessment and Testing Report published for the Department of Education and Science by the Central Office of information (March 1988)

primary level, was a pretty haphazard affair and depended very much on the teacher's personal interests. Most secondary schools had history specialists on the staff and their courses were more structured but often duplicated ground that had already been covered in primary school. It was not uncommon for instance for pupils to be taught the Vikings at primary school only to be taught the Vikings yet again at secondary school. The need for a basic history syllabus common to all was clear.

Amongst the contents of my mailbag, which was beginning to increase daily, was a book by one of the members of the group, Henry (Tom) Hobhouse. It was entitled *The Seeds of Change*[*]. In the accompanying note, Tom described it as 'the intellectual baggage he would be bringing to the Group'. It was a remarkable book by a remarkable person. Taking various seeds such as quinine, tea or potatoes, Tom proceeded to show how they had altered the face of history. A clue to Tom's character lay in the quality and quantity of footnotes at the end of each chapter, some of which were barely relevant to the text. Tom had a fascination for facts, and an elephantine knowledge of almost any subject under the sun. This had its advantages when we came to develop the programmes of study where his knowledge was invaluable, but it did mean that, whatever the subject under discussion, Tom would be reminded of some equally interesting but irrelevant fact, and I had to be on guard against 'red herrings'.

Throughout December I had frequent meetings with Roger, Jenny and the secretariat as we discussed our proposed method of working. We decided to meet on a fortnightly basis with two day meetings in London followed by a two/three day residential meeting out of London. We felt it was very important that we should meet as many people as possible across the country and hear their views. We also hoped to travel to one or two foreign countries to see how they handled the teaching of history. This approach which enabled us to hold discussions with a wide range of people from teachers in Belfast or Selly Oak to leading academics and the Speaker of the House of Commons, gave us valuable insight into other viewpoints which we were able to take into account. Such visits to foreign countries that we were able to arrange were similarly helpful in giving us yet another perspective of British history as well as their own.

Fairly early on I was invited to meet the Secretary of State, Kenneth Baker with his junior ministers. An historian himself, Ken made it clear that he was looking for a course which would capture the interest of the pupil within a disciplined environment. He underlined the points that had already been made in the supplementary guidance. The word 'empathy' was out; 'rigour' was in. British history was to be at the core of the programmes of study. He

---

[*] *The Seeds of Change* by Henry Hobhouse, Harper and Row 1985

confessed to being rather envious of my job. It was something he would dearly have loved to do himself and he would therefore be taking a close interest in the work of the group.

The first meeting of the working group (HWG) took place at Elizabeth House on 24th January. As I prepared for the meeting, I found myself becoming increasingly nervous at the prospect of confronting this team of experts. Jenny was encouraging.

'Don't worry,' she said, 'you are the chairman. They will be far more scared of you!'

We duly met in one of those bleak conference rooms and for the first time I was able to put faces to the names. Jenny was right. I very soon found that while the members of the group were experts in their own individual fields, I was probably one lap ahead of them as far as the national curriculum was concerned and, of course, being in the chair does give one a head start.

I have always believed that while the chairman of a meeting needs to have a good knowledge of the subject under discussion and a clear idea of the direction in which the discussion should proceed, his job is essentially to extract the views of the group rather than air his own, making sure they keep to the point and, when everyone has had their say, make his own contribution, sum up, and hopefully reach a conclusion. This is not as easy as it sounds and there were moments in our work which I used to dread when the clock ticked on, the discussion became more and more convoluted, and the conclusion ever more elusive.

On this occasion things went off reasonably well and I was very encouraged by our initial discussions. The subject matter was relatively straightforward and concerned mainly with methodology and work patterns, but it rapidly became clear from the start that there were no shrinking violets; every member of the group had something to say and was not afraid of saying it. Furthermore they were all fired with enthusiasm for history and though as individuals they came at it from a number of different directions, there was much goodwill and a common desire to do our subject justice. Many months later towards the end of our time together, I was chatting to our Welsh representative Dr Gareth Elwyn Jones and he said:

'Do you know, Michael, I have sat on a number of educational bodies in my time but none has maintained such a high intellectual level of discussion as this one, and furthermore we seem to have kept it up all day and sometimes half the night!'

In between our formal meetings we planned a series of fact finding visits, the first of which was to the BBC's educational division at Ealing Broadway. We were met by a very enthusiastic team and shown some excellent videos backed up by printed material for follow on work. Clearly much effort and considerable funds were being devoted to this work but, while it had great potential as a teaching aid, the choice of subject was governed more by its suitability for dramatic presentation than its historical value and in its current form was of limited use. For instance there was a perfectly splendid video on the 'Mysteries of History' which in this case focussed on the legend of the *Mary Celeste*. It was all good stuff with monsters devouring the hapless crew; the children would have loved it but it was not history.

This was the group's first appearance in public since its appointment had been announced, and we suddenly became aware of the public interest in our work with the corresponding need for confidentiality. There were many people out there, including the BBC, who would have given anything to know what we were going to say. It was of the utmost importance therefore that we gave no hint of how our minds might be working to the outside world. This was not easy for it came naturally to our able, experienced and intelligent members to criticise bodies like the BBC and to want to suggest how they might improve. We all had to learn to hold our tongues.

If any of us had harboured thoughts that we might be on to a pleasant intellectual excursion into the realms of school history, we were sharply brought down to earth by Michael Phipps, our DES minder, who briefed us on the assessment process which was to form the basis of our recommendations. Our first task would be to decide on the definition and number of attainment targets, and their grouping into profile components. In this we should have to take careful account of the recommendations of other subject working groups to ensure consistency and avoid duplication. We were then to develop a 'criterion-referenced' set of 10 levels for each attainment target accompanied by statements of attainment for each level. These statements had to be progressive and explicit in order that the pupils' performance could be assessed as accurately as possible at each key stage.

It all sounded very complicated and in due course common sense was to prevail and it was indeed simplified. At this time, however, we had no option but to plunge in at the deep end with profile components.

I asked the group for their suggestions and it was agreed that 'Historical Knowledge and Understanding' should head the list with 'Historical Investigation and Communication' as a second. We then went on to consider the attainment targets to fit the profile components, and agreed that there should be three: 'A Sense of Time and Place', 'Historical Information in its Setting', and 'Interpretations'. On the second, a further three attainment targets were identified: 'Acquisition and Enquiry', 'Evaluation and Analysis of a Wide Range of Evidence', and 'Organising and Expressing'.

Having tested the water, so to speak, we then indulged in what I can only describe as a certain amount of horseplay. Under the eagle eye of our facilitator, Ms Jane Henry from the Open University, we devoted the session to 'creative' thinking about how to make history interesting, exciting and enjoyable. The minutes go silent at this point which is probably just as well as people caught onto the idea and relaxed, so their thoughts of how to make history interesting etc. grew ever more imaginative. Our facilitator captured these odd strokes of genius on a flip chart which towards the end resembled a large whale with a mass of harpoons stuck into it. Each harpoon contained a bubble with an idea in it. These started with the more obvious approaches such as site visits or dramatic reconstructions (always in context) but the standard rapidly deteriorated as the afternoon proceeded to include such items as pop singers and carnal sex. It was all good fun and as a group I am sure it helped break down barriers between us. As we packed up to go home, I looked back at the flip chart and nearly had a fit. If the cleaner found that next morning what would she think? I could imagine the headlines:'The history curriculum is in the hands of a group of perverts'. Jenny quickly removed the offending chart.

Our first residential visit to Malvern was something of a watershed. We had set ourselves the task of agreeing the statements of attainment for the four key ages: 7, 11, 14 and 16. This at once brought us face to face with the problem of finding the right phraseology which would enable a teacher to measure a pupil's progress within an attainment target, an exercise in mental gymnastics which made *The Times* crossword seem child's play by comparison. It was necessary first to decide what standard the pupil should have acquired at the various levels and then to express it in language which was simple, clear and explicit. While on the face of it this might seem a relatively easy task, in practice it took up an inordinate amount of our time, particularly when attempting to measure historical knowledge and understanding.

We decided that it would be easier to focus in the first instance on the attainment targets within the second profile component which were essentially 'skills' orientated.

After a good deal of sweat and brainstorming, during which my chairmanship was sorely tested, we arrived at a set of statements with which we were moderately happy and it appeared that we were making good progress. I was conscious, however, that we had barely scratched the surface of the problem and we had some very steep hills to climb.

The meeting over, members took the opportunity to visit museums in the area while I met Professor Robert Rees Davies, the chairman of the History Committee for Wales (HCW), a very eminent Welsh historian, Professor of History and Vice Principal of University College, Aberystwyth. Despite some apprehension on the part of our officials, we got on very well and, I believe, established a very important bond of trust. His was the rather frustrating task of having to wait to see which way HWG jumped before his committee could start work. I was determined to be as open as I could and to let them have all our working papers provided they had been approved by HWG. The Welsh responded with comments and suggestions which were invariably helpful. Naturally they were keen to know our initial ideas about content because this would govern much of their work. I assured them that just as soon as we had something to say on content, they would have it. We agreed that our management teams should meet on a regular basis; meanwhile Gareth Jones would keep them fully informed of HWG progress or otherwise.

I greatly valued this Welsh connection and when later we came under attack from various quarters, HCW gave us very solid support and it was good to have that strong, academic backing behind us.

At our next meeting in London we were to address the purposes of school history, and to determine criteria for the structure and selection of historical content. This would then lead us on to the much more problematic area of drafting the statements for attainment targets relating to historical knowledge and understanding.

I opened the meeting by remarking that this was probably the most critical and controversial aspect of our work, and certainly the debate that followed was seminal in setting the direction down which we were to go. One of the first areas to come under the microscope was the whole question of historical knowledge, its nature and purpose. As the discussion continued it became clear that knowledge of a range of historical facts alone without understanding was meaningless, and that the two were inseparable. Roger Hennessey then introduced what became known as his 'carrot', an inverted cone designed to illustrate how a pupil would progress through a course of history. The vertical element indicating increasing knowledge and skills while the horizontal dimension indicated a deepening understanding.

For me this was a revelation. I had been taught history in the traditional way at Eton and then Dartmouth. While the individual teaching was sometimes excellent, such quality was not uniform and there was little or no attempt at any chronological sequence. On the whole we were introduced to set sources which we read and on which we answered questions. There was no question of doubt or enquiry and certainly no hint that our sources might be biased. Now it appeared that the certainty which this form of teaching engendered was to be replaced by doubt or more precisely by a process of enquiry, evaluation and analysis through which the pupil would arrive at the answer on the basis of the evidence. While this might be thought to be a somewhat sophisticated approach for a five year old, or any school child for that matter, it certainly underlined the importance of history as a subject in that historical knowledge and understanding would teach pupils about their past, while the development of historical skills was a very real and important training for life. If we could design a syllabus along these lines which could realistically be taught in schools what an achievement that would be. I was at once fired with enthusiasm for the potential offered by this challenge.

I do not propose to go into the details of our discussions. These have all been painstakingly recorded in the minutes which are a matter of public record, and also in a number of publications, in particular *History Teaching, Nationhood, and The State* by Robert Phillips[*] which gives a comprehensive description of the group's work. I shall simply attempt to rehearse the principal arguments which led us to draw certain conclusions which we published in our interim report.

With the aid of Roger's carrot we were able to agree on the purpose of history, and the criteria for the selection of content. We laid particular stress on the wide range of benefits that history can offer both in terms of knowledge and skills. It helps pupils to understand the present in the context of the past; it gives them a sense of identity and an understanding of their cultural roots; it helps them to understand other countries and cultures, and by training the mind in disciplined study it is an excellent preparation for life.

The following month, in April, we met for another residential meeting, this time on the familiar ground (for me anyway) of Portsmouth. Our principal task was to agree the statements for the four key ages in respect of attainment targets relating to Historical Knowledge and Understanding. These had now been reduced to two, one dealing with knowledge and understanding, and the other with interpretations. At once we hit a problem. What is meant by the expression 'historical knowledge'? Does it specifically mean a range of historical facts learned possibly by rote from some textbook or dictated notes and recalled for assessment purposes, or does it mean an acquaintance with a range of historical facts, some of which should be learned and all of which should be understood. The dictionary supports both interpretations.

The group were in no doubt that historical knowledge involved the ability to recall salient facts and events but this ability was valueless unless the facts were learned in context and properly understood. Understanding was at the root of this attainment target.

Besides there was another problem affecting history in particular. If the

---

[*] *History Teaching, Nationhood, and the State*. Robert Phillips. Cassell 1998.

word knowledge is taken to mean factual recall alone, how is it to be expressed in ten progressive levels? Should levels be chronologically based starting, say, at level one with the Romans and ending up at level 10 with the late 20th century, or should they be expressed in quantified form – pupils should know the dates of ten battles by level three? The statements within the attainment target had to be brief, concise, clear and progressive. They could not contain subject detail unless in the form of examples.

We struggled with this issue at Portsmouth and subsequently for many days as we felt instinctively that historical knowledge should at least form part of an attainment target and that its omission could face considerable opposition when we published our Interim Report. The more we wrestled with the problem however, the more it became clear that knowledge per se as an attainment target simply would not work unless it was linked to assessable understanding. Ultimately, we were forced to conclude that it was not feasible to include specific areas of historical knowledge in the attainment targets, but that this was best placed in the programmes of study, where it could be broken down into 'knowledge to be learned' and 'knowledge for guidance and general background'.

This enabled us to focus the statements of attainment on the pupil's increasing level of understanding of historical information contained in the programmes of study which they would have to demonstrate through recalling significant areas. We felt that by this means we had ensured that the important points of history would be learned and properly assessed in context. We therefore amended the first Profile Component to read 'Historical Understanding' omitting the word knowledge. While logically correct, it left us open to criticism when our interim report was published by giving the impression to those who were not prepared to study the report in depth that we were not concerned with any form of factual recall. Perhaps with the benefit of hindsight we should have made our thinking clearer and retained the word 'knowledge' in the attainment target. Its omission certainly proved to be a hostage to fortune.

It was with a sense of relief that we put the mind-bending exercise of the attainment targets behind us and turned to the programmes of study at our next meeting in London. At last, we thought, we can forget the semantics and concentrate on real history – but it was a false hope. The programmes of study had, of course, to be closely linked to the attainment targets. The former must support the latter and be specifically related to the levels of attainment, in each key stage. They had to be designed in such a way that teachers could select material appropriate for pupils of different abilities within the key stage.

Our meeting was attended for the first time by Jenny Bacon, Head of the

DES Schools Branch Three and responsible for the national curriculum. We had a useful discussion. She accepted that our attainment targets were 'not data-based but founded in skills and understanding' and that for the purposes of assessment the data would be in the programmes of study. Therefore it was all the more important that they related closely to the attainment targets, and that the content was framed in such a way that the pupils could learn the basic historical knowledge they needed to achieve all the targets.

In our earlier discussions we had already decided that the programmes of study for each key stage should comprise a series of core subjects supported by options. We took this idea to the next stage and agreed that the core, which should be prescribed and learned, should be focussed on British history but include areas of European and World history. There was some reluctance among members of the group to accept the principle of prescription, particularly of non- British history, as they felt that this might tie the teachers' hands. Eventually it was agreed that provided the rationale for the selection of material to be prescribed was clearly spelt out, this was the best way of ensuring that pupils 'would be able to fulfil their entitlement to learn history'[*].

I was very pleased about this as I knew it was a tricky subject but having decided to omit historical knowledge from the attainment targets, we would not have a leg to stand on if we did not insist on salient parts of the core programmes of study being prescribed and learned. We were much helped here by the sensible view of the Welsh committee who had already agreed in principle that some form of prescription would be necessary.

We next addressed the issue of chronology and had no difficulty in agreeing its importance. In order to cover the ground at the different key stages however we saw the core being taught in a broadly chronological pattern over each key stage with opportunities for revisiting earlier periods in more depth as the course proceeded and when pupils were ready. The options menu would be designed to support the core and enrich the chronological period under study. The aim was that by the end of key stage 3, aged 14, the pupil would have covered a broad chronological span leaving the final key stage 4 for revisiting or, as it turned out, concentrating on the 20th century.

With these important decisions behind us we were now nearly ready to embark on drafting the actual programmes of study, and for this we headed north to Corby. The members of the group were gaining in confidence and working well together. The battle over the attainment targets had provided a 'baptism of fire' from which we had all benefited.

[*]   The Minutes of the Sixth Meeting of HWG on 20 April 1989 para 7.8.

In the intervening periods between meetings I took the opportunity of a visit to Scotland to meet Professor Keith Robbins, at that time Professor of Modern History at Glasgow University and President of the Historical Association. While in this capacity he was clearly an important ally, he was also particularly interested in British and in local history, and promised to let us have his thoughts on both. Jenny and I then went on to a conference organised by my Heritage Education Trust at Culzean Castle. This provided an interesting opportunity to meet a group of Scottish teachers who welcomed our work and hoped that it might stimulate the Scottish authorities into doing something similar as they felt that there was a need for more direction in the teaching of history in Scottish schools.

A visit to Wales followed to meet Professor Rees Davies and the History Committee for Wales (HCW) at St Fagan's, the Welsh Folk Museum near Cardiff. They seemed to be moving faster than us, possibly because they did not spend so long battling with the statements of attainment, and they were now keen to progress with the programmes of study. To do so they needed to know HWG's thinking which was still at the preliminary stage. I could well understand their frustration and we hoped to have something more definite for them to work on after Corby. The late Professor Rees Davies was renowned as an eminent academic historian but he was also very practical and I always found his comments to the point, perspicacious and helpful. He was already concerned at the amount that the authorities were endeavouring to cram into the timetable, and sounded a warning note about the size of our programmes of study.

As we embarked on the programmes of study we were conscious that we were breaking new ground. We had to define a period or aspect of history in terms of what a teacher should teach. First we needed a name and we coined the expression History Study Unit or HSU. It might not be very felicitous but at least it was neutral, all-embracing, and could not be confused with any other expression already in use such as 'topic'. An HSU could be a core history unit of British, European or World history, or it could be a longterm theme designed to support the core. Schools would be encouraged to design their own themes some of which should be based on local history. The core units would be compulsory but choices would be available for the themes.

We then designed a standard format which would apply to all study units to ensure that the unit was studied in depth and related to the attainment targets. In particular we identified four specific aspects which should be covered in each unit: Political, Economic and Technological, Social and Religious, and Cultural and Aesthetic (PESC). We were concerned that traditionally there has been a tendency to focus almost exclusively on the political aspects of an area of history and, whilst we accepted that political events inevitably dominate a period of history, they can only be properly understood against a wider background which includes the economic, social and cultural aspects of the period.

Naturally some units would be stronger on some aspects than others, and this was where we would seek a balance, particularly where the core was concerned. This format, applied to each study unit, adjusted for the age and level of the pupil, would form the basis of our programmes of study and, we hoped, reflect our self-imposed mission to ensure that our course of history was broad in its coverage, balanced in content and coherent in its delivery.

Outside the formal meetings various subgroups had been working on the subjects for study and we now had a fairly well defined idea of the core subjects for Key Stages 1, 2, and 3. Generally speaking KS1 was concerned with an understanding of time and the relationship between the past and the present. KS2 covered a broad chronological period of British history from the 'Invaders' to the twentieth century. KS3 we saw as the critical period in that pupils at this first stage of secondary schooling would have achieved a degree of sophistication which would enable them to study history in some depth. We brought them back to the medieval period and looked in more detail at certain selected areas of British and some world history in chronological order up to the 19th century, but possibly including one or two items from the twentieth century. KS4 would concentrate primarily on 20th century studies.

We had covered a lot of ground, very fast, and I think some of us were a bit breathless by the end of the meeting – but time was moving on. It was now the middle of May and our interim report was due to be submitted before the end of June. We still had a good deal of work to do to flesh out our ideas on attainment targets and programmes of study and there were one or two items we still had to discuss such as our views on assessment and pupils with special needs. I was not unduly worried however. I felt we had made great strides into virgin territory and had something really important to say.

We concluded our meeting at Corby with a dinner at Rockingham to which we invited a number of local educationalists from both the public and the private sector. This was one of several occasions on which we met those at the coal face of school education and it was always helpful to hear their views while keeping quiet ourselves.

At the end of May we found ourselves heading north to Bronte country, where we stayed in a converted warehouse at Hebden Bridge. The object of this meeting was to take the first draft of our interim report labelled by Jenny as A TRY. We would also have an opportunity to look at the many submissions and letters we had received from members of the public and take stock generally of the position we had reached.

In practice we did not manage to reach the draft report because nearly the whole of the two day meeting was taken up with the programmes of study. There was a certain amount of debate once more about the ratio of prescribed work to options, with some members of the group, interestingly from the academic side, feeling that we should increase the latter at the expense of the former. I could understand and sympathise with the point but I knew that we were likely to be accused of going soft on our attainment targets by placing 'knowledge' in the programmes of study and if we were too generous with our 'options' we could well find our work being redone by the National Curriculum Council (NCC). That was something none of us wanted.

My abiding memory of Hebden Bridge is not its bleak outlook in a cold late May or the wildness of the moors behind, but the discussion we had on the last day, and night, on the content for the programmes of study. As I have already mentioned, much work had been done on this by the subgroups and indeed we had little difficulty agreeing the HSUs for key stages 1, 2 and 3. Things became more problematic when we came to key stage 4, the final two years at school when much of the pupil's time would be taken up studying for GCSE.

We had decided to concentrate on mainly twentieth century studies so that pupils would leave school with a broad understanding of the immediate historical background to contemporary world events. The question we now faced was how we were going to do this. There was some doubt about the time available, particularly for those not taking history GCSE, but that was a minor problem compared to deciding how to teach 100 years which have seen more change than any other century, and about which we knew more. Furthermore where should we start and where should we stop? History was being made while we sat there. No sooner had we designed an HSU on Europe post second world war entitled 'East meets West' than the Berlin Wall came down and everything changed. Similarly we had an optional HSU in KS4 entitled 'Modernisation of China post 1945'. Then we heard about Tiananmen Square.

All day we wrestled with first one idea, then another; there was so much important ground and so little time in which to cover it. Finally, exhausted, we broke for dinner with nothing resolved. We met again after dinner and looked at each other in silence. Then Dr John Roberts, Warden of Merton, and author of *A History of the World* said:

'Shall I tell you about the 20th century?'

Dumbly we nodded assent. He went to the flip chart and for two hours held us spellbound with a most lucid, comprehensive and succinct view of the 20th century in macro terms. It was a virtuoso performance. He told us of Europe coming together in the late 19th century only to throw itself apart in the First World War. Revolution in Russia echoed in China; Europe in turmoil again in the Second World War, then the Cold War, independence and political change in India and Africa, economic change as manufacturing moved to cheap labour in the East. Through John's words we saw the century unroll like a giant tapestry with patches of colour here and there. This was clearly the answer and, fired with a new enthusiasm, we wrote a broad brush History Study Unit entitled 'Modern Britain: Politics, Warfare and Social Change'. We thought it a splendid solution to a complex problem,

In our enthusiasm, however, we failed to see that such a general approach might be seen as giving too little emphasis to such seminal events as the two world wars. Roger Hennessey indeed warned me that such an approach could lead to serious difficulty. He was right – as we soon discovered when we published our interim report.

The 1988 Act called for the setting up of two educational bodies, the National Curriculum Council (NCC), who were responsible for implementing the national curriculum and the School Examination and Assessment Council (SEAC). NCC in particular were very interested in our work which they would have to take on and implement or not in due course. We were due to visit them at their new offices in York following our meeting at Hebden Bridge.

There had been some fluttering in the DES dovecotes at the prospect of this meeting. The chairman of NCC, Duncan Graham, was a forceful Scot who was currently engaged in building a substantial empire in York. Not only was he thus regarded by Elizabeth House with some suspicion mixed with alarm but they were also afraid that he would squeeze information out of us before we were ready to give it. I was highly amused; it was so typical of Whitehall. They set up these quangos for whatever reason, give them a measure of independence, and then spend their time second-guessing the quango's agenda wishing they were still in control.

The group spent a light-hearted half hour thinking up false trails for NCC to pursue one of which was a long term theme that we thought had much mileage entitled 'Sex and Sewage'. Actually it would have made a very good HSU.

Of course in the event we all related extremely well. Duncan was an historian himself before becoming Chief Executive Officer of Humberside. He was supported by a high powered team with Chris Woodhead as Chief Executive (subsequently the controversial Head of OFSTED) and Nick Tate (later headmaster of Winchester) in charge of history. We had a constructive discussion and despite some probing questions nothing important was given away.

The interim report which now dominated our thinking was the product of a number of minds. Individuals and subgroups had been tasked to produce sections and Jenny and her secretariat did the editing. In the end it read rather well. I particularly liked the enthusiastic opening sentence to Chapter 1:'History is a splendid subject for study at any age but particularly so at school.' In the introduction we asked that readers should read the whole report and not skip bits because every word counted. It was not long, and we stressed in the introduction that ... 'Our aim is not to produce historians but to give all children a knowledge and sense of history that will contribute to their general understanding and development.'

In my covering letter I restated our aim to ' devise a course of school history which will equip pupils with the historical knowledge, understanding, and skills to enable them to play their part as informed citizens of the 21st century'. I went on to say that 'In particular we stress the importance of historical knowledge...'. Rees Davies also wrote a most helpful covering letter in which he spelt out in detail the arguments that we were putting forward for the inclusion of historical knowledge in the programmes of study as opposed to the attainment targets. After all this you would have thought that without even reading the report, no one could be in any doubt as to where we stood on the importance of historical knowledge learned in context.

CHAPTER 11

The History Working Goup – Reaping the Whirlwind

Our interim report was submitted to ministers on 28th July 1989, two days ahead of schedule. About ten days later I received a summons to see the Secretary of State, and found him indeed sitting in state at a long table on a sort of raised platform flanked by Angela Rumbold, Minister of State, and senior civil servants.

From this eminence Ken Baker welcomed the report and both he and Angela Rumbold gave every indication that they were pleased with it. They expressed reservations about our decision not to include historical knowledge in the attainment targets and needed to be convinced that knowledge could be properly assessed in this way. They were also concerned that there was insufficient emphasis on British history.

I explained that it was not for want of trying but that we had been unable to find a sensible formula which would enable us to express knowledge in terms of historical facts, dates and events, within the progressive structure of the attainment targets. It was possible, if clumsy, physically to list the content that pupils should know at a certain level of attainment but the place for content is the programmes of study, and in any case it was not the content alone that we wanted to assess but the pupil's understanding of it. We were adamant that knowledge and understanding could and should go hand in hand and that the former should not be taught in isolation from the latter.

We thought that we had found the ideal solution whereby pupils would be assessed on their understanding of historical knowledge learned from the programmes of study. The attainment target would only be achieved if pupils could demonstrate accurate recall of historical knowledge which would be specified and prescribed in the programmes of study. While we were against learning by rote, preferring the expression 'memorising of facts', there was nothing to prevent teachers, if they so wished, as a teaching aid, to encourage their pupils to learn, for example, the dates of the kings' and queens' reigns. This was essentially a matter for the teacher and we had interpreted our remit as recommending what history should be taught, not how it should be taught.

On the second point about being insufficiently focused on Britishness, I explained that this was really a question of choosing the right examples which we would look at again.

Ministers appeared reassured on both points. Kenneth Baker in particular seemed to accept our arguments for basing the attainment target on understanding rather then on historical knowledge alone and asked us to demonstrate in the programmes of study that they were capable of being assessed. All in all it was a very satisfactory meeting and I reported back to the group accordingly.

I have described this meeting, which was the last I was to have with Kenneth Baker as Secretary of State, at some length for two reasons: first, because the argument about knowledge and the attainment targets will come up again and again and to repeat it at such length would be very boring. Second and more interesting, is the contrast between my notes of the meeting and Kenneth Baker's recollection as stated in his autobiography[*] where he expresses disappointment 'with the lack of emphasis on the teaching of hard facts and their chronology'. If he was that disappointed with the report, he certainly did not convey it to me in those terms at the time - rather the opposite in fact.

The original plan had been to publish the interim report on 13th July, but unfortunately this fell foul of Mrs Thatcher's summer cabinet reshuffle. Mrs Thatcher seldom seemed to like to leave ministers in post for more than two years - which is barely long enough for them to see through any changes for which they might be responsible. In this particular round of 'musical chairs' Kenneth Baker went off to be Chairman of the Conservative party and was replaced at the DES by a reluctant John MacGregor who had been dragged out of the Ministry of Agriculture where he was doing good things. I knew John of old. We had sat together on the Country Landowners Association Executive Committee and I had met him once or twice in his MAFF hat. Publication of our report was therefore delayed to allow him time to read it and form his own opinions. At least that was what I was told.

---

[*] *The Turbulent Years, My Life in Politics* by Kenneth Baker - published by Faber and Faber 1998

In fact the truth was somewhat different. I came into the office one morning to find Jenny ashen faced.

'What's the matter?' I asked.

'It's bad news,' she replied.

It appeared that, for some reason, Kenneth Baker had sent our report across the road to Number Ten. There was no requirement to do this, and no one seemed to know why he had done so. It then came into the hands of Professor Griffiths, Head of the Policy Unit, who seemed to think that it had been written by a bunch of way out left wingers, and briefed Mrs Thatcher accordingly. The message came back that the report was badly flawed and there was some question whether it should be published at all. It was of course all to do with the fact that we had declined to include knowledge in the attainment targets. The fact that the attainment targets could only be achieved through the recall of knowledge learned from the programmes of study did not seem to register. No attempt was made to seek any explanation of what we were trying to say in a very complex and difficult area and I rather suspect that we were dealing with closed minds from the start.

There was a very vigorous, articulate and influential lobby coming from the right among the more vocal of whom were Professor Robert Skidelsky, of Warwick University and Dr Sheila Lawlor from the Centre of Policy Studies. I was amazed at some of the things they were saying. It was as if they saw history in purely mathematical terms, as a series of facts and dates which pupils should know by heart. Whether or not pupils understood what they were learning did not seem to matter. These critics also failed to address the problems that we had faced over the statements of attainment, or if they did, they did not publicise their solutions. Furthermore there was no love lost between Number Ten and the DES. The former assumed that the latter was a hot bed of near communists and that anything that emerged from the DES was almost certainly tainted. Given all this it was disappointing, if hardly surprising, that our report received the 'thumbs down' from Mrs T.

Mrs Thatcher was very keen on history. Kenneth Baker in his autobiography describes how she saw history as a pageant of glorious events and significant developments, with our small country giving the world parliamentary democracy, an independent judiciary and a tradition of incorrupt administration.

In her autobiography[*] Mrs Thatcher describes history as the 'hardest battle' she fought on the national curriculum. She felt strongly that 'learning history required knowledge of events and that it was impossible to make

---

[*] *The Downing Street Years* by Margaret Thatcher. Harper Collins 1993

sense of such events without absorbing sufficient factual information and without being able to place matters in a clear chronological framework – which means knowing dates.' I cannot think that there is anything here with which HWG would disagree, and indeed this is what we were attempting to achieve in our report within the straitjacket of the assessment system. She then goes on to record that when she saw our interim report in July, she was appalled. 'It put the emphasis on interpretation and enquiry as against content and knowledge.... There was not enough emphasis on history as a chronological study .... I considered the document comprehensively flawed and told Ken that there must be major, not just minor changes. In particular I wanted to see a clearly set out chronological framework for the whole history curriculum.'

While HWG might think Mrs Thatcher's views on history were somewhat simplistic, it is fairly clear from the above that the difference between us was not as wide as she might think but that she had not properly understood what we were trying to say. The briefing she received, to put it mildly, was itself 'comprehensively flawed' and skewed heavily to the right.

At the time I was not supposed to know that the report had gone to Downing Street, but I did and felt sure that if I had been allowed to see the Prime Minister in person I could have persuaded her that what we were proposing was the only way forward and that it included plenty of good history which would be learned and tested. I recalled the moment when we went to see her in opposition about heritage matters and she had seen our point well ahead of her colleagues. Possibly I was wrong and that she too had developed a similar inflexible mindset as her staff. Anyway I was not allowed to see her and had to wait another month until John MacGregor asked me to go and see him at his cottage in Norfolk.

It was a lovely summer day and I took my old Bentley out of the garage to give it some exercise. Rather embarrassingly when we reached John's house, I could not get it through the gates and had to leave it parked in the road. John met me walking up the drive and, after a short interruption while we looked for the dog, we sat down in the orchard over a cup of tea and some of Mrs MacGregor's excellent cake. John went straight to the point.

'I have now had a chance to study your report and broadly speaking, I like it. I am however unhappy with two important areas. I am not convinced that historical knowledge can be properly learned and assessed in the programmes of study and would have preferred to see 'knowledge' in the attainment targets. Secondly I would like to see more emphasis on British history'.

I accepted the point about Britishness which Kenneth Baker had made before him and which raised no problems for us. The treatment of knowledge was far more problematic and had he studied the arguments spelled out in the report which led us to place knowledge in the programmes of study rather than the attainment targets? He had but he was not convinced by them.

I then, impertinently, asked whether these were his views or those of the Prime Minister. He gave me an old-fashioned look and said they were his of course, but that the Prime Minister was extremely interested in our work.

I then rehearsed the problems we had faced over knowledge in more detail and emphasised the benefits to be obtained from placing it in the programmes of study. John listened with great care and appeared to understand the point I was making. He then asked me a direct question: 'Would the group reconsider placing historical knowledge in the attainment targets?'

My reply was that the group would look at anything again but it would not accept any directive regarding its recommendations.

John then showed me the draft of a letter he proposed to write to me which would be published at the same time as the interim report. In effect it was asking us to look again at our treatment of knowledge, and to place more emphasis on chronology and British history. I do not recall the precise contents of the draft, but while it was perhaps worded rather more strongly than the final letter, there was nothing in it requiring the group to take this view or that, which would of course have been quite unacceptable and lead to resignations, mine amongst them. The nearest the final letter came to a directive was in the following paragraph:

'I understand that the group has considered this aspect of its approach (historical knowledge in the programmes of study) in some detail, but I am not convinced that the case has been made for knowledge remaining only in the programmes of study. I should be grateful if the group would look again at this matter with a view to including essential knowledge in the attainment targets.'[*]

I then returned to Mrs Thatcher's hostility to the report of which I was well aware, and asked whether I could go and see her to explain in plain words what the issues were about knowledge and why we had taken the course we had. John felt that direct contact with the Prime Minister was better left to him. All we had to do now was to convince him of our arguments and he would back us to the hilt. He was in fact as good as his word and when the time came, fought our corner against huge Prime Ministerial pressure.

While all the politics was being played out at a high level, the group's

---

[*] Letter from Secretary of State to Chairman HWG dated 10th August 1989 published with Interim Report.

work continued. Sadly we lost the services of Dr John Roberts who had been having difficulty attending meetings and felt that he no longer had the time to do the subject justice. He stressed that his departure had nothing to do with the publication of the interim report which he fully supported. I was very sorry to see him go. His clear mind, his immense knowledge and worldly-wise experience had been invaluable and his presence had given the group weight in academic circles

He was replaced by Professor Peter Marshall, Rhodes Professor of History at King's College, London, an expert on the British Empire. Peter made a delightful addition to the group, contributing strongly in a number of ways.

We took the opportunity of this relatively quiet period to carry out a number of useful visits. In early July some of us visited Birmingham where there are a number of schools with a high percentage of pupils from the ethnic minorities. We needed to see for ourselves what history they were being taught and to form a view on whether the ethnic minorities should receive special treatment in respect of their own personal histories.

We visited one very unpromising looking primary school made out of what appeared to be temporary buildings. We entered the tiny hall, a group of strangers somewhat formally dressed, and a door to our left burst open to release an avalanche of children. Quite unfazed by the rather stuffy party in the hall they seized us by the hand and with spontaneous shouts of welcome led us into their classroom where they proceeded to entertain us with songs like *Any Old Iron*.

Their enthusiasm was infectious. I was approached by a Vietnamese boy who could not have been more than ten. He spoke excellent English and explained that he and his family had been 'boat people'. I asked him where he had learned his English and understood him to say in Vietnam. I then asked him what a Vietnamese school was like. He did not reply but went off and came back with a print of a Dickensian classroom scene with some wretched child being beaten in front of the class.

'That's what it was like in Vietnam,' he said. He went on to say how happy he and his family were in England. The headteacher, himself of Afro-Caribbean origin, told us that 56 different native languages were spoken in his school. He was determined that his pupils should be taught the history of the country of their adoption. While the ancestors of a number of his pupils had been slaves, he did not feel it was necessary to over-emphasise the role of slavery. There was one problem. British history is mainly about white people and black pupils needed to be able to identify with one of their own ethnic group. Fortunately someone discovered a nurse of African origin who served in the Crimean War with Florence Nightingale, and her picture cropped up all over the place.

It is easy to think of the 'ethnic minorities' as one homogeneous mass, but of course this could not be more wrong. In practice they represent a range of cultures from all over the world and the contrast between them was underlined by our next visit to a secondary school where we attended a class consisting largely of pupils from Bangladesh being taught about the Second World War and Hitler in particular. Bangladesh is an agricultural country and its people live a subsistence life lurching from crisis to crisis always on the margins of survival. Their language reflects this essentially practical existence. It is therefore a major culture shock for them to find themselves in a strange country being taught in a strange language about concepts which do not easily translate into their own native language. Nevertheless I felt heartened by our visits and encouraged to think that on balance our already multicultural tolerant society could be further enhanced by the input of these young people. The general theme of the British identity and the position of the ethnic minorities within it cropped up on numerous occasions subsequently, particularly when discussing the question of British history, and indeed it was in the forefront of our minds when we visited Switzerland in July.

Switzerland is unusual for a number of reasons, but in particular we wanted to learn how they dealt with the three cultures and languages, French, German and Italian, which co-exist, apparently happily. The answer was interesting. Switzerland is run principally by local government, and the federal government plays a relatively small part. For instance there is no federal parliament, only a committee which run the country of which the chairman as *primus inter pares* is the equivalent of both Head of State and Chief Executive. In educational terms therefore each 'canton' was given a degree of independence which allowed for the cultural differences to be addressed.

The interim report was finally published on 10th August including an upbeat covering letter from me in which I expressed the hope that "the report conveys some of the excitement we feel at this opportunity to restore history to its rightful place in the school curriculum', and the Secretary of State's response, generally welcoming the report but listing a number of issues which he wanted us to address, in particular a chronological framework, more emphasis on British history, and, of course, to look again at the question of including historical knowledge in the attainment targets.

With the publication of the interim report, the work of the group changed gear. Indeed at times it seemed to go into overdrive. Whereas hitherto we had done all our work in camera and had been able to concentrate our minds on the matters under discussion, now everything was out in the open and no more could we hide behind a veil of secrecy. First there was the press interest which was very strong and took up a lot of time with interviews and so on. One of our members, Professor Gareth Elwyn Jones, has written an excellent piece in the *Curriculum Journal* on the role of the press in the debate on the national curriculum for history in England and Wales.[*] He concluded that the activities of the History Working Group generated more column inches than any of the other curriculum working groups.

The headlines ranged from 'Back to 1066 and all that for history class of 1990'[**] to 'This history is bunk.'[†] The education editor of the *Daily Telegraph*, under the headline 'Clash over the way to teach history' wrote, 'The first official attempt to define the history that children should learn.....has been largely rejected by Mr MacGregor...'[††] and went on to state that John MacGregor was firmly on the side of the traditionalists. The *Guardian*, on the contrary, maintained that 'the report was welcomed by supporters of more traditional history teaching and by Mr John MacGregor...'[‡] It seemed from these contrasting views that we had indeed achieved what we had set out to do and found a middle way between the two extremes.

The Times, in a long leader,[‡‡] gave the report a particularly warm welcome, calling it 'balanced and coherent' and vindicating the 'eccentric' appointment of a retired naval officer as chairman . My background as an 'Old Etonian naval commander-turned-landowner in whose castle (Kenneth Baker) happened to stay"[#] came in for comment in a number of papers, notably the *Guardian*, which had expected a strongly traditionalist approach and were therefore somewhat surprised to find the reverse.

While at this early stage press comment focussed mainly on Mr MacGregor's request for British history to be given more prominence, it was not long before the Prime Minister's role reached the public domain. Ten days after publication of the report, the *Observer* carried a story[##] on its front page headlined 'Thatcher changes course of history'. In it, the Prime

---

[*] The Debate over the National Curriculum for history in England and Wales 1989-90:the role of the press. The Curriculum Journal VoII No.3 Autumn 2000 299-322 by Gareth Elwyn Jones , University of Wales Swansea.

[**] *Today* August 11 1989.

[†] The *Evening Standard* August 10 1989.

[††] The *Daily Telegraph* August 11 1989.

[‡] The *Guardian* August 1989.

[‡‡] *The Times* August 12 1989.

[#] The *Guardian* August 1989.

[##] The *Observer* August 20 1989.

Minister apparently refused to endorse the report and told the new Secretary of State, John MacGregor to take a tougher line, with greater emphasis on facts rather than skills and understanding. With hindsight, it was a remarkably accurate piece of reporting, presumably leaked from Downing Street.

While all this media interest was not unhelpful in publicising the report, our real concern was to receive comments not just from politicians and pressure groups but from historians, teachers and members of the public. Unfortunately the DES underestimated the interest that the report would arouse, and there were not nearly enough copies to go round. We felt it was important that every school had a copy but some did not receive theirs until well into the autumn. Notwithstanding this, we were swamped with over 1000 submissions from every possible source. Each one had to be acknowledged, logged in and read by a member of the group. It was a colossal task and our small secretariat performed magnificently.

Through the good offices of the Historical Association a number of conferences were arranged across the country which members of the group attended, and a colloquy of senior historians was arranged at Chatham House. Chatham House rules forbid publication of the proceedings and no record was kept, but it was an illuminating exercise. Some thirty to forty eminent historians attended and the chair was taken by the Deputy Director, Mr William Wallace. It rapidly became apparent that when two or three or more academics are gathered together and the subject is the teaching of history there will be little if any common ground other than a passionate interest in the subject. The issues raised by the interim report were soon forgotten as the debate raged back and forth. Eventually I tried to bring the discussion back to reality by saying that fascinating though the debate was, the buck had to stop somewhere and decisions had to be made. It was of little avail however and I hazarded the irreverent opinion that in the academic world it is the debate that matters. Decisions are unwelcome because they bring the debate to an end. Seriously though it was a most useful and generally supportive meeting despite the contrary advice that the group were given.

Taken as a whole HWG could be well satisfied with the reception given to the interim report. There was plenty of criticism but the general thrust of the report was welcomed, particularly by the Historical Association and the teaching profession. Thus encouraged the group resumed its task at the end of August at Bournemouth.

In the intervening period a number of us had visited Edinburgh to learn about the teaching and assessment of history in schools in Scotland and to discuss the Scottish dimension of British history. The Scots gave us a warm welcome and an excellent presentation, as one might expect from a country which has rightly prided itself on the high standards both set and achieved in education over the years. Rather to our surprise, however, it appeared that, as far as history was concerned, for once the south was ahead of the north, and their curriculum was still at the theoretical stage. They were thus following our discussions and those of our Welsh colleagues with great interest.

Back in sunny Bournemouth we found ourselves confronting the mammoth task of putting the detailed flesh and bones on the principles expressed in our interim report. To help us grapple with the thorny problem of drafting ten statements of attainment for each attainment targets we had co-opted Tim Lomas, a history adviser from Lincolnshire, who had been a history teacher, and was apparently an expert in this difficult area. In due course we co-opted another ex-history teacher turned author, Chris Culpin, to help us draft the programmes of study. Both made a major contribution to our work but, even with their help, it was becoming clear that with all the delays in publishing the report and the sheer complexity of the detail with which we were now faced, we were not going to be able to deliver our final report within the required timescale. I therefore asked for and was granted an additional month so we had until the end of January to complete our work and answer the criticisms made by our respondents, not least of course those of the Secretary of State.

At about this time there were two senior staff changes at the DES affecting the group. Jenny Bacon, Head of Schools Branch Three and the development of the national curriculum, left to be Chief Executive of the Health and Safety Commission and was replaced by Anthony Chamier. Michael Phipps, our so-called assessor, was replaced by Barney Baker. We were sorry to see them go. Both were unfailingly helpful and supportive. Michael Phipps, in particular, took great pains to explain the technical detail of the more arcane areas of the Education Reform Act and advise us on what was expected of us, but never for one minute attempted to influence our thinking or interfere with our discussions.

The only political influence which bore on our work followed from the Secretary of State's observations on the interim report. We had no difficulty with emphasising British history though we had yet to discuss what it would comprise. Neither were we concerned about his point on chronology; but we were desperately worried that if we lost the argument on historical knowledge, our recommendations might be overridden with disastrous effect. If we were to succeed in persuading government that the right place for historical knowledge to be learned was in the programmes of study then the latter had to be comprehensive and rigorous. As a result we probably tried to include too much.

From Bournemouth we went north to West Auckland for our October meeting. In the meantime some of us visited Ireland, spending a day in Dublin and a day in Belfast. I found Dublin enlightening and the teachers we met were confident, enthusiastic and proud of their profession. Ireland sets great store by education and the teacher enjoys a status in the community on a par with the priest. Furthermore in the south they were provided with enviable resources and high quality curriculum materials.

We asked them what they would like to see taught as the Irish dimension of British history. They were keen that we should avoid using the stereotyped events in Ireland's history. In particular we should include the 'golden' period in Ireland's early history when the Celts exported literacy and Christianity to Scotland and also their modern day role in Europe.

The Irish enthusiasm for Europe came across in several ways. At lunch one day I found myself sitting next to a senior inspector who was also a member of the Anglo Irish Council. He was firmly of the view that the only way we would sort out the Northern Ireland issue was under the umbrella of a European Federation of which Eire, Northern Ireland and Great Britain would all be constituent members.

Again in Belfast we were met by enthusiastic teachers from both protestant and catholic communities. They were adamant that there should be no sectarian bias in their teaching. Welcoming the new ideas in our draft programmes of study there were no moans about insufficient resources, rather

'If we do not have the resources, then we shall make them ourselves.'

We were addressed by a diminutive young lady in forceful tones. She turned out to be the Head of History in a large Catholic girls school on the Falls Road. Her pupils were immaculate and the school was spotless.

The principal object of the meeting at West Auckland was to review the responses to the interim report and to thrash out in more detail the subjects to be included in the programmes of study. To date 500 responses had been received, mostly supportive of the report with criticism concentrated on the selection of content and lack of resources for new subjects. Almost without exception every respondent urged the group to stand by its proposals to put knowledge in the programmes of study and not in the attainment targets.

We then had a long and detailed discussion on the study units of key stage three, probably the most important key stage for learning history, and one or two disagreements began to appear between members. A particularly contentious issue was whether the study of Islam should be treated as a compulsory 'core' item as recommended in the interim report or not. Strong views were held on this issue both for and against, and I needed all my diplomatic skills to prevent a scene possibly leading to resignation. In the final report it emerged as optional.

We were on stronger ground when it came to the question of British history. We all agreed that it was of fundamental importance, but what was British history? Much of what had hitherto been accepted as British history had in fact been English history or at least an Anglocentric version. To be truly British we should take account of the histories of the four countries that make up the British Isles. This at once opened up whole new areas of study. For example, while every pupil in England (one hoped) would be taught about King John and the Magna Carta as the first 'bill of rights', how many would know about the Declaration of Arbroath which performed a not dissimilar function in Scotland?

As the debate continued, we found ourselves once more drawn into discussing the British identity and the many different cultures which have contributed to and enriched it over the years. While our course of school history could not hope to accommodate all the individual inheritances 'specific to country, region, ethnic grouping, religion, gender, and social class', at least we should make pupils aware of the 'richness and variety of British culture and its historical origins'.[*]

Now, eight years on, the 'war against terrorism' and the divided loyalties of some British Muslims give this debate a special relevance. There are many, particularly on the right, who regard the multicultural issue as an anathema and lay today's troubles at its feet. The multicultural nature of British society is however a fact which has to be faced. Most of us have some foreign blood in our veins. My father was a Scot, my mother was half English and a quarter Greek and Austrian with a touch of Irish. As a race we have benefited from this infusion of foreign blood over the years and shall continue to do so, provided those who come to our shores are prepared to accept the culture of the country of their adoption and abide by its essential values of tolerance, justice and honesty. Equally we for our part must make them feel welcome as British citizens. As far as history is concerned the group felt that our ethnically diverse population 'strengthened rather then weakened the argument for including a substantial amount of British history'.[**] If they wish to study their own cultural background then they would be welcome to make their own arrangements outside school hours. The French in their pragmatic way provide for ethnic studies on Saturday afternoon paid for by the pupil's country of origin.

We learned this on a visit to Paris, the last of our foreign visits. We found

---

[*] National Curriculum History Working Group Final – Report. Paragraph 4.22.

[**] National Curriculum History Working Group – Final Report. Paragraph 11.25.

these visits astonishingly helpful in giving us the opportunity to view our history from the perspective of a foreign country and to hear from their educationalists how they were tackling the problems we faced. We had hoped to include India on our itinerary but unfortunately the money ran out and we had to be content with France instead.

France has had a national curriculum since 1808 and a mighty tome it is. We were just beginning to become aware of the temptation and danger of including too much in the curriculum but this book was vast.

'Does all this have to be taught?' I asked my host.

'Mais oui, c'est la loi,' he replied.

'Then how on earth do you fit it all in ?'

He shrugged his shoulders in a typically Gallic fashion: 'Oh, personne n'applique pas!'

In these few words my host had put his finger on the essential difference between France and Britain. The French accept the spirit of the law but do little about it while the British religiously obey every letter of the law and become very frustrated as a result. On a more serious note, they then outlined the five main areas of French history which they felt should be taught to British pupils as follows:

Colonisation by the Romans

The reign of Louis XIV

The industrial revolution in France influenced by that of Britain

Britain's role in World War 2 as the pillar of freedom

The relationship between Britain and France, described as 'cousins'.

Interestingly there was no mention of Napoleon.

French history is taught in parallel with civics and geography which makes a great deal of sense provided the separate identities of each subject are respected. I had hoped that we might have been able to do the same with our geography curriculum. The Geography Working Group started six months after us and could, if they wished, have adopted our approach. We could have liaised over study units and, I believe, found much in common which might have enabled us to reduce the burden of content which our separate and entirely unrelated reports brought to bear on the curriculum.

I put this idea to their chairman, a wily ex-diplomat, Sir Leslie Fielding, who was Vice Chancellor of Sussex University. He had observed the treatment meted out to us on our interim report and was not going to buck the system. Much to the disgust of some members of his group and of geographers at large, he insisted on putting knowledge in the attainment targets. While this pleased Kenneth Baker and Mrs Thatcher, my understanding is that it created considerable difficulties for the National Curriculum Council who had to implement it.

Our November meeting in Great Yarmouth was memorable for two reasons. On my way there I was conscious of an itching sensation in my foot. This became more and more uncomfortable as the meeting progressed. Finally I could stand it no longer, and Jenny took me to the local hospital where I was diagnosed as suffering from gout. It was nothing that a few pills could not cure but it caused much amusement in the group to find the chairman empathising so successfully with life in the 18th century!

No sooner was this sorted out than I was called to the telephone by Nick Stewart, one of the deputy secretaries at the DES. For sometime there had been rumblings of dissatisfaction emanating from the House of Commons, that our treatment of the Holocaust in the interim report was inadequate. Now someone had put down a question to the Minister of State, Mrs Rumbold, seeking confirmation that the Holocaust would receive proper attention in the final report. Mrs Rumbold had accepted the point and what were we going to do about it? I replied that certainly we would give the Holocaust serious consideration but I could not of course predict the outcome and it was in any case quite improper for the minister to anticipate the group's thinking. Poor Nick was, I think, hoping that I would let him off the hook with his dilemma but I could not compromise the group in that way, otherwise our independence, and with it our credibility, would have disappeared overnight.

With barely two months to go to the submission of the final report, the group's discussions took on a new urgency. There was much detailed work still to be done on the programmes of study and some hard decisions to be made on which study units to include in each key stage. Not before time, the DES had had a change of heart and was now seeking to simplify the assessment process. Profile components were dispensed with and we reduced our attainment targets from five to four. There was no escaping the drafting of the statements of attainment, however, on which Tim Lomas, our co-opted wordsmith was burning the midnight oil producing paper after paper with remarkable good humour. Thanks to his hard work there was a glimmer of light at the end of this particularly long tunnel.

The whole question of 'bringing history to life' was a subject close to my heart and in particular the use of properly organised site visits along the lines I had been promoting through the Heritage Education Trust and the Sandford Award. In view of my personal interest I did not want to lead on this subject and was therefore delighted when the group raised the value of such visits without any prompting from me. There are all sorts of ways that the study of history can be both enjoyable and interesting. For example education programmes in the media, literature (including good historical fiction) and of course drama and role play – provided that in every case proper regard is had to the evidence. This is where the importance of our second attainment target of 'understanding points of view and interpretations...' came in. At the time of writing our report, information technology was still in its infancy but we recognised it as a powerful teaching aid of the future.

December found us in Exeter confronting a huge pile of paper which Jenny had warned us would require not just wet towels but ice packs. It was the first draft of the final report and indeed the fruit of a herculean effort by Jenny and her staff. By the end of the meeting we had a second draft which, while it still needed more detailed work on the programmes of study and statements of attainment, was in a form that I felt I could send to the Secretary of State to advise him of the way our minds were working and to prepare him for the final draft due at the end of January. I noted in particular the care with which we had addressed the question of including knowledge in the attainment targets and that it was 'not just a matter of principle but of sheer practicality' that we had held to our view that knowledge should be in the programmes of study.

We concluded our meeting at Exeter with a very pleasant dinner hosted by Tom (Henry) Hobhouse, one of our members, who had become Chairman of Somerset County Council. Tom had been a source of great strength throughout the work of the group but I was aware that at times he was far from happy with the views of some of the group. He was broad minded enough not to rock the boat too strongly and when he had said his piece he accepted the general view. I was grateful for this as it would have made my job infinitely more difficult, and substantially weakened the impact of our report, if we had not managed to reach a consensus.

Early in the new year I was summoned to see the Secretary of State who had read our final draft. He told me that he was content with the group's response to the issues of British history and chronology and that we had convinced him of our arguments that pupil's acquisition of historical knowledge was best assessed by an attainment target focussing on understanding , but drawing on content from the programmes of study. He warned that the report would face considerable opposition in that Downing Street were expecting a different approach and suggested certain minor amendments to the draft report with which I knew the group would have no difficulty.

The group met once more in January at Cheltenham to work through the programmes of study, check out the statements of attainment and take any last thoughts on the final report. It was our last formal residential meeting but it was no less pressured than any of its predecessors as there was an immense amount of detail to be covered. Despite serious rationing of time for comment by the chairman, we had to work well into the night to cover the ground.

We met finally on 29th January for lunch at Corby to check the programmes of study once more. It was vital that the enormous amount of detail in the 40 History Study Units was 100% accurate. One date wrong and the press would have a field day. By Tuesday evening we agreed that we had done all we could. Our programmes of study and indeed the report itself could be improved in places given more time but we had already had an extra month and it was time to close the shop and let others have a go.

Exhausted but reasonably satisfied we repaired across the road to the castle where I hosted a final dinner. We had all worked very closely for a year, with almost 100% turnout at every meeting and, while we had some disagreements, they were remarkably few considering the controversial nature of the subject. They were all resolved somehow and at the end of the day the report was a truly joint effort of which we all shared ownership and of which we were all proud. The occasion of our final dinner was therefore a moment of triumph mixed with sadness as we each went our separate ways after what had been a demanding but most stimulating task.

It was appropriate that it should take place in the great hall at Rockingham which has been the site of many historical events and I reminded the group of a less satisfactory occasion almost 900 years ago in 1095 when King William II held a council with his barons and bishops to decide whether the Archbishop of Canterbury, Anselm, should accept the pallium, the symbol of spiritual authority, from the Pope. The meeting took three days. The King and his barons sat in the hall; with the Archbishop in the chapel. The bishops, appointed by the King, and owing spiritual allegiance to the Archbishop, went backwards and forwards between the two attempting to achieve an agreement. As the meeting wore on, this looked increasingly unlikely so, as Anselm's scribe, Eadmer, records, 'they split up into groups and went into separate rooms better to find a form of words acceptable to both parties'.[*] They failed. *Plus ça change.*

The final report was submitted to the Secretaries of State for Education and Science, and for Wales on 31st January with a covering letter from me and a supporting letter from my Welsh opposite number, Professor Rees Davies, chairman of the History Committee for Wales. Looking through my correspondence files, I am struck by the number of letters in beautiful copperplate from Rees Davies, each one full of sensible practical comment and support. The role of HCW in the drafting of the national curriculum history has been very underplayed. At every meeting of HWG we received a verbal report of HCW's work together with the minutes of their last

---

[*] *Dictionary of National Biography*

meeting and on a number of occasions our thinking was influenced by their comments. Above all I was immensely grateful once more for the robust stance taken by the Welsh chairman in support of our decision to resist pressure to place historical knowledge in the attainment targets.

As the group's work moved towards a conclusion, we were vividly reminded of the strength of the opposition in the form of a pamphlet written by Dr Sheila Lawlor of the Centre for Policy Studies. It was a lengthy document containing detailed criticism of the interim report, the gist of which was that our recommended course of history was more suited to a graduate than for teaching in schools. The author had clearly taken a lot of trouble and the paper undoubtedly contained some useful points but she weakened her case by misrepresenting the report in places and adopting such a polemical style that I found it hard to believe that anyone could take it seriously.

Another critic, Professor Robert (now Lord) Skidelsky, wrote a more thoughtful paper arguing that knowledge should be an attainment target on its own. His argument would have been more convincing if he had given us some examples of what his statements of attainment would look like. None of our critics ever did show how they would have fitted their ideas into the TGAT formula.

I knew that John MacGregor was now much more sympathetic to our case but I felt he needed some support with the Prime Minister, and I therefore went to see Kenneth Baker, now the Conservative Party Chairman, to enlist his aid. As an historian who understood what was at stake, would he go and see the Prime Minister and explain to her the problem and that our proposed solution would meet all her concerns. Sadly he was not too keen on the idea and did not want to tread upon John MacGregor's territory. I also wrote, off the record, to Professor Griffiths, Head of the Prime Minister's Policy Unit to ask him to lunch but received no reply.

As the final report disappeared into the maw of government and we waited for the explosion that was bound to come when Downing Street found that their requirement was not being met in the way they had expected, the press started to speculate, and academia prepared for battle.

The normal procedure for processing curriculum working group reports was for the Secretary of State to amend the report as he saw fit and then publish the amended report as his statutory proposals for consultation. On completion of the consultation period, the National Curriculum Council (NCC) would be tasked to produce the statutory orders have taken account of the comments on the proposals.

Things happened rather differently with history. Our final report went to the Secretaries of State on 30th January and a deafening silence ensued.

February passed without a murmur, and by the middle of March the press began to become restive. Everyone knew that Mrs Thatcher wanted 'facts'. Would the working group change their minds or would they persist with an 'empathy' orientated approach? Members of the working group and I were constantly being lobbied by journalists and unable to give any response. It was becoming embarrassing and I asked to see the Secretary of State to clarify the position and seek guidance on handling the press.

Meanwhile a new body appeared on the scene calling itself the History Curriculum Association (HCA). Founded by two teachers, Chris McGovern and Dr Tony Freeman, who had managed to recruit to their cause a number of prominent academic historians such as Lords Beloff, Blake and Thomas of Swynnerton, Robert Skidelsky and Sir Geoffrey Elton. As might have been expected this group was concerned that too much emphasis had been placed in the interim report on historical skills at the expense of knowledge and they achieved a certain amount of press coverage for their views. By and large the press maintained a balance by matching this with other stories by senior historians like Raphael Samuel of Ruskin College, or Lord (Conrad) Russell, who were strong supporters of HWG's line.

Finally I was sent for to see the Secretary of State on 26th March to be informed that Mrs Thatcher was unhappy with the report for no clear reason. He had persuaded her that the argument to place knowledge in the programmes of study was unassailable but she was concerned at the quantity of detail and proscription. He agreed with her about the detail and had decided to put the report out for a further round of consultation before issuing his statutory proposals. He planned to publish the report in its original form on 4th April.

This was good news as it meant that everyone would have a chance to judge the report on its merits. The consultation lasted two months and while I was not allowed to see any of the responses, I was firmly under the impression that the final report had been favourably received in a whole range of areas, particularly in schools. The Secretary of State then produced his statutory proposals and to our delight it emerged that the Schools Examination and Assessment Council (SEAC) had advised that our proposals offered a sound and workable basis for assessment. While they had reservations, which I shared, on whether our statements of attainment had succeeded in differentiating the ten levels, they commented that our recommended assessment structure was likely to provide an effective, economical and practicable basis of assessment. They contrasted the relatively small number of statements of attainment in each key stage with the number already prescribed by order for the core subjects and recommended for geography. The Secretary of State therefore accepted our recommendation that a pupil's knowledge and understanding of historical content specified in the programmes of study can and should be assessed against attainment targets and statements of attainment which do not themselves specify content.

He went on to announce that he proposed to amend the first attainment target to read 'knowledge and understanding of history' rather than simply 'understanding history in its setting'. He did not however think it necessary to alter the statements under this target. There were a number of other proposals aimed at simplifying the recommendations, but in general terms our report had been vindicated and school history saved from being relegated to a stultifying recitation of meaningless dates and facts.

Meanwhile the 'enemy' was in chaos. To emphasise their point, the HCA published a large advertisement in the *Daily Telegraph* criticising the report and appending the names of a number of eminent historians, many of whom had not been asked to participate nor, as they made clear, did they wish to be associated with the sentiments expressed.

The Final Orders for history in the national curriculum were published in March 1991. At first sight they bore little actual resemblance to our report, but on closer examination they were clearly based on the principles which we had established, and, while greatly simplified, the attainment targets and the programmes of study were essentially those we recommended.

Now, almost two decades later, the debate continues but the space available for the teaching of history has been eroded in the drive to improve the teaching of basic subjects. I entirely accept that top priority must go to the core subjects of mathematics, science and English language, but for school pupils to study serious history only at key stage three (years 7-10) is to deprive them of an opportunity to understand the world they live in and to learn the skills of research, analysis and expression.

As a postscript, Lady Thatcher and her husband came to lunch at Rockingham many years later. It was a simple family occasion and we lunched in the great hall. She was charming, provided one kept off politics. I could not resist mentioning that I had had something to do with the history curriculum which had caused her so much grief. I had meant to go on to say that I was sure I could have convinced her that her requirements were being met but she forestalled me with an exclamation.

'Oh, the history curriculum, the Left got hold of it - but we trounced them in the end!'

CHAPTER 12

The British Library

As 1989 drew to a close and we were putting the finishing touches to the final HWG report, I started to wonder what I might do next. I rather hoped that there might be a chance to work in museums and galleries. I could see this becoming an increasingly important area as interpretation and display techniques improved and, encouraged by the national curriculum, concepts like heritage education gained ground. Indeed there was a strong similarity between museums and historic houses in that both were being challenged with the need for enhanced accessibility. Besides, my experience with the Washington exhibition and with the National Heritage Memorial Fund had given me an insight into this field.

I was not to have long to wait, but the call, when it came, was a totally unexpected one. My cousin, Richard Luce having resigned as Minister of State at the Foreign and Commonwealth Office over the Falklands had been brought back into Mrs Thatcher's third administration as Minister for the Arts. At his mother's memorial service on 25th November Richard was holding court in a room at the rear of the house and he asked me to see him.

'What are you going to do now?' he asked.

'I have not the faintest idea but I hope something will turn up.'

'Well don't take on anything without letting me know as I have something in mind for you. Incidentally are you interested in libraries?'

I had to confess that libraries as such had not featured prominently in my mind. I had of course used them from time to time and we had a library at Rockingham so I was familiar with some of the problems of cataloguing and conservation. I was fond of books and though my first love was art and painting in particular I recognised the importance of libraries as sources of information, wisdom and pleasure. If there was a chance of doing something useful in that field I should be happy to have a go.

No more was said at the time but a fortnight later I was sent for by Richard's office in the Cabinet offices overlooking Green Park. As I waited in the hallway I noticed on the walls a drawing of the new British Library building at St Pancras and suddenly the penny dropped. I had heard of the British Library only as a controversial project under attack for the design and location of its new building. Of the British Library itself and its origins I knew little and if questioned would have responded that it was housed in the British Museum under the magnificent dome of the round reading room. In common with many others who were not frequent users of its facilities, I was completely ignorant of the scope, depth and wealth of its collections.

Richard emerged from behind his desk. Tall and willowy, few people are aware that he has a serious disability, and much of his life has been spent in pain and discomfort. You would not have guessed it from his relaxed manner, nor would you have guessed that you were facing probably one of the toughest negotiators on the government front bench. His subsequent appointments as Vice Chancellor of Buckingham University, Governor and Commander-in-Chief, Gibraltar, and ultimately the first commoner Lord Chamberlain crown an unusually distinguished life of true public service.

'Would you be prepared to take on the British Library?' he asked.

'I cannot imagine anyone less qualified than I, who has not been to university and seldom darkened the door of any library let alone the British Library.'

'That's by the way,' said Richard. 'The British Library is currently scattered all over London and in Yorkshire. The different parts, which were brought together to form the British Library under the Act of 1972[*], need to be given a focus, a sense of corporate identity preparatory to the huge operation of moving into the new building at St Pancras. It needs leadership rather than scholarship at this time and that you can give them.'

'But won't people accuse you of nepotism – appointing your cousin to this job?'

'On the contrary I think you are the best person I know to do it. My view is confirmed by Kenneth Baker whom of course you know. I shall clear the appointment through the Prime Minister's office. I do not have to as it is my appointment. I do not anticipate any problems.'

Richard went on to explain more of what the library was about and I could see a fascinating challenge emerging. The thought of chairing the body responsible for holding and making available the entire English speaking culture represented by the printed word was awe inspiring in itself. The opportunities offered by the commissioning of the new building,

---

[*] The British Library Act 1972

and by the developments in information technology gave the job a new and exciting technical dimension to which I could relate from my naval experience in the field of communications. Above all, there was the human factor with over 2400 members of staff needing to be given a lead.

In its scale and potential the job greatly exceeded any expectations I might have had. I knew that I should be sailing into uncharted waters and that the question 'Why You?' would be raised once again but chairing the History Working Group had given me the confidence that I could do these things, and I might never have another such opportunity again. I accepted without further hesitation.

As I left the room, Richard added, 'It's paid, you know. It is the only job in my power that is.'

'Oh,' I said, 'I am sure that is not necessary. I have never been paid for doing anything like this before.'

Luckily Richard took no notice and I was more than happy to be offered a salary of around £20,000 a year for two days per week, my first regular salary since leaving the Royal Navy eighteen years earlier. Not only was the money very welcome but it also gave me a stimulus to put in at least three days per week and often more.

Surprisingly, in the light of our earlier encounter over the history curriculum, the Prime Minister's office raised no objection to my appointment and it was arranged that I should succeed Lord Quinton in March 1990. The first phase of the new British Library building was due to open in 1993 and Richard proposed that I should be appointed initially for five years so that I could see the Library into its new home.

Somewhere along the line however this admirable idea was intercepted and I found myself appointed for three years only which would bring my term of office to a close a month before the building was due to open.

I suspected that the civil service had intervened and wished to hedge their bets, particularly with such an unknown and untried figure as myself. Nevertheless it was not a satisfactory situation and I told Charles Henderson, Head of the Office of Arts and Libraries, as much – but nothing was done about it. In fact, as it turned out, even if I had served the full five years, I would still not have seen the Library into the new building.

It was now early December and the appointment was to be announced in the new year. In the meantime, I thought that I ought to learn something about my new job. I therefore went along to the British Museum and asked to visit the round reading room.

'Where's your pass?'

'I am afraid I do not have one.'

'In that case please step inside the admissions office and they will help you.'

In the admissions office I was put through a very polite form of third degree on my reasons for wishing to visit the round reading room. I searched my brain frantically for some research objective and came up with some drawings by Tillemans of Rockingham which I knew were in the Library somewhere.

'Oh that's prints and drawings,' said my interrogator. 'You must ring ...'

I gave up. A few weeks later, when I was visiting the manuscripts department of the Library as chairman, the drawings were laid out for me to see. They were in the Library after all.

Early in the new year I met Lord Quinton for lunch at the Garrick. A distinguished philosopher, Tony Quinton was Master of Trinity College, Oxford, elevated to the peerage by Margaret Thatcher. Erudite, urbane and friendly, we had a delightful lunch of sausages and mash but I ended it not much wiser as to what my new job entailed.

I then met Lord Dainton. Fred Dainton had chaired the committee set up by Viscount Eccles, the then Minister of the Arts, to look into the creation of a single national library by bringing together a number of existing libraries and library services, which were operating independently of each other under different government departments and sited in various locations across London and in Yorkshire. The British Library was thus established under the British Library Act 1972 and Lord Eccles, by then no longer a minister, became the first chairman of the board. He was succeeded in due course by Lord Dainton. These two men, Eccles, the cultured politician with his vision, and Dainton, the scientist with his practical sense and forceful personality, were effectively the godfathers of the British Library, this great and unique institution which, now housed in its purpose-built building, ranks with the Library of Congress as undoubtedly one of the finest in the world.

Fred Dainton was fond of telling how his father could not read and Fred, the youngest of the family was sent to the local library to draw out books which he read to his father, clearly himself a remarkable man. This experience had given Fred a lifelong love of books and a huge respect for libraries. His report was not universally welcomed, particularly in its recommendation that responsibility for the books and manuscripts in the British Museum library, which had hitherto been regarded as the national library, should be removed from the trustees of the British Museum and vested in the new British Library board. His powerful logic won the day, and plans were commissioned for the biggest and probably most controversial government civic building project in the 20th century. I found Fred immensely helpful and supportive right from the beginning. He and his wife

Barbara became good friends and I greatly valued their advice.

As I contemplated the heavy responsibility that I was about to undertake, I saw the chairman's role as having two principal functions, to chair and direct the proceedings of the board itself and to fight the Library's corner in the outside world. I had three very distinguished predecessors as chairman of the British Library board who in their time had adopted distinctly different management styles. David Eccles and Fred Dainton in particular were 'hands on' chairmen who believed in direct management. Tony Quinton *per contra* was 'hands off' and left everyone to get on with their job, making himself available as and when he was needed. I felt I needed to aim somewhere between the two. It is not a non executive chairman's job to manage. Put simply he should 'know' everything and 'do' nothing. That is in the executive sense of course. There is plenty that a non executive chairman can do, working through and with management without becoming directly involved, but to be an effective chairman he does need to have a very clear idea of the functions of the institution – how it works both politically and practically.

I certainly intended to make the most of this wonderful opportunity and I saw my first priority being to learn about the Library's many activities and in the process to get to know and be known by as many of the 2400 staff as possible. With my own experience in mind, I was struck by the almost total ignorance of the role and functions of the British Library amongst people of influence in politics, industry, commerce and the professions – and even in some cases academia. My second priority was therefore to inform and, I hoped, enthuse as many of these people as possible with the huge importance, the wealth, and the potential of the Library and its collections.

My appointment was to take effect from Tuesday 13th March 1990. Looking at my diary of that time I am amazed at the number of other commitments I had. I was a trustee of the Royal Botanic Gardens, Kew, and of the National Heritage Memorial Fund; I was in the process of issuing the report of my History Working Group with one or two meetings still to come. I chaired the Heritage Education Trust; still had some residual interest in the Historic Houses Association as ex-president and I was a member of the executive committee of the Country Landowners Association. Back at home we were deeply into a controversial scheme to build a new village on Desborough aerodrome which mercifully came to nothing. All this on top of a number of local commitments: which included chairman of the Tourism Development Advisory Panel to the County Council, chairman of the Northamptonshire Association of Youth Clubs, chairman of the Ironstone Royalty Owners' Association, director of the Lamport Hall Charitable Trust and the English Sinfonia Orchestra, not to mention our local Parochial

Church Council and Parish Meeting.

Something had to go and I cut a swathe through these commitments in order to concentrate as much time as possible on the British Library which was clearly going to be one of the biggest challenges I faced in my life.

At 0830 precisely on Tuesday 13th March, the door buzzer in my London flat went and a voice said,

'Good morning sir, it's Bernard here, your driver.' I went downstairs to find Bernard holding open the door of a bright blue Ford Granada, the official car which I was to share with the chief executive. Bernard offered me front or back. I chose front and off we swept.

Bernard was to be my constant companion for the next two years and I could not wish for better. Born and bred in East London he was a cockney through and through, and a fund of information on any subject under the sun. He had served for a time in the Navy as an aircraft handler which at once gave us a common interest. Most of his adult life had been spent 'hauling meat' for Smithfield market. I suggested that his job had not changed that much but Bernard, the perfect gentleman, refused to be drawn.

As I settled into my seat I suddenly realised that I was seeing London for the first time from the viewpoint of a passenger in the front seat of a private car and thus able to see the buildings above first floor level. You cannot do this from a taxi and my wife seldom, if ever, drives in London. As we drove across London to the Library's temporary offices in Soho I much enjoyed my new and constantly changing view of London's varied architecture. Cubitt's elegant Belgravia gave way to the more solid imperial grandeur of Whitehall before we dived into the maze of small streets of Soho. Then, as we approached the Library's offices in Sheraton Street, I was struck by the number of red lights burning at first floor level at 8.45 in the morning!

The administrative offices of the British Library were housed in a building known as Novello House. It had been built by the Novello music publishers and it boasted a very grand entrance up a marble staircase into a splendidly bogus 'Jacobean' hall. It was found by Fred Dainton, who was so pleased with his new offices that he asked the Prime Minister, Mrs Thatcher to lunch. Far from being impressed, her immediate reaction was to tell Fred that the building was far too grand for him and that he should find something smaller and more modest – a task that proved to be easier said then done and was in any case overtaken by subsequent events.

Bernard deposited me at a side entrance where I was met by a security guard who swept me up to the first floor to be greeted by Ken Cooper, the chief executive, Denise Martin, secretary to the chairman and chief executive, and Cathy, Bernard's daughter who made the coffee and kept everybody cheerful. I was shown to my office where I was immediately struck by the desk which resembled a full size ping-pong table. On it were a blotter, a pen set, two keys, a telephone and a large computer screen.

I sat down behind it and Denise showed me round: 'Here is your computer screen; Kevin will show you how to work it. Here is the key to your executive toilet, and here is the key to your bar.'

'Fine,' I said. 'Now I am beginning to feel like a chairman. Where's the paper?'

'What paper?'

'Well work; I mean papers to work on.'

'There isn't any... I can get you a copy of the newspaper if that is what you want.'

'There must be something for me to do. What did my predecessor do?'

'He read the newspapers.'

This sounds rather stark but, as I was to find out, there really was not a lot of correspondence for the chairman which was not of his own making. It was all, quite properly, handled by the chief executive, whose office was next door to mine. A tall, good-looking man with a commanding presence and a powerful voice, Ken Cooper took immense trouble to explain to me how the Library worked and to arrange a comprehensive programme of visits by way of an induction course. Despite his kindness, I gained the distinct impression that he was used to dealing with a non interventionist chairman whose function was to chair the board but take little part in the day-to-day running of the Library. This made me all the more determined to be involved not in an executive capacity but in order to learn about the issues with which the Library was faced. From the beginning therefore I was aware of a certain tension in our relationship which eased as we came to know each other better.

My arrival at the British Library coincided with the publication of the final report of the History Working Group and much of my first two or three days in office was taken up by press interviews and photographs. For a brief moment I became a national celebrity with profiles in the national newspapers and much public comment, mainly favourable from the press and public but distinctly unfavourable from the Prime Minister's office who regarded the report as the product of a left wing cabal and insisted that it should, exceptionally, be circulated for further consultation. If Downing Street's hope was that the academic world would suddenly become 'converted' to the view that school history should consist solely of dates and 'facts' and throw out the principal recommendations of the report, they were disappointed. The report was generally well received and rather to my surprise I found myself being regarded in certain circles as a 'hero' who had 'saved' history. The historians at Warwick University even went so far as to award me an honorary doctorate. The issue rumbled on for a year or more and I found myself addressing seminars and conferences across the country but mentally I had now moved on to concentrate on my new command, learning about its many different functions, visiting, meeting, and being seen by as many of its staff as possible.

The British Library is an amazing place. No one who has not been directly involved with it can have any idea of the diversity, scope and scale of its operations spread at this time over nineteen buildings in London and an industrial site in Yorkshire. The following statistics taken from the 1989 annual report[*] give something of the flavour. The combined London collections occupied 233 miles of shelving, those in Yorkshire, 91 miles. Both collections were growing annually at the rate of 5.1 and 3.3 miles respectively. In terms of books and serials alone, the holdings amounted to in excess of 14 million items. When the newspapers, philatelic collections, manuscripts, maps, music scores, prints, drawings and other items were added in, the total holdings for which the Library was responsible amounted to a staggering 63,393,000 items.

No statistic can however do justice to the quality and diversity of the collections. My induction tour was a journey of constant wonder and surprise. To see and hold the original manuscript score of Beethoven's ninth symphony and feel this great outpouring of music from a deaf and almost blind man as the notes soared off the printed staves up into the right hand corner of the paper was a very special experience. Then deep in the bowels of the British Museum, in a secure vault among the 'penny blacks' in the philatelic collections I was shown with pride a couple of pieces of wood hollowed out and strapped together with leather thongs. It was the last 'mail boat' from St Kilda!

I gloried in the delights of the Luttrell Psalter; I was shown Mogul drawings of outstanding beauty, and ancient Chinese manuscripts from time immemorial. The Newspaper Library revealed the announcement of Nelson's victory at Trafalgar in *The Times*. I heard what was reputed to be Queen Victoria's voice on a wax cylinder. In the patent office I was shown the original patent for the first biro, while at the Document Supply Centre I saw a request from South Korea for the papers from a conference on AIDS being handled with expedition.

The British Library had expanded since it commenced operations in 1973. It now comprised principally the British Museum collections of humanities material focussed on the round reading room and the King's library, including the official publications, manuscripts, music, philatelic and map collections - together with a range of support functions such as

---

[*]   The British Library Seventeenth Annual Report 1989-90.

preservation and reprographic services, conservation binderies and workshops, all of which were housed in the rabbit warrens of the British Museum.

Then there were the scientific collections and the patent library at the Science Reference Information Service in Chancery Lane, the environmental sciences in Keene Street, the oriental collections in Store Street, the India Office collections south of the Thames, the Sound Archive in Kensington, and the Newspaper Library in Colindale. Finally at Boston Spa in Yorkshire, on a disused ammunition site, stood a large purpose-built building at the centre of a massive world-wide information and lending service, the Document Supply Centre. In addition to these libraries the British Library Act embraced other library-related bodies including the Research and Development Department, and the National Bibliographic Service.

Thus, not only were these libraries and other bodies physically separated, prior to the British Library Act they were administered by different government departments and different sections within a department. Now, still physically separated, they were administered centrally from Sheraton Street, but it was not surprising that some members of staff, particularly those working in the British Museum, found it difficult to identify with this newly created body known as the British Library.

It would be different of course when they were all together under one roof in the new building now under construction at St Pancras, and it was this controversial project which dominated my three years at the Library. For most people outside the world of libraries, led by the media, the building and the institution were synonymous. It was certainly the most visible and politically sensitive area of my responsibility but taken in context with the work and development of the Library as a leading international institution poised on the cusp of an information technology revolution, it was almost an irrelevance and certainly a complication that the Library could well have done without. That being said, the building was essential to the development of the Library. It was the biggest single cultural building project undertaken in the UK in the twentieth century and for me personally it presented an exciting challenge which, though acutely frustrating at times, was immensely important and worthwhile.

The saga of the construction of this great building has been well documented elsewhere[*]. As far as I was concerned when I took over as chairman in 1990 the construction of the first phase, or Phase 1AB as it had now become, was well under way but no decision had been taken on the

---

[*] The issues are very elegantly set out in a pamphlet 'The British Library and the St Pancras Building' by my successor Sir Anthony Kenny published by the British Library in 1994 at the height of the controversy over construction delays.

next, and possibly final, stage of the building. All along, the design and construction process had been dogged by indecision over funding, but now the intention was to complete this first phase ready for public access in 1993. This would give the Library the full storage facilities of the four basements, some humanities reading rooms, the Science Reference Library, sundry offices and a vast entrance hall.

Access to the bookstacks in the basements would be available from the middle of 1992, enabling the Library to start moving books with a view to opening the reading rooms in spring 1993. In order to make up the shortage in reading room space, a dual operation would be run between St Pancras and Bloomsbury pending completion of the final phase. In fact the Completion Phase, as it became known, was announced in June 1990.

The management of the construction of the building was firmly in the hands of the Government. It had had a chequered career. The brief had been prepared by the British Library and worked up into detailed drawings in conjunction with the architect, Sir Colin 'Sandy' Wilson, his wife, M.J Long and their design team. Once the brief had been approved, the Office of Arts and Libraries (OAL), as the sponsoring department, assumed overall responsibility for funding and developing the project.

Supervision of the construction was vested in the Property Services Agency (PSA) who appointed Laing Management as construction management contractor. The construction project was thus run by a triumvirate,* a project director appointed by the OAL, and a representative of both the PSA and Laing Management. The latter was responsible for managing the construction programme and overseeing the work of the numerous contractors, while the contracts were with the PSA. After a number of changes this was broadly the structure which was in place at the time of my arrival. It was not one calculated to inspire confidence in that no one appeared to have or take overall responsibility and 'the buck' remained in perpetual motion.

Touring the building site shortly after my arrival in March 1990, I was assured that the project was on time and everything was set for the Library's occupation of the basements in June 1992, but I had my doubts even at that early stage. My experience as chairman of the Buildings Committee at Kew had taught me that even relatively simple buildings run into difficulties as the date for completion approaches – and the library building was certainly not simple.

The British Library's responsibilities at this stage were restricted to planning the occupation of the building and its subsequent operation,

---

* In a lighter moment I likened them to the three wise monkeys 'seeing no evil, speaking no evil, and doing no evil'

together with the design and development of the On Line Public Access Computer (OPAC). These were nevertheless substantial tasks undertaken by specific departments within the Library and in parallel with its normal work. The Occupation Planning Office was responsible firstly, for assuming control of the building from the Government when the handover took place and secondly for planning and supervising the biggest book move ever undertaken. The Operational Planning Office was concerned with the way the building would be run and services provided after the Library had been installed. The OPAC, a complex interactive computer retrieval system which would take the place of the printed catalogues, was being handled within the Computing and Telecommunications Directorate alongside a number of other new programmes.

The controversial decision having been taken to replace the printed catalogues with a computer system, the latter had to be reader proof and totally accessible in a range of languages and characters including Greek, Hebrew and Cyrillic. The intention was that the reader without any special knowledge of computers would be able to identify the book he wished to read, call it up using the OPAC and it should be on his desk within twenty minutes.

The books themselves, which included some of the most valuable in the world, would be kept in air-conditioned bookstacks in one of the four gigantic cellar storage areas and brought automatically to the reader's desk in the reading room by means of a complex conveyor belt system – the Mechanical Book Handling System.

All this was a huge improvement both in terms of service and conservation on the current facilities at the British Museum where it could take several hours for the reader to receive the book of his choice, and the books were kept on iron bookstacks under leaky skylights in a space more like the boiler room of the *Queen Mary* than a modern bookstore. Notwithstanding these advances the new building at St Pancras had many critics.

Some were unhappy with Colin St John Wilson's squat asymmetric design. Prominent among these was HRH the Prince of Wales who, having laid the foundation stone, described the building as 'looking more like the assembly hall of an academy for secret police'. Others were deeply concerned at the loss of the round reading room and the King's library in the British Museum, arguing that there would not be enough reader seats in St Pancras and therefore the round reading room should be retained to make up the balance.

I was sympathetic to both viewpoints. To me the design of the building resembled an aircraft carrier poised to launch its 'jump jet 'into the Euston Road. As I came to know it better, however, I began to appreciate the quality of the construction and the initially harsh, angular horizontals of the exterior softened with familiarity. It is purposeful rather than beautiful but the interior is magnificent and the building as a whole sits comfortably on its site, complementing Gilbert Scott's fantasy, the Midland Hotel at St Pancras station. With the passage of time it will come to be regarded as a building of major architectural importance and a fine example of its period. Furthermore it is essentially a practical building designed for a specific purpose with its modular construction illuminated by clerestory windows allowing for the inevitable expansion without affecting the fundamental design of the building. This stands in marked contrast to other great libraries such as the Library of Congress in Washington, or the more recently constructed Cambridge University Library, both of which had been designed on classic lines which draw much of their natural light from quadrangles behind the grand classical facade. In the course of time these are gradually filled with bookstacks and the natural light is lost.

It also stands in marked contrast to another big contemporary library project across the Channel, the Bibliothèque Nationale de France, and President Mitterand's final monument to his presidency. In this case the books were to be housed in four huge glass towers standing at the four corners of a large subterranean space which was to contain the readers. Magnificent though the structure might be, it could hardly be less suited to a library where the books need to be stored in darkness and the readers need natural light to read. Once this home truth had become apparent, the glass towers had to be coated with a special substance to render them opaque, adding considerably to the cost.

Concerned at the rising costs, the Finance Committee of the French Senate, who were responsible for voting the funds, came over to see how we were managing. A tour of the new building quickly convinced them that they were enmeshed in an expensive project which might not be entirely suitable for the purpose for which it was designed. Lunching at the French embassy after the tour, I found myself next to the chairman, a lugubrious gentleman who spoke no English. I was able to follow the gist of his conversation, which appeared to be a diatribe on the president and his *folies de grandeur*. When he paused for breath, I asked him, 'If you so disapprove of the project, why do you not turn off the tap and withdraw the funding?' To which he replied: 'C'est impossible. M le Président a dit et c'est ça.'

I wished our funding problems could be resolved so simply.

The inevitable loss of Smirke's much loved round reading room in the British Museum as a result of the move to St Pancras aroused much passion. It is indeed a remarkable space and it was perfectly understandable that there should be strong feelings about its demise as a reading room.

So strong was the feeling that, a few weeks after my arrival, I received a scholarly deputation from the House of Lords led by Lord Jenkins of Hillhead. They argued strongly for the retention of the round reading room in the British Museum, with special arrangements being made to transport books from St Pancras to Bloomsbury and back. I heard them out sympathetically, but the die was cast and it was too late even if such a change were desirable – which it was not. The fact was that not only was the round reading room in the wrong place, but there was insufficient space for the new technology and the arrangements for the storage and delivery of books were hopelessly inefficient and out of date.

This did not deter an articulate body calling themselves the Regular Readers Group who fought tooth and nail against the new building and were always ready with a quotation for the press whenever a piece of bad publicity emerged – an increasingly frequent occurrence as the saga of the building process unfolded.

I had a month in which to familiarise myself with the British Library and its people before my first board meeting and a fascinating time it was too. I visited all the outlying areas including the book stores in Micawber Street, and at the Duke of Wellington's old barracks at Woolwich, where among several miles of material could be found all the transcripts of the BBC news broadcasts from the Second World War. I spent a day with the Sound Archive in Exhibition Road and the Newspaper Library at Colindale.

At the Science Reference Information Service (SRIS) in Chancery Lane and in the Patent Library next door, the atmosphere was quite different to that at the British Museum. Scientists know what they want, and want it quickly, and furthermore it is generally available in serial or magazine form. The material is therefore made available on 'open access' which enables the reader to browse the shelves himself and select his material to read as required. At Bloomsbury, the home of the humanities and social sciences, closed access was the order of the day. The reader had to order his material to be brought to him to read in the reading room and was never permitted to see the books on the shelves.

The arrival of a book in the reading room is the final stage in a process involving a number of people starting with the expert scholar whose job it is to acquire such books as the Library can afford from its acquisition budget which are not supplied under the legal deposit[*]. On receipt all books, including those received under the legal deposit, have then to be checked,

---

[*] Legal deposit requires a copy of every book or serial published in the UK to be offered free of charge to the six copyright libraries, The British Library, The National Libraries of Scotland , and Wales , The University Libraries at Oxford, Cambridge and Trinity College, Dublin

stamped, placed and catalogued.

The placers sat under a high ceiling in a large room each confronted with several piles of books of every sort and kind. Georgette Heyer rubbed shoulders with Dickens; an autobiography of some politician with an encyclopaedia. I asked the girl at one of the desks how she decided where these books should go.

'Simple,' she said holding up a ruler. 'They are all placed by size.'

'But what about the subject matter and the author, surely this must play some part in where they go?'

'That is the job of the catalogue.'

It came as something of a shock to realise that while the Library was the guardian of the nation's wisdom in the form of printed material, it was not concerned so much with the subject matter but rather with how best to store, conserve and make it available. In other words it was a gigantic warehouse in which every item was unique.

When I attempted humorously to make this point, I was rapidly told that it was a gross over-simplification, which of course it was, and that in any case placing by ruler only applied where the books were on closed access.

It is a commonly held view that a librarian is a quiet sober type living a sheltered and secluded life among his books and catalogues. This concept was given some substance by a recently published survey which stated that of all professionals the librarian was least likely to suffer from stress. My induction tour soon exploded this myth; the staff I met were splendid people who were deeply committed to their work and enjoyed a good party, but the impending move, the continuing organisational change and the financial uncertainty had taken their toll. Their lives were certainly not without stress, and they needed to know that the board was on their side. One way of achieving this would be to make the board and its members more visible.

I took this message to my first board meeting which I viewed with some apprehension. As was to be expected the board consisted of a number of distinguished people from a range of backgrounds. They included two heads of colleges at Cambridge, two university principals, two senior librarians, a chairman of a major publishing company, and two chairmen of large industrial companies together with the chief executive and two directors general of the British Library. Altogether they were an impressive bunch but if they were surprised to find themselves presided over by a relatively junior retired naval officer, they did not show it and right from the start gave me their full support.

A major preoccupation of the board at this time came under the general heading of 'Relocation North'. Essentially this covered a rationalisation of the Library's estate in anticipation of the move to St Pancras, and sprang from an earlier decision by the board that activities which were not being accommodated in St Pancras and did not need to be carried out in London should move to the Library's site at Boston Spa in Yorkshire where they could be carried out more cheaply and efficiently. These included most of the administrative functions, some technical departments, and storage capacity, all of which would require new buildings at Boston Spa and involve the relocation of some 300 members of staff from London to Yorkshire.

As the scheme rolled out, various buildings in London would become surplus to requirements and be disposed of – including Novello House.

The finance for this operation, which would lead to considerable savings in the long term, was to come from the sale of a freehold building in Store Street, currently the home of the Oriental Collections. The first step in this process therefore was the integration of the Oriental Collections with the India Office Library and Records at Orbit House south of the Thames where there was surplus capacity. Store Street could then be sold and the proceeds earmarked for a new building at Boston Spa.

We hoped that this scheme would be entirely self-financing without drawing on the Library's budget. Things are never that simple in government, and it soon emerged that the Treasury would only allow the Library to retain half the proceeds of this sale. Despite this setback, we were convinced that the investment was essential if we were to achieve our dual aims of reducing accommodation costs and uniting all the Library's activities on one site.

The most sensitive part of this exercise was the relocation of 300 staff from London to Yorkshire. Our hope was to achieve this by voluntary means, and in order to sweeten the pill for sophisticated Londoners invited to move to the 'wastelands' of Leeds and Bradford, prospective volunteers were invited to take their partners for a free weekend to discover for themselves the undoubted charms of the area. We also offered a service to facilitate the sale of their London home. Ultimately the relocation was achieved with no one being moved against their will.

As an early gesture of confidence and example, the chief executive's office (and of course the chairman's) was relocated from Novello House into a Portakabin at the rear of the building site at St Pancras. This had the undoubted advantage of being on site for visits to the new building, but it meant that we were no longer at the hub of the administration and as a result felt somewhat isolated. The area itself was far from salubrious with few watering holes worthy of the name.

It did however give me an opportunity to embark on my idea of publicising the Library through what became known as Library Lunches.

Every fortnight or so we would invite up to a dozen leaders of society, the 'movers and shakers' from industry, the city, politics and academia. The object of these occasions was to introduce people of influence to the riches of the Library and the scale of the new building, in the hope that they might pass the message on and gradually build up a body of informed support in place of the almost universal ignorance which seemed at that time to prevail.

An enthusiastic briefing by me or the chief executive would be followed by a tour of the building which with its huge basements and entrance hall even in half completed state could not fail to impress. Then there was a buffet lunch in the Portakabin followed by questions and debate. In all during my three years in the chair we entertained over four hundred people in this way and I am sure it paid dividends later on when the Library came under attack because of delays to the new building.

Another issue which caused concern during my time at the Library and subsequently was the question of the land at the rear of the site occupied by the new building. When the new building was first mooted, an area of twelve acres was purchased next to St Pancras. In the event when the final phase of the building was agreed some five acres remained surplus to requirements and of course there was pressure from the Treasury to sell it. Libraries are essentially organic beasts. They grow and grow and grow. Having acquired this valuable site all in one piece and built this magnificent building, it would be madness to throw away any prospect of expansion on the same site.

The Treasury returned to this issue from time to time like a terrier with an old sock. Our position that the land should be retained for future expansion cut very little ice because we had no clear idea of what we wanted to do with it nor did we have the money. Eventually the issue was kicked into touch by the temporary utilisation of the land for accommodation units concerned with the huge railway project at St Pancras. Hopefully when that is completed in a few years time the Library will be in a position to make a strong case for the use of part of this land on the grounds of proven expansion. I would have hoped that it might also include the Newspaper Library, currently out in the 'sticks' at Colindale together with my dream of a multimedia centre bringing together in electronic form the gems from the sound archives with the original manuscript scores. There was also the question of the bindery at the British Museum which had still to find a new home. This particular issue has now been resolved and a new state-of-the-art Conservation Centre opened earlier this year on the St Pancras site (2007).

For me, a particularly interesting dimension of the Library's activities was its overseas operations. Information is universal and transcends national boundaries. Even in this age before the internet became commonplace, libraries throughout the world kept in constant touch, and there were various international bodies on which the British Library was represented which met in different countries over the world. On one occasion an international conference of librarians in Russia coincided with the Yeltsin revolution and the conferees abandoned their syndicate rooms to dance in the street round a burning White House.

We had particularly close links with the USA, the Library of Congress and the Research Libraries Group who were pioneers in the area of digital transmission. I took an early opportunity to visit the USA with Ken Cooper to meet the personalities concerned and see some of the things they were doing. I was particularly interested in a visit to the National Library of Medicine in Washington. This very impressive organisation had links with just about every hospital and general practice in the USA and was able to provide them with up-to-the-minute data on diagnosis and treatment. The Library supplied the hardware, and the recipient paid for the use of the net. Clearly we had much to learn in the NHS where few if any GPs had computers of any sort, and there was in any case no standard medical network other then the telephone and fax machine.

We saw experiments in medical training using multimedia techniques. A class was working with an interactive video computer on some abdominal operation. The student plunged the knife onto the screen, the patient writhed in agony and blood went everywhere. Another class, presumably in psychology, were interviewing a potential suicide case. Depending on the way the interview went the patient either emerged smiling or took a rope out of his pocket and hanged himself!

Another very important American connection was the American Trust for the British Library. Under the enthusiastic leadership of the late Douglas Bryant, ex-Harvard librarian, a number of American philanthropists came together and formed the trust aimed at replacing the material lost when a bomb on the British Museum devastated the American department in the Second World War. They raised huge sums and by the end of my time at the Library had virtually achieved this goal. It was indeed a remarkable act of generosity which underlined the value our American friends placed upon libraries and the British Library in particular.

I was struck once again by this enthusiasm for libraries in the USA, which stands in such marked contrast to attitudes in UK, when we visited the New York Public Library, a truly remarkable institution funded entirely by private donations.

On the whole the overseas conferences were the province of the chief executive and the relevant specialist staff. Very occasionally an invitation would come for the chairman. One such was an all-expenses-paid invitation to a conference in Taiwan. The Nationalist Chinese were very keen to be accepted as a world-class country and mounting prestigious conferences was part of this policy. Certainly they pulled out the stops. Every night there was a banquet chaired by a minister and while the food became rather monotonous, and the speeches worse, it was interesting to meet so many highly intelligent and articulate people.

Two particular memories stand out. One was of a visit to the National Library which contained some of the most priceless items in the world. The highlight of the visit was to be lunch with a very distinguished Chinese professor who was one of the leading world experts on early Chinese manuscripts. As the tour came to an end we were shown into a room where there was a large low table with what appeared to be beer glasses on it. There was a gentleman in the room in a very dirty white T shirt and khaki shorts fussing about with some bottles in a holdall.

It transpired that this was the professor and his chief concern was that we had not been provided with adequate alcoholic refreshment. Finally a waiter appeared with a tray of small glasses which were distributed round the table. We were invited to fill the tumblers with beer while the professor filled our glasses with some strong spirit from the bottles in his bag. He then demonstrated a strange technique by raising his glass to a toast, then dropping the glass into the tumbler of beer and consuming the contents. As one of two visiting 'chairmen' I was placed on the professor's right; we squatted down and the meal began. Soon the whole place was awash, and with the professor speaking not a word of English, I could see I was in for a sticky time as toast succeeded toast.

Luckily I spotted a German delegate who spoke Chinese and invited him to take my place which he did with great enthusiasm. A little time later, however, he was to be observed sinking slowly under the table into the sea of beer and spirit which were clearly the hallmarks of a good Chinese party.

The other memory was of a delegate from South Korea who came up to me tentatively and said, 'Please, is it true that the capital of England is Boston Spa?'

It was the only place he knew in England and it brought home to me the importance with which the Document Supply Centre is viewed abroad while in Britain few are even aware of its existence.

The Document Supply Centre at Boston Spa is the largest document supply organisation in the world. Indeed I believe that both in its range and its approach to handling information using state-of-the-art technology it was at one time unique. Now I suspect that international competition particularly from the USA has taken the lead, in quantitative if not qualitative terms. In my time the chief function of the DSC was to receive requests from all over the world chiefly for scientific or medical information, to which it responded by fax or post. The exercise was run on commercial lines and it generated revenue of just under £15m in the year 1992/93[*].

The concept of a world-class lending library was the brainchild of Dr Donald Urquhart who conceived the idea in the late 1950s, selected a site, designed and built the building and established it as a world leader in the provision of information. It is a remarkable story which he relates in a book entitled *Mr Boston Spa*[**].

The DSC's supremacy in this field was however under threat from two directions. Firstly the advances in electronic transmission using high quality cables was gaining ground, particularly amongst our rivals in the USA. We visualised a situation where if we were unable to keep pace with these changes we should soon lose out on the lucrative market of supplying information in regular use and be left with the much less economic prospect of supplying only material used once every so often.

We estimated it would cost £20m to scan the material at DSC and there was no way we could produce that figure from our own resources. It had either to come from government or through private finance. There was little chance of the former so we opened discussions with Cable & Wireless and with British Telecom, but it was before the days when institutions like the Library were encouraged to go down the private route under what was known as the Private Finance Initiative, and the scheme foundered.

The other threat to the DSC and the Library more generally was the lack of any legal deposit legislation on non-print material. The great strength of the Library to date was its ability to acquire all printed material published in Britain through the legal deposit free of charge[†]. Increasingly material was being published either on disc or tape which we then had to acquire through our meagre acquisition funds and there was a serious danger that unless suitable legislation was introduced soon, the Library would be failing in its duties as the national archive of published material. There were copyright problems but these were being resolved and the fundamental problem was to get the government to act and grant parliamentary time to pass the necessary if not very exciting legislation.

Towards the end of my first year at the British Library I found myself engaged in finding a relief for Ken Cooper who was due to retire as chief

[*]   The British Library Annual Report 1992-93

[**] *Mr Boston Spa* written and published by *Donald Urquhart* CBE DSc FLA, Wood Garth, 15 First Avenue, Bardsey, Leeds LS17 9BE

[†] See note on page 209 for an explanation of the legal deposit system

executive in June 1991. The job description was impressive. With a staff of 2400, and a turnover in excess of £90m, one-third of which was generated by the Library itself – to say nothing of the national and international dimension, and of course the fact that the new chief executive would be responsible for accepting and moving into the new building – we were indeed looking for an exceptional person. Management experience ranked high in the qualities for which we were looking but above all I wanted someone with a forceful personality, vision, and an intellectual capacity that would carry weight with politicians, academics, and businessmen at the highest level at home and abroad.

We were very limited on what we could offer as a salary for this paragon and I took advice from a consultant on what sort of salary we should be offering potential chief executives for a similar commercial company. He found it difficult to make a comparison. Ostensibly the Library equated to a medium-sized business turning over £100m a year for which the salary in those days might be around the £75,000 mark plus share options. Of course the Library could not offer share options and furthermore the straight comparison took no account of the national and international dimension of what was a unique institution. Against that could be set the kudos with which the job endowed its occupant, particularly in the academic world, which just about made up for the lack of share options. In the event I could not persuade the OAL to move very far from their basic figure for the grade involved. Exceptionally, I was given some flexibility within the bracket but even then it would bring the salary and perks nowhere near that of a comparable commercial body.

Some years previously I had met Dr Brian Lang at a heritage conference at Leeds Castle. We made friends and used to lunch together regularly. He was at that point Secretary to the Historic Buildings Council for Scotland. He was then selected as the first director of the National Heritage Memorial Fund, where he did an outstanding job under the chairmanship of Lord Charteris. I was fortunate to be appointed a trustee and was able to observe Brian working at close quarters. He then surprised us all by resigning from the NHMF to become marketing director of the National Trust thus exchanging a post with a small staff but considerable influence for a job with more staff but less influence. As things turned out, however, it was a wise move.

Brian and I related well. He was tough, intellectually strong and ambitious. I felt that he needed stretch and cast a fly over him one day at lunch. He had never thought about the Library. I took him round the building at St Pancras and at once he was fired with the challenge. I was therefore delighted when he applied and was subsequently appointed to succeed Ken Cooper as chief executive.

Some years before at one of our lunches we had speculated that we might do something together. Little did we realise that this dream would come to pass in such a way. Dream it may have been but in my case it did not have long to last. For Brian it was sometimes a nightmare but I am sure it was an experience he will not regret and having finally moved the Library into the new building it did lead him ultimately on to the rather more congenial post of Vice Chancellor of St Andrews University.

Ken Cooper retired in June 1991, having done a major job in preparation for a move that never took place – work which was far from wasted when the time came for the move. He virtually completed the relocation programme, and prepared the Library for a period of inevitable financial stringency as the delays in the building construction fouled up our carefully calculated three year funding pattern.

An issue which occupied much of my time was the question of works of art for the new building. The architect, Sandy Wilson, himself a major collector of modern British art, had incorporated within his plans three major works of art. There was to be an enormous bronze sculpture by the Scottish sculptor, Paolozzi, based on William Blake's satirical painting of Newton surveying the world, prominently placed on the piazza opposite the great entrance gate. It was meant to bring together the humanities and the sciences in some symbolic way which I never quite followed. Furthermore there were already several versions of this theme about. While I should have preferred an original commission for such an important site, I have to say that the finished work stands most impressively and entirely justifies Sandy's persistence.

The other big work on which he had set his heart was also not entirely original. This was to be an enormous tapestry, to be hung in the vast entrance hall, based on a painting by R. B. Kitaj, itself based on T. S. Eliot's poem *The Waste Land*. Again the strong allegorical message escaped me but the colours were bright and cheerful even if the subject matter was a little gloomy and the tapestry itself performed a vital function in preserving the acoustics of the entrance hall.

The third project was not so far advanced and I was able to intervene. A circular area like a small arena had been created in the piazza to be known as the 'Poets Circle' and to be used ostensibly for readings. The original concept was for this to be surrounded by poets' heads on plinths. I did not much care for this idea and said that it smacked of the Bastille. Fortunately the Advisory Committee on Works of Art took the same view and commissioned a sculpture from Anthony Gormley.

The question was who was to pay for these works? Initially an allowance was made in the original estimate for a sum set aside for the provision of works of art. Then as time went on the Treasury's enthusiasm waned and we were told that the government was only prepared to make a partial, matching donation. Now the message was 'Find it yourselves'.

At this time the Library had no central fundraising organisation. Each department did its own and some were more successful than others. They guarded their 'networks' with great care. Not only were we now looking for sponsors for these three works of art, the new building was going to have three exhibition spaces, one permanent and two temporary. The spaces came with the building but we had to find sponsors for the exhibitions. Some form of centralised fundraising was essential and I formed a board working party to look at the problem.

The issue was closely linked to public relations which was not one of the Library's strong points. People will give money to save some great work of art for the nation but the concept of private patronage applying to a public building, particularly a controversial new library building, was clearly going to be hard to sell. It became even harder as the opening date for the building receded into the mists of the future.

The first intimation that there might be problems with our carefully planned book move into the new building at St Pancras emerged in early May. Shelving similar to that being installed in the St Pancras basements had been erected in the bowels of the British Museum to enable staff to practise loading the shelves prior to the actual move. The shelves were mounted on rollers and could be moved singly or together to create space for access. It is a system of proven design but with the essential difference that shelves themselves had to be specially lengthened to fit into the space provided in the basement. Our staff found that the loaded shelves had a tendency to whip causing movement and potential damage to the books.

This was duly reported to the St Pancras building team whose initial reaction was that the shelves in the British Museum were of a different specification to those in the St Pancras basements. Some modifications were however carried out to strengthen the shelving in St Pancras and the book move planned for June 1992 was put back six weeks.

As the date for the handover of Basement Four approached and the Library's engineers were allowed access to the space, more problems began to emerge. Some were trivial but some were more serious indicating a general lack of proper supervision and quality control. For instance it was reported that the removal of a one metre square panel in the ceiling of Basement Four had revealed eighty wiring faults.

Worse was to come when a test run of the book move resulted in the shelves jamming under a full load as the gearing was simply not up to the job. It had apparently not been modified to accept the additional weight of the lengthened shelves. Then a closer examination of the shelves themselves revealed that they had not been properly painted and were liable to deteriorate well within their specified lifespan with corresponding danger to the books. In some cases the uprights were simply not strong enough and buckled under load.

Samples taken from the shelving were tabled before the board. As we examined these pieces of twisted metal it was difficult to avoid a feeling of acute frustration and anger that such poor material should have been accepted from the contractors and installed at St Pancras. If this was an indication of the state of the rest of the building, we faced a very serious situation indeed. There could be no question of the Library taking responsibility for the building until all the defects had been rectified and the quality control over the remainder of the work massively improved.

I proposed to write to the minister in strong terms expressing our deep concern at the failure to provide adequate supervision and quality control, and to suggest a meeting of the principals involved to discuss the way forward. In so doing I recalled a similar situation when I was a trustee of the Royal Botanic Gardens, Kew. Delays were being experienced to the restoration of the Palm House and we invited the chairman of the contractors to come to Kew and see the problem himself. The effect was electric. The number of workers on site doubled overnight and the work was completed well within schedule.

Charles Henderson, Head of the Office of Arts and Libraries, who was present, assured us that the department fully supported our position and they were enforcing more stringent quality control. He added that the PSA were sensitive to the Library's concerns and feared that a meeting of principals might upset working relations. I felt that the time for sensitivity was past. What was required was action. The board supported me and I wrote to the minister accordingly.

In the meantime it so happened that a visit by the Secretary of State for the Environment, Michael Heseltine, took place. The visit had been planned some time before these problems emerged, and it had been hoped that he would see the actual book move taking place. In fact the timing of his visit was propitious. As the minister responsible for the Property Services Agency, who were managing the project for the government, he was able to see at first hand evidence of incompetent supervision.

I took the party round the basement and explained the problem. I do not know to what extent, if at all, Michael Heseltine had been briefed but he expressed considerable surprise and concern. Turning to the representative from PSA he asked whether the shelving had been tested and examined before installation. The reply was in the negative. As I recall it, the following exchange then took place:

'Why not?'

'Well, when you buy a new car you do not expect to have to examine it in detail before taking delivery.'

I could not resist adding at that point, 'At least you make sure that it actually works.'

The Minister for the Arts was now Tim Renton. Richard Luce had decided to leave politics and resigned to be succeeded for a brief spell by David Mellor who was followed in turn by Tim Renton. He agreed to convene a meeting of principals which duly took place in his office in November 1992. Amongst those present were Martin Laing, chairman of John Laing, the managing contractors, Tim Yeo, the junior environment minister with responsibility for the PSA, a senior man from PSA, Brian Lang, and myself. Tim Renton took the chair, gave a résumé of the situation and called for comment. Both Martin Laing and the man from the PSA took a bullish line the gist of which was as follows:

'We are building a great building and it is going to be very good indeed. There are bound to be snags with a new building especially one as big and technically complex as the British Library. Once these are sorted out everything will be fine.'

I expressed the Library's concern at the lack of proper supervision and quality control evident in the space that we had been invited to accept. What were they going to do about it, and when would the building be ready for occupation? There then followed what I believe is termed in diplomatic language as a 'useful exchange' which certainly cleared the air. We all agreed that there was a problem which had to be addressed, and that we should all work more closely together. I was not convinced that we all shared the same view on what the problem was or that I had managed to impart to those present the sense of urgency and frustration that we were feeling as our carefully laid plans for moving into and opening the building fell apart.

The book move was postponed indefinitely pending the remedial work to bring the shelving up to standard. We were determined not to compromise on quality even if it involved further delays. The negotiations between the PSA and the contractor for the shelving took some time but were ultimately successful in that the defects in the shelving were put right at the contractor's expense. As we had feared, more serious problems came to light with the mechanical and wiring systems throughout Phase 1A and it became clear that there was no question of the building opening as planned in 1993.

The knock-on effects of these delays and the uncertainties they created had serious implications for our finances, our relocation plans, for the morale of our staff and for our readers. Buildings due to be vacated had to be reoccupied for an indefinite length of time. One of the worst affected was the British Museum which had plans and the promise of funding for the occupation of spaces vacated by the Library which were dependant on the dates being adhered to.

The media of course had a ball. Drawing no distinction between the British Library construction project and the British Library as an institution, they went to town on what they saw as a major failure. Here was a great pink elephant that no one wanted, consuming huge public funds, and wallowing in a sea of incompetence. Their approach was widespread and the Library came in for as much flak as the government. The fact that the Library had no direct responsibility for the building project was seldom recognised and it did nothing for our staff, already demoralised by the constant changes and uncertainties surrounding the move, to find their organisation being slated in the press.

Towards the end of the year Lord Annan came to see me. He was very concerned about the situation and wanted to raise it in the House of Lords. I was anxious that he should not be too controversial. In fact he and his colleagues on all sides of the House were most supportive of the Library and the well informed debate gave staff morale a much needed boost.

The situation continued into 1991 without much apparent change in the project management's attitudes, but with more and more defects coming to light as the Library's engineers penetrated further into the building. Dr Ruth Coman, the director of the Occupation Project was assiduous in ensuring that her staff examined every pipe and cable run to ensure that all defects were identified and remedied. At board level we gave her our full support. We were determined that the Library should not be fobbed off with a half-finished building which would be a constant drain on our resources at the expense of the central purposes of the Library – notably acquisition and conservation of the collections.

I sensed that there was beginning to be a suspicion on the part of our political masters that in our quest for quality we were aiming for an unrealistically high standard. This became more apparent after the General Election in March 1992 when we found ourselves being administered by the new Department of National Heritage (DNH), with a Secretary of State, David Mellor. I sought an early meeting with Mellor who had been Minister for the Arts for a short time in 1991 before he was promoted to Chief Secretary to the Treasury – and of course before the problems emerged with the building.

The meeting took place in the grand office overlooking St James's Park used by the Ministers for the Arts. The grandeur of the office is not matched by the comfort of the furniture; visitors have to perch on the edge of a very low and deep sofa while the minister sits in an equally low armchair with large arms. David is not a big chap and he almost disappeared into the chair so that his head was barely visible.

From this undignified position he proceeded to harangue me at some length, the gist of which was that he was determined not to allow his new so called 'Ministry of Fun' to be dragged down by the bad publicity surrounding the British Library building. When at last he drew breath, I remonstrated that the construction project was his responsibility and not mine but if he wished the Library to take on responsibility for the project then that was something we could certainly consider. My concern was that the Library should not accept the building until all the defects had been remedied. I made the point that we were determined not to compromise on quality and to make no announcement about opening until we were satisfied that the building was ready in all respects. He agreed and said that he was appointing independent consultants to look into the management of the building project to ensure that it was on a sound footing and to introduce clearer lines of authority. I welcomed this, encouraged that at last we might see some tightening up of the project management, and that the Library itself might be more closely involved.

In fact, for reasons unconnected with the review or St Pancras, the project management arrangements were due to change once again. PSA was reorganised and then privatised towards the end of 1992 which in turn led to the contracts being taken over by the DNH. Eventually the Library appointed its own project director and took a much closer part in the project management – but this was after my time. Meanwhile the Completion Phase was now well under way with a much simpler, tighter management structure, so at least some lessons had been learned.

The press campaign against the Library continued throughout the year. John Major's Government, his rubric of 'Back to Basics' not helped by our Secretary of State's indiscretions, was under attack and any shaky government project was fair game. The Library and its new building was a soft target and as I went on my 'parish visits' I could sense the growing frustration of staff who felt that they were being wrongly blamed for the delays and cost overruns of the building. Things reached a head in October when Brian Lang held a press conference in my absence on leave abroad to launch the annual report. Such occasions were normally pretty anodyne affairs and the problem was to raise any press interest at all. Not so on this one. Under increasingly aggressive questioning as to why the Library was accepting these delays in such a supine way, Brian laid the responsibility where it belonged, with government.

I returned from leave to find a furious letter from the Permanent Secretary, Hayden Phillips, on my desk accusing the Library of breaking ranks at a time when we were all trying to pull together. He had a point but I supported Brian. We may have made ourselves unpopular with the Department but our responsibility was first and foremost to our staffs who were delighted to see their management standing up for the Library. We both agreed however that it was an episode which could have been handled with more tact.

Meanwhile normal Library business had to continue complicated by the need for additional storage to compensate for the delays in the availability of the St Pancras basement. Books taken to St Pancras had to be returned to the British Museum, where our continued occupation of substantial areas which should have been vacated was causing major inconvenience. The Museum had raised substantial funds for its own programme of refurbishment, following the departure of the Library, which were now placed at risk.

Another issue arising from the delays to occupation of the building concerned finance. In order to enable arts bodies to plan ahead, Richard Luce had somehow managed to persuade the Treasury to agree to funding the arts on a three year basis. This was an excellent arrangement for most art organisations but in the case of the Library it was very nearly disastrous. An allowance had been made for extra funding to meet the costs of the move to St Pancras in the years 1991 to 1993. With the move on hold, these funds also needed to be placed on hold, but that is not the way the Treasury works. Under-spending is very dangerous for any public body. The Treasury could take the view that the money was not required in the first instance and not only would it not be available in future years when it was needed but the organisation concerned could find the sum underspent actually deducted from its future grant-in-aid.

Our financial worries were not just restricted to the move. We were also becoming increasingly concerned at the costs of maintaining the new building out of our existing budget. I wrote to David Mellor in August setting out the position and seeking his support in the September expenditure round. Unfortunately he had other things on his mind at the time which led to his resignation and I do not know whether he ever saw the letter. Mellor's successor was Peter Brooke, fresh from Ireland, our fifth minister in three years, and I prepared to brief him but in the event fortune dictated otherwise.

As 1992 drew to a close I was conscious that my three-year appointment was due to terminate in March of the following year. While I hoped, and indeed expected to be reappointed, I was surprised not to be told one way or the other and as the days passed hoped that no news was good news.

The building apart, there were three items on my agenda that I wanted to accomplish. I wanted to see a firm bid from the Library for the use that it wished to make of the land to the rear of the new building. Provision for the bindery from the British Museum was one essential item. Then I visualised something which went by the name of a 'mediathèque' which was essentially an electronic library in which readers would be able to access material from anywhere in the World in digital form, including material from the Newspaper Library and the DSC.

First however we needed to ensure that the Library was receiving copies of all material published in electronic form and this meant persuading the government to introduce the necessary legislation to extend the legal deposit.

The third item on my agenda was the modernisation of the DSC at Boston Spa. Substantial investment was needed to bring it up to standard ready for the electronic revolution which in 1992 still lay around the corner, and to enable it to continue to compete on commercial terms with the electronic libraries in the USA.

At my request I arranged a meeting on 21st January with Hayden Phillips, the Permanent Secretary to discuss the appointment of new board members. Shortly before it was due to take place I was informed that the Secretary of State wished to see me. I found myself once again on that uncomfortable sofa that I knew so well while Peter Brook disappeared into the armchair which not long before had consumed David Mellor.

'You have done very well at the Library,' he said, 'and there is a very warm feeling for you there. I want to make an academic appointment however, to demonstrate my confidence that the British Library building at St Pancras will open. I have asked Tony Kenny if he will take over from you when your appointment terminates on 11th March and he has agreed.'

My response to what was in effect my dismissal for no particular reason was to accept that I was of course expendable, but if he wanted to see the new building open then he would do well to make changes in his own arrangements for supervising the project, because this in my view was where the problem lay.

'Those are salutary words,' he replied, but it took a further six months before he acted on them.

It was a shattering blow. Not only did I feel cut off in midstride when there was still so much that I felt I could do for the Library but I was infuriated at the suggestion, and I do not know whether it was intended or not, that I had somehow contributed to the delays .

I never did discover the real reason for my removal. I suspect that it was a combination of academic pressure for what has always been seen as an academic post coupled with the hope that an academic chairman might be easier to deal with.

At least I knew the Library would be in good hands with Sir Anthony Kenny, warden of the Rhodes Trust, recently retired president of the British Academy and ex-master of Balliol. I had invited him onto the board a year or so earlier, when I felt the academic representation on the board needed stiffening, and he had been very supportive over the problems with the shelves. He would not be pushed around.

Sadly I returned to the Portakabin which had been my home for the past two and a half years and told the staff. They were all rather shocked. I then embarked on a series of farewell visits to all the departments. It was particularly pleasing to go to Boston Spa and find so many members of staff clearly enjoying the novel experience of working together on the same site.

By way of a postscript I went with Brian on a prearranged visit to the USA in February. The object was to meet the American Trust for the British Library whom I had entertained at Rockingham when they visited UK in 1992. Doug Bryant, the redoubtable founder, was retiring and we needed to find a new role for the trust now that the original task for which the trust was set up was complete.

We then paid a visit to the National Archive Center, which was just moving into a newly-built building of similar size but less complexity than ours. The difference between their project and ours was that they, the client, prepared the specification, and the Senate put up the money. The Center then managed the project themselves, hiring a top-class project manager who was responsible for the project from the design stage right through to completion. There was no question where the buck stopped; it stopped with him. The building was completed well within the timescale, and under budget.

We went on to spend a night with David and Mary Eccles at her delightful farm in New Jersey. David Eccles was not the easiest man to deal with but we seemed to get on well. He had great vision and saw the British Library as the cultural stepping stone between Europe and the USA. Mary herself was a very considerable scholar and together they gave £1m to endow a Centre for American Studies based in the library.

Finally we visited the Multimedia Laboratory at the Massachusetts Institute of Technology and saw some of the work they were doing at the cutting edge of information technology. We flew home with plenty of food for thought.

Looking back on those three years I felt very privileged to have had the opportunity of heading up one of the world's greatest institutions at a critical time in its development. It was sad not to be able to see the project through to its completion but I am certain that if I had been able to achieve what had originally been intended and opened Phase 1A in the spring of 1993, the result might have been disastrous. In the event the additional time meant that all the technology was fully tested and working when the building opened. More important was the fact that the public saw the whole building with its soaring ceilings and great glass tower containing the King's Library from the word go. Phase 1A on its own would not have been nearly so impressive and the bad publicity would have lingered on.

In this chapter I have concentrated on the principal issues which arose during my time at the helm. There was a personal side to the job which I had not expected but which greatly added to the quality of the experience. By virtue of being chairman of the board of the British Library I was invited to all sorts of interesting functions. These included a lunch at Buckingham Palace, dinners at Claridge's hosted by the Atlantic Richfield Company and attended by no fewer than three ex-Presidents of the USA. Of these three, Nixon, Carter and Reagan, Nixon was by far the most impressive. He took us on a succinct *tour d'horizon* across the globe with no notes and complete mastery of his subject. Then there were numerous publishing occasions, soirees at the Royal Society, and the British Academy.

I left the Library in March 1993. Two years later I was asked to succeed Lord Wardington as Chairman of the Friends of the British Library. While there was a good deal to do to build the organization up preparatory to the move I was most ably supported by my vice chairman, Colin Tite and Hugh Cobbe, the music librarian, as secretary. It was good to be involved with the Library, if only peripherally, when, with the project finally completed, the day came when the Library opened the doors of its magnificent new building to the public with everything working. Attitudes changed overnight. The traumas of the past were quickly forgotten as critics came out of the woodwork claiming they had supported the project all along. Those of us who had lived through those traumas knew that the patent success of the building from the moment of opening made it all worthwhile.

CHAPTER 13

Twenty-five Years at Rockingham

Looking back over our twenty-nine years at Rockingham from the comfort of retirement, the events, the excitements and the traumas fuse into one steadily evolving pattern of development leading up to our departure in 1999. In practice of course this is entirely delusory and at the time our life at Rockingham felt more like riding a roller coaster with its high moments and its low ones. The first three years from 1971 to 1974, covered in chapter 4, were without doubt the most critical; dominated by the need to increase the income flow and reduce costs so that the estate could be run and maintained on a balanced budget without drawing on capital to fund revenue items. They were also years in which we took a number of decisions as to the way forward for the various estate enterprises, and indeed for our own lives. In general terms the policies which emerged in those early years held good for the rest of out time at Rockingham.

Probably the most important economic decision was to concentrate on building up the farm as the principal business of the estate. As explained in chapter 4 a number of the bigger tenants on the estate were reaching retirement age, and we were able to expand the farm by taking this land in hand. Fortunately this coincided with the rising tide in cereal prices which helped to finance this expansion.

Ray Dalton, our new farm manager, arrived in the nick of time and straightaway set about simplifying the farm structure. The dairy herd, with all its problems of brucellosis and juxtaposition with the public opening, was an early casualty followed in turn by the beef enterprise. Prior to Ray's arrival, I tried to improve the beef suckler herd by introducing half a dozen

Friesian cross Charolais heifers in calf to a Charolais bull. They were quite cheap and I thought I had done rather well. This was a big mistake, as my cowman, Albert Caunt, lost no time in telling me.

'You'll rue the day you bought these beasts, Commander,' he said.

He was right, and whenever one of the heifers calved, which was generally in the middle of the night, Albert made sure I was present to assist. It was a nightmare. The poor beast had a terrible time. The calf's head was too big and we had to haul it out with the aid of a Spanish Windlass. They all survived, however, and for a time we had some rather jolly little Charolais bull calves on the place, but I realised very quickly that I should never make a good stockman .

It soon became clear that our permanent pasture in the park was not good enough to fatten cattle so we concentrated our stocking efforts on sheep. Working closely with the Agricultural Breeding Research Organisation we built up the flock to 1000 ewes which were put to different rams and the results carefully recorded. With a gross margin of £60 per acre we thought we were doing rather well until the computer arrived and told us that our fixed costs were £120 per acre. I did not believe it but you cannot argue with a computer and out the sheep had to go. With them went one and a half men, a Landrover, and a whole mass of 'vet and med' bills. We let off the grazing, concentrated on the arable land, and for the first time the farm started to show a profit after a notional payment of rent. The computer was right.

With the aid of drainage and with minimum cultivation techniques enabling earlier drilling, yields began to creep up from thirty hundredweight to two ton and more of wheat to the acre. Burning the stubble provided a disease break which enabled us to grow continuous crops on the same soil and further increased the yield.

Desborough aerodrome, a disused wartime site most of which we now farmed in hand, had on it four hangars which were retained by the government after the land was handed back. The government offered them to us for £1500 each in 1973. So parlous were our finances that while we bought all four we had to sell two to pay for the other two. We lost one by fire, which we replaced and a third which we built ourselves. The high point came when we were able to let all three for a considerable sum to the Cereals Intervention Board. That year was a good one, and we sold all our arable crops to the board into our own hangars for the unheard of price of £130 per tonne.

Those days were not to last, however, and it was becoming rapidly clear that straw burning was a seriously antisocial exercise. We therefore invested our profits in equipment which would enable us to chop the straw off the combine and bury it with the stubble. Initially yields fell as the breaking down of the straw consumed much of the nitrogen, but once the cycle was established, soil which had been heavy and hard to work became much lighter, and yields began to climb again. Mono-cropping was out because of the carry over of disease which had previously been disinfected by burning. So we reverted to the traditional system of rotation based on one crop of wheat and breaking it with potatoes, field beans and oilseed rape.

Towards the end of the 1980s prices stabilised, then began to fall but under these techniques wheat yields grew till one year the farm averaged the amazing figure of over four tons to the acre, with the soil in better shape than ever before.

Now, ten years later, with the focus of farming under the European Community changing from production to preservation of the environment, it is very sad to think that all this hard work over the years to improve the quality of the soil may go to waste and once more the fields will be a haven for wild oats, twitch and black grass, when they could be producing food not only for ourselves but for the many other people starving in the world.

It was drummed into me during my naval training that however sophisticated the ship and its equipment might be, it is only as good as the men who serve in it and the officers who lead them. Of course this applies to any walk of life, but particularly so in modern agriculture where a farm worker can find himself operating high technology equipment worth literally hundreds of thousands of pounds. Ray gathered round him a core of enthusiastic young men: the Norman brothers, born and bred in Rockingham, joined us from industry where they had started their working life; Bryan Beauchamp, our engineer, came with Ray from Stoneleigh; Derrick Chambers our principal tractor driver came with Tony Hill from Charles Champion's farm when he retired. There were others who came and went; Peter Robinson came as a trainee and stayed. They were a good team who worked all hours of the day and night when it was necessary, which was most of the time.

We had many laughs. It became customary to hold an estate supper in the great hall in the run-up to Christmas and this was an occasion for remembering some of the more ridiculous things that happened during the year as well as the triumphs. For a number of years I adopted an idea I picked up at sea of playing Father Christmas with a sting in the tail, a toy watch for the late comer, a pocket compass for Derrick to help him find his way to the fields without demolishing the bus station (which or course he had just done). I was not exempt from this and my shelf is stacked with reminders of those days. Early on when I was struggling to learn to plough I was given a model tractor over the motto ' For those in peril on the land'.

It was not just the farm that took part in this jollity. We were very keen to create a family feeling on the estate where everyone, the cleaners, the gardens staff, the woods staff and estate maintenance staff all felt part of a team and worked together.

The biggest single department after the farm was devoted to estate maintenance. My uncle had adopted the traditional practice of employing a small direct labour force under a foreman to cater for routine maintenance with major works put out to contract. There did not seem to be a budget nor any specific costed repair programme and I suspected that a good deal of time was being wasted. In our present financial state we really could not afford to keep a full time skilled labour force waiting for something to happen.

The excellent and much liked estate foreman and mason, Jack Smith, died tragically just before we arrived and the carpenter went his way which reduced the maintenance staff to two, Chris Tkotz, and Bill Burbidge. An ex-German prisoner of war from East Germany, Chris liked it so much over here that he stayed on at the end of the war. It was in any case impossible for him to go home to East Germany. Virtually illiterate, he would turn his hand to anything. In particular he had an elephantine knowledge of the layout and run of the drains and when, somewhat unexpectedly, he died, this knowledge died with him. Bill Burbidge, a veteran of Dunkirk, used at one stage to work in the woods but when that became too arduous for his failing health he was transferred to estate maintenance. A pillar of the village meeting, Bill kept us all in line. In this he was aided by another strong village character, Winkie Lewin. Winkie was a man with strong views and a countryman through and through. He was not a man to be trifled with, but equally he was not averse to having a little fun and could be guaranteed to 'stir the pot' from time to time.

Bill Burbidge's son Trevor ran the housing division of Corby District Council, and combined the roles of clerk to the Parish Meeting and secretary to the Parochial Church Council. Winkie's son, Brian, succeeded him as head woodman.

Brian and I are of a similar age; we may even have attended the village school together for a time. He spent his National Service in the army as a dog handler, serving in Britain and Germany. On his return home, my uncle sent him on a forestry course: armed with this knowledge, he then assumed the role of head woodman over his father – an unusual arrangement which appeared to work very well.

There were about 450 acres of dedicated woodland which we managed through a plan of operations drawn up with the Forestry Commission. Much of the mature timber on the estate had been felled in the first half of the century, with little or no replanting. This is fatal for a hardwood timber operation as each tree can take 150 years to mature and a gap in the planting cycle means a gap in output 150 years later.

This was the position in the latter half of the 20th century and we faced considerable outgoings as we tried to restore the balance with little or no income. It was only made possible by a favourable tax regime specifically designed to deal with the long-term economics of forestry. Unfortunately this excellent arrangement became associated with a number of rich celebrities who were being attracted into forestry by the tax reliefs – and giving the industry a bad name. The Inland Revenue needed no encouragement to simplify tax structures by cutting out extraneous reliefs and Nigel Lawson, the then Chancellor, seized the opportunity to throw the baby out with the bath-water and remove forestry from the tax system altogether. This was all very well for the big commercial conifer forests in the uplands which had trees to sell and a cash flow, but it was no help to those small lowland owners of traditional mixed woodlands like ourselves whose losses far exceeded income and who now faced financing their woodland maintenance out of income after tax.

Trying to run a commercial forestry operation in these circumstances was clearly impossible, but the woods were an important amenity which we were keen to preserve. We also did not want to lose ground on what had already been achieved. I therefore determined to retain the woods staff if I possibly could, using them not only in the woods but as a reserve of labour to help in other areas such as the gardens where our two staff were at certain times of the year under great pressure.

Furthermore, in addition to being head woodman, Brian Lewin had assumed the duties of head keeper in which he was supported by his two colleagues, John Nicholls and Gerry Anderson. My uncle had refused to rear any birds and, while he retained a full-time keeper, there were years when in order to preserve the wild stock he did not shoot at all. Admirable though this system was, I simply could not afford to run the shoot in this way. I therefore allowed the keeper to rear the birds, which he had been longing to do and invited a number of local friends to become paying guests. I appreciated that this arrangement would not cover all the costs but it would leave me with control.

All went well for a couple of years until the keeper, driven mad by vandalism from Corby, resigned, and his successor fared no better. I then resolved to put the shoot, which was becoming an expensive worry, into care and maintenance. At this point Brian Lewin came forward and suggested that we should buy some adult birds and that he and his colleagues would each take responsibility for a wood in which these birds would be released. This seemed an excellent idea, particularly coming from 'the bottom up' and the shoot developed from that point. With the help of the Game Conservancy we were able to show some sporting birds off the escarpment and had a lot of fun over the years.

The most difficult post to fill was without doubt that of head gardener. When I was a child, Mr Gildon, the then head gardener, resplendent in grey waistcoat and watch chain, presided over a staff of fourteen – four of whom worked in the pleasure gardens under Mr Walpole, and the remainder in the kitchen garden. Gildon, as he was called by my grandmother, was rather an austere and frightening figure. It was not until we returned to live at the castle and found Gildon living in retirement in the village that I discovered he had a tremendous sense of humour. The formal gardens at Rockingham are large and extensive, based on the fortifications of the Norman castle. There are seven miles of edging. Then there is a ravine garden known as the Grove with over two hundred different species of tree or shrub. The head gardener, who now only had himself and possibly two others to do the job of fourteen, had to be not only a knowledgeable plantsman but a very good organiser and prepared to do a lot of hard work him or herself. It was not so difficult to find someone with two of these qualities, but to have all three was rare. Finally Richard Stribley joined us from Cornwall. With the strength of an ox and determination to boot, he would carry the big Ransome motor-mower across the path rather then drive it rattling across. He is still running the gardens today, assisted now by his son Ben and Diane Carr.

On the estate side Rob Gardiner of Strutt and Parker continued to act as our agent for a number of years. Rob was a true friend and his advice was always sound, but inevitably as his responsibilities within the firm increased so we saw less of him and more of his assistants. These came and went until one day a young man called Rupert West was introduced. He stayed and has been a pillar of support over the years. In particular he excelled in the planning and execution of the complex handover of the estate to James.

I have always believed that in estate management it is the man that matters and not the firm. This was put to the test towards the end of our time at Rockingham when Rupert decided to break away from Strutt and Parker and set up on his own with a colleague. After all he had done for us – for by then the estate was nominally James's and I was in a caretaker role – I had no hesitation in recommending that we should go with him. It was not the easiest time for anybody; Strutt and Parker were furious and dug up all kinds of old accounts for work done on potential future developments which had long since been forgotten. The new firm is now well established, and neither James nor I have had any cause to regret that decision.

That being said, Strutt and Parker served the estate well for many years, becoming closely involved in various mad ideas that I had from time to time. One such was the Stoke Griffin scheme. Holidaying in Scotland one day I received a telephone call from the chairman of the County Planning Committee who was also at that time the senior partner of the firm of architects we retained in respect of the castle.

'How would you like a village on Desborough airfield? We have been told to provide for 1000 new dwellings in the rural areas to the north of the county in our new County Structure Plan, including the possibility of a new stand-alone settlement of 750 units in the Kettering district. Desborough airfield could be a potential site.'

I have to confess that I was excited by the idea of designing a new village from scratch. The 1980s building boom was at its height and, little realizing the up-front costs of infrastructure and community gain, e.g. schools, surgeries, recreation centres, all of which the developer could expect to have to provide free of charge, I fondly visualized a scheme whereby half the development would be sold off to pay for the other half which would be built by the estate. The latter would be sold on long leases and their rents would go to maintain the estate for all time.

Not only was it financially attractive to my naïve eyes, but there was an interesting social challenge. I wanted the master plan to reflect those features which make villages so popular. There would need to be a mix of houses, of all sizes and income groups, and I was keen to avoid the 'ghetto' atmosphere of the modern housing estate. In order to control the development I resolved to produce the master plan myself rather than put the whole thing in the hands of a developer.

The problem was to find an architect who shared my views. As I looked around, I could find only one example of a village designed along the lines I had in mind. This was a scheme near Newbury designed by the architect John Simpson. It had many of the ingredients that I was looking for but the design itself was flamboyantly Palladian, and looked more appropriate for the Veneto with its domes and urns than the decidedly severe building environment of Northampton.

I saw John at his office in London, and he was enthusiastic, promising faithfully to follow our local vernacular style of high roof pitch with positively no urns. My sister, Elizabeth Banks, who was well on her way to becoming one of the top landscape architects in the country, agreed to do the landscape plans and with Peter Banks of Strutt and Parker's London office co-ordinating and Rupert West, our agent, we went to work.

It soon became clear that we were not the only candidate, and there were in fact six other areas being considered. As the scheme evolved with the production of an elegant brochure under the name of Stoke Griffin, local opinion became concerned and mounted a very effective protest. Suddenly the bleak treeless ex-wartime airfield became endowed with special environmental features which would be lost if the development went ahead.

Meanwhile we were begining to appreciate the financial realities of the scheme.

The brief called for a 350 unit or a 750 unit settlement. What the council really wanted and what they ultimately chose was a scheme which started with 350 units but could grow to 750 in due course. Our scheme needed at least 750 units to justify the expense of the infrastructure.

In the event our scheme was not chosen. While disappointing at the time, it was in fact a relief. If we had been chosen the momentum would have inevitably carried us on into more and more expense only to find the price of development land tumbling round our ears. Land worth £400,000 one day was worth nothing the next.

It was a salutary exercise. Perhaps we should have involved a developer from the start but it is easy to say that with hindsight and our flexibility would have been greatly curtailed. We should almost certainly have lost control at an early stage in the development.

There was an unexpected sequel to this saga. At some stage John's initial drawings appeared in the *Daily Telegraph* where they were seen by the Prince of Wales who wrote me an enthusiastic letter of support. He was himself in the process of designing a village style development at Poundsbury on the edge of Dorchester and he was concerned to extend the concept and bring the benefits of village life into the inner city areas. To this end he invited a group of developers to look into the practicality of developing inner city areas along village lines. They were due to hold a seminar to report progress and I was invited to speak about Stoke Griffin. In fact there were only two speakers at the seminar, Leon Krier, the architect for Poundsbury, and myself, neither of whose subject had anything to do with inner cities.

Another policy decision made in those early years was to concentrate the estate's residential property on Rockingham village. In principle, any residential property outside the village which came in hand and was not required to house estate staff would be sold and the proceeds invested in land. With rents taxed as investment income at up to 98%, there was no future in owning residential property for letting where the money could be put to better use elsewhere. The village, all of which was owned by the estate with the exception of the old rectory and six council houses, was different. Its close historical, social and archaeological relationship with the castle was something very special and I felt it was important that it should all be retained in the same ownership as long as possible.

The village of Rockingham as it stands today winding up the hill below the castle dates from the late 17th century after the Civil War when it was moved from the immediate vicinity of the castle. While there are one or two earlier buildings, most of the cottages and farmhouses are 18th or 19th century. Until recently the only 20th century contribution was six stone-built council houses at the bottom of the village set to one side.

My uncle had carried out a major modernisation scheme on the village in the 1950s, raising roofs to provide more headroom, installing bathrooms and indoor sanitation. There was no central heating but every house was provided with a solid-fuel cooker of the Rayburn variety. As a result of this, most of the village was in a reasonable state of repair when we arrived in 1971 and we were able to concentrate on building up the income flow without the burden of a major repair programme. The repair bill is one of the few items of expenditure that can be controlled but it cannot be held off for ever. Old houses need serious attention at least once every thirty years, and the longer they are left, the bigger the bill at the end of the day.

It was a great relief therefore and a sense of achievement when our investment in the farm began to bear fruit, and at last with the help of our consultant architect, David Allsop of Gotch , Saunders and Surridge, we were able to set in train a programme of major repairs, tackling on average two cottages per year, all funded out of income, sometimes with the aid of a small grant from the local authority. Where possible, the structural repairs would be accompanied by improvements to the layout to meet the needs of contemporary lifestyle.

Rockingham might be very picturesque with its two rows of cottages glowing in their golden ironstone, some with thatched roofs and some with Collyweston slates, but by modern standards their accommodation was pretty mean. Ceilings, particularly on the ground floor, were low, windows small and staircases steep. The bathroom would have been added on plus a scullery area in the 1950s, but space was limited. My Victorian ancestors built on at the back of each cottage a sort of brick unit containing an earth closet, a wash place and a pigsty. Sometimes it was possible to incorporate this into the scullery to make a modern kitchen

In the early seventies roughly two-thirds of the occupants lived in the village by virtue of their relationship with the castle or estate. The practice was that anyone who worked for the estate was offered a rent-free cottage, if one was available, for the duration of their employment. If they served for a substantial period of time, such as twenty-five years, then they and their spouse could continue to live in that cottage rent free for the rest of their lives. The remaining third rented their cottages in the normal way, but rents were low and controlled. The general effect of this state of affairs was that in terms of cash flow, the village cost a good deal more to maintain then it produced in cash.

This situation was changing, however, as the number of people directly employed by the estate reduced, and the elderly died or went to live in sheltered accommodation* elsewhere. The effect of this movement was to throw up more houses to let, and that, with the relaxation of controls and the ability to charge realistic rents, has transformed the economic situation – but it has altered the social balance of the village. Whereas in the past the majority of the village population were permanent residents, their successors who have no links with the estate tend to be more transient and less inclined to become involved with the village institutions such as the Parish Meeting, or the Village Hall Committee.

Georgina and I kept in close touch with the village. We sat on the Parochial Church Council (I was a churchwarden) and attended the Parish Meeting when we could.

My uncle had chaired it and I was expected to follow suit but I refused, believing that it was important that the chairman should be drawn from those people who actually lived in the village. I attended as a resident and we discussed the shortcomings of the estate when they arose as if it were a third party without any embarrassment.

If you really wanted to know what was going on in the village, the best source of gossip was the tearoom kitchen. There under the benign but nevertheless sharp eye of Mrs Smith, widow of the late Jack Smith, estate foreman, the village girls and their friends acted as waitresses, while the more mature ladies did the washing up, or supervised the tea urn. Georgina would sit at the receipt of custom by the door and keep an eye on the waitresses. It was very much a family affair. This went also for the castle itself. We wanted our visitors to feel that they were our guests in our family home.

There were two things on which we were not prepared to compromise. We would not have private parties in the house hosted by individuals, which ruled out weddings, and we did not want any gimmicks or things on display which we would not have chosen to have in our home. We ran the place ourselves and inevitably by the demanding standards of today our efforts would have looked decidedly amateur.

Keeping the numbers up to scratch was a continual worry. I am not at my

---

* I tried for a number of years to build accommodation for the elderly so that they could remain in the village but the additional expense of building in stone made the cost prohibitive. Now at last it has happened and six bungalows designed for the elderly have been built in an old farmyard, separated from the main road by a wall.

best thinking up new headline gripping one liners for the press. We therefore retained the services of Norman Hudson, who subsequently became Technical Adviser to the Historic Houses Association, to handle our publicity. I first met Norman when he was working for Savills. An elected member of the National Trust Council he had specialised in the management of leisure attractions and Historic Houses. I was at once struck by his interest in the smaller house lived in by its owner and open to the public. This at a time when those firms who were interested in leisure and tourism management were really only prepared to consider large scale operations. He seemed to be just the man we required not only at Rockingham but with the HHA as well. Now, thirty years later, countless owners have benefited from his wise advice, not least myself.

The designation by the English Tourist Board of 1981 as Maritime England Year gave us an opportunity to celebrate our naval connections and put on show our considerable collection of naval memorabilia. It also gave us an opportunity to clear out the space known as the 'undercroft'. This was a substantial space under the tearooms (Walkers' House) which had once been the kitchen of the Tudor house above. Its most recent use had been as a sort of coal hole combined with a dry timber store. Opening out onto the front courtyard it made an ideal space for mounting exhibitions outside the house itself. All we needed was someone to design the exhibition for us.

The hour produced the man and into our lives swam Arnold Rattenbury, who not only designed for us four superbly original exhibitions but became, with his wife Sim, very close friends. By nature a poet, he designed exhibitions to keep body and soul together. He started his life as a committed communist but gradually became disillusioned first with the communists, and then 'New Labour'. Loyal to his faith he would say to us, sadly,

'I love you very much, my dears, but when the revolution comes, I shall be the first to string you up in the village square.'

It so happened that the Naval exhibition coincided with the Falklands War, and among the exhibits was an abstract from the ship's log of *HMS Challenger*, which, under the command of Captain Michael Seymour, landed the first British Governor of the Falklands, Mr Smith in 1832. Altogether, we had four exhibitions each lasting two or three years: The Naval Connections, Charles Dickens, The Civil War and The Castle through the Centuries. These provided useful added value to the garden tour, and to some extent made up for not having a bedroom on view.

Another activity which became and still is a popular event was open-air Shakespeare. We tried it first in the fourecourt which is a natural amphitheatre with the house providing a backdrop on three sides, but it faces north and tends to be rather cold. The terrace which is open to the west, worked better. People come with tables and chairs and have supper before the show; everything is very informal. In the ten years or so that I was involved I only remember it raining once, but so hot was the scene of Othello in bed with Desdemona that no one noticed. On another occasion we did *Romeo and Juliet* in the forecourt, but the only window suitable for Juliet was in fact the kitchen of the nursery flat. Poor Juliet had to sit in the sink in order to be seen by the audience. A true professional, no one would have guessed her discomfort.

One day I received a phone call from a neighbour. His name was John Hawkesworth, the producer and originator of *Upstairs Downstairs*. He asked if he could come and see me as a matter of urgency. He explained that he was working on a series for the BBC about the Civil War. It was to be called *By the Sword Divided* and would focus on the divided loyalties of families during the period leading up to the war and during the war itself. He was looking for a suitable location and did I know of anywhere which might do. An important feature was that the building had to be capable of withstanding a siege or at least give the visual impression that it could do so.

I was naturally on tenterhooks. What a wonderful opportunity this would be to get Rockingham on the map. So I said:

'What about Rockingham? Presumably you must have considered it?'

'Rockingham would be marvellous if you were prepared to put up with us. It is a frightful imposition, you know. Filming will take upwards of fifteen weeks, and during that time you will be isolated from the outside world. The road may give the sound people a problem but this is not insoluble.'

'I think it would be the most tremendous fun. We can easily arrange that when filming takes place on public open days our visitors keep clear.'

And so it came about that Rockingham was selected as the principal location for *By the Sword Divided*, a twelve part series, to be followed possibly by another the following year. It was all very exciting but we had much to learn.

At an early stage we found ourselves locked in negotiations with the associate producer, Richard Cox. Richard was in charge of the money and very tight it was. All the filming at Rockingham was to take place out of doors for which we were to be paid a daily rate, with the interiors being filmed in the studio. Occasionally filming would take place from within the castle of some scene outside. This was known as a POV (point of view), for which we would be paid a supplementary fee. I tried to persuade Richard that a few more POVs would greatly improve presentation, but he had it all worked out in advance and was not going to fall for that one.

I retained Norman Hudson to act for us in the negotiations with the BBC which he did splendidly. The BBC made much of the number of additional visitors that we should receive as a result of the publicity, a point which would have carried more weight if they had agreed to include Rockingham in the credits. This they eventually did and our numbers increased by 60% in the first year (1985) with the general effect lasting almost ten years. Finally a fee was agreed, and the contract signed. We were then invaded by an army of designers determined to remove the slightest trace of anything dated after 1650. Victorian Tudor was all right but anything remotely Georgian such as sash windows had to be blanked out. The retaining wall on the ramparts acquired polystyrene battlements and a forge appeared below the towers.

I was amused to see when we visited the studio that the designer's version of the great hall at Arnsecote (Rockingham) bore no resemblance to ours. It was a very grand state-of-the-art 17th century hall with painted columns, and if there had been a ceiling I am sure it would have been painted too. I tried to point out that Arnescote would be much more likely to have had a medieval or a Tudor hall like ours, but the brief was 17th century and so 17th century it had to be.

There was another issue over the drive. Clearly tarmac would not do and we were invited to cover it with some suitable substance. We chose mushroom compost which we could use in the gardens afterwards. The designers then wanted turf down the middle. We had a turf company at the time so we were more than happy to provide this – but I did wonder why. As it happened it looked fine until the first horse-drawn vehicle passed over it and the turf was kicked aside never to reappear.

The filming schedule for the first series involved two periods of three weeks in June and September (1984). During these periods we had to keep all cars away from the castle which meant not only our own but the postman, milkman and all other deliveries. Luckily it was a very dry summer and we were able to park vehicles on the Tilting Lawn and approach the castle through the gardens. We were committed to our already announced opening times and somehow had to arrange for the filming to take place on one side of the castle while keeping the public on the other. The BBC were very co-operative and the public thoroughly enjoyed it all.

While none of the cast or crew were accommodated on site, they had to be fed and watered during the day and a large marquee was erected for this purpose alongside the stables. It was a popular spot not just with the film crew but for our people as well.

We gave the cast dinner in the great hall on each of their visits. I made out a seating plan for the first occasion and placed the lady of the house in the film on my right. Luckily I had the presence of mind to show the plan to

Richard Cox. I was about to commit a serious social error. Once filming was over the actors shed their parts and in the subsequent pecking order the lady in question was relatively junior. Her place was taken by the 'cook', a well known character actress of considerable girth.

I took a very close interest in all the filming which was just as well as it was easy for staff to be seduced by the excitement and immediacy of the filming to do or permit something drastic. One morning I was sitting in my office overlooking the front court when I saw Charlie Woods, our expert master mason, advancing on the 12th century stonework around the Gothic front door with a drill in his hand.

'Good morning, Charlie. Where are you going with that thing?'

'Oh, they want a ring attached to the wall to hold a horse.'

'Well they cannot have one there. Why don't they have an ostler holding the horses head?'

This they did without demur but the episode itself led to one of the more comic incidents in this hectic period. The scene involved the departure of Prince Rupert from Arnescote where he had been spending the night. The front door was to open. The Prince was to embrace Lucy, the daughter of the house, leap on his horse which was being held for him by a groom and, accompanied by his favourite poodle, gallop out through the towers – a fairly straightforward scene, one might imagine.

The horse and the poodle arrived on the scene. The man with the boards said, 'Episode XXX Take One – Action', the cameras rolled, Prince Rupert emerged from the door, leapt on his horse and galloped out through the towers, but the poodle stayed put, much to the consternation of the girl handler who was silently but frantically beckoning to the dog. After two or three takes without the dog budging, John Hawkesworth, the executive producer, finally lost his temper and threw a stone at the dog which got up, stretched, and lifted its leg on the camera tripod.

On another occasion when the castle was under siege, a cannon had been set up on the ramparts. It was the genuine article, very heavy and mounted on sleepers to enable it to fire over the wall. The story line had this cannon being taken out by a mortar. The programme for this episode, which was to take all day, concentrated during the morning on the firing of the mortar while the afternoon was given over to the arrival of the bomb on the cannon. After lunch I wandered out onto the terrace and climbed up onto the gun platform from which I had witnessed the morning's filming. The structure did not seem quite as firm as I had expected but I did not have time to investigate before a voice from behind called out: 'Get off that platform at once!'

It was of course not the original cannon on its heavy sleepers but a polystyrene version wired up to explode and be blown over the wall. I was very lucky not to set it off. As the bogus cannon cost £3000, it would not have been a popular move.

There were many other such vignettes during the course of the filming which including the second series amounted to around twelve weeks on location at Rockingham and it was an education for us. We were left with the abiding impression that there is a lot of hard grinding work and precious little glamour in acting for television.

When it was all over we celebrated our twenty-fifth wedding anniversary, James's twenty-first and Fiona's eighteenth birthday with a ball, largely financed out of the BBC's fee. We entertained 400 people with dinner in a marquee on the terrace, dancing in the panel room, and a disco in the square tower. I arranged for the gardens to be illuminated hoping that guests would be able to enjoy a balmy summer evening out of doors. September is an unreliable month, however, and it blew a gale for most of the evening. I put my nose outside about midnight and the rain had stopped but the effect of the illuminations was somewhat marred by a convoy of caterers' vans. The party was the first and only one if its kind we held during our time at Rockingham and it was a memorable occasion.

The first twelve episodes of the television series were shown in the autumn of 1985. They had an immediate effect on our end of season's numbers. The following Easter weekend of 1986 we topped 2000 visitors on the one day. This meant queues extending almost to the ramparts. Luckily it was fine and I wandered up and down the line murmuring that William the Conqueror designed the castle to keep people out. On the whole the public were very understanding and helpful. There were the odd one or two who complained. There was one man who looked rather out of place in a city suit:

'You really ought to get things better organised,' he said.

'I am sorry,' I replied, 'but if you choose to visit a small historic house which has received some publicity on a Bank Holiday Monday, you have to expect queues.'

The additional numbers produced a very welcome improvement in our cash-flow which enabled us to undertake some much-needed conservation. We had already been setting aside, when funds allowed, a modest sum per year for the cleaning of pictures and conservation of books, but this was really only a drop in the ocean. There were three areas which needed urgent attention: the long gallery, the library, and the archives.

My uncle and aunt had decorated most of the parts of the house which they used but they stopped short at the long gallery because they simply did not know what to do with it. They had a horror of anything Victorian and could not therefore bring themselves to restore it, nor could they face stripping it out and redecorating it with modern materials as they had done elsewhere. So they left it for us.

This fine room was last done up the mid 19th centruy by Richard and Lavinia Watson, following the construction of the flag tower by the architect, Anthony Salvin, which gave the long gallery a large bay window looking west over the valley. The crimson silk damask curtains were in ribbons due to the effects of light and the Puginesque wallpaper stained and blackened over the years. Despite this shabbiness the long room with its three magnificent Venetian chandeliers, its elegant French furniture, and fine family portraits, still retained a mature dignity and was undoubtedly the show room of the house.

Nevertheless something had to be done and the question was – what? While the current decorations were Victorian, the room itself was much earlier. The wing which contained the long gallery was in fact started by Edward Watson in 1553 and extended right out to the curtain wall, but the money ran out and its rafters spent eighty years exposed to the elements until his grandson Lewis Watson finished the wing in 1631 – only to have it knocked down twelve years later in the Civil War. The wing that stands today, thirty feet short of its original design, is essentially a 17th century construction. By this time the Tudor idea of the long gallery as an exercise chamber had been superseded by the concept of a gallery as a show place which is, by and large, the role it fulfils today. In between, the Victorians used it as a drawing room, mainly in the summer. When not in use, the furniture would be covered with dustsheets and the blinds lowered. This sensible practice used to infuriate my grandmother who had no idea why it was done. Then one day the old housekeeper who had ruled the house (and, remarkably, my grandmother) with a rod of iron, died, and I recall my grandmother announcing this sad fact with inappropriate glee.

'Rosina is dead. Hooray, now we can throw away those dreadful blinds which remind me of death.'

From that moment the light started to eat away at the fabrics in the library and long gallery. The old housekeeper knew what she was about. Her skills had been handed down from generation to generation but with no one to follow on, they died with her. Our generation, who are now responsible, had to learn these skills afresh the hard way. Back went the blinds and, with the windows treated with ultraviolet screening, we hoped we had at least bought time while we worked out what we were going to do with the room.

I contacted the Victoria and Albert Museum for advice and Clive Wainwright, Keeper of Woodwork and an expert in the Victorian period, came to visit us. He was very excited about the room and took from his pocket a photostat copy of an invoice to Mr Richard Watson from Messers Cowtan, attached to which was a sample of the wallpaper.

'There's so little of this left,' he said, referring to the decoration of the room generally, 'You simply must keep it as it is. We shall do what we can to help you with the restoration of the fabrics. The wallpaper is a problem but maybe we can clean it.'

In the face of such enthusiasm it was impossible to refuse and we embarked on a restoration programme which was to take us the best part of five years. Trestle tables were set up at the far end of the long gallery, and Georgina gathered around her a team of volunteers. Each curtain (and there were twenty) had to be taken down, and all the threads that successive seamstresses had sewn in a desperate but futile attempt to arrest the effect of the ultra-violet rays of the sun on the silk, had to be unpicked. Similarly interlining and the gimp round the edges had to be taken off. Finally the silk damask, or what was left of it, was sent off to the textile workshops at Osterley Park where, under the supervision of Sheila Landi, Keeper of Textiles at the museum, it was washed, treated and pressed carefully onto Japanese silk backing of matching hue. The curtain was then sent back to Rockingham where it was reunited with its interlining and gimp and rehung to look almost like new.

Attempts to clean the wallpaper were ineffective but, with the help of my sister-in-law, Joanna Saunders, an interior decorator, we found a young man with an exotic girl friend and a Ferrari who took away a sample and reprinted the wallpaper so well that it was an almost perfect match with the original paper, the only difference being that former was made with gold leaf while the latter had to make do with printed gold – but it was hard to tell the difference. Indeed once the restoration had been completed it was hard to tell that it had taken place at all, and we left one ragged curtain to give some idea of before and after.

The library at Rockingham consists of about 5000 leather-bound books dating from the early 17th century formed out of two collections, that of the 1st Earl of Rockingham and that of the Right Honourable Sir Henry Pelham, whose daughter married the 1st Lord Sondes. In the days when the castle was properly staffed, each book would be taken from the shelf and dusted at least once per year – it was part of the spring cleaning routine. Books not only need to be kept clean and dry but from time to time the leather requires treating in order to keep it from cracking, particularly down the spine. We had a survey carried out which indicated that the environmental conditions could be much improved and that many of the books needed attention. We did what we could to improve the environment with dehumidifiers and creating air passages behind the shelves, but tackling the books themselves was a huge task.

Fortunately we were able to obtain a grant from the British Library (before I became involved!) for cataloguing the books and identifying those which were in urgent need of conservation. Then, with the aid of our local NADFAS* branch, the books were cleaned, dusted and treated. There is still a considerable amount of conservation work needed but at least the situation is, I hope, temporarily under control.

Rockingham's close proximity to Corby had both advantages and disadvantages. On the one hand there was the possibility of selling off agricultural land for development, which was balanced and indeed limited by the need to prevent Corby encroaching upon the amenity of the castle. On the other was the ever-present threat of vandalism and disruption, generally by children aged between ten and twelve operating in gangs. As far as I was concerned, by far the greatest advantage of being so closely associated with Corby and its predominantly Labour council was the opportunity it gave to keep in touch with contemporary Britain – an opportunity which would not have existed if we had been in the wilds of Cumbria or even nearer home, in east Northamptonshire. I made it my business at an early stage to get to know some of the leading figures in the council and found them helpful and generally sympathetic to what we were trying to do. I supported our local Labour councillor who stood for Rockingham and Gretton and was assiduous in looking after the interests of the villagers. I was careful, however, not to identify myself closely with any political party as I wanted to be able to talk on equal terms with politicians of all parties.

Corby's brief history as a steel town began in the 1930s when Stewarts and Lloyds moved their steel works from Glasgow down to the ore fields of north Northamptonshire. This move followed a recently discovered process for converting locally mined ore into steel which had hitherto not been possible. Accommodation for the workforce was built in the vicinity of the works, and for white collar staff in the grounds of a nearby country house, East Carlton Hall. This had the unintended effect of making Corby appear a one-class town which post-war New Town development and subsequent regeneration efforts have so far failed to alter.

From the start therefore Corby was heavily dependent for employment on the steel works and its associated tube works. Furthermore it was government policy to keep it that way and companies wishing to move to Corby who could have widened Corby's industrial base were refused the necessary Industrial Development Certificates.

When it was announced in 1970 that the steel works would close in ten

* National Association of Decorative and Fine Arts Societies

years, no one took much notice, and it was not until the announcement became a reality in the summer of 1980 that the full implications for Corby became apparent. Out of a work force of some 30,000 at least half were to be made redundant, bringing unemployment in the town to over 30%, about three times the national average.

At once Corby came to life. Action Groups were formed and various demonstrations were mounted including a large rally in Glebe Park. This was addressed by, amongst others, the leftwing firebrand MP for Bolsover, Dennis Skinner, and was followed by a march to London; there were threats of sit-ins and sit-outs. While the overall objective of these demonstrations was to persuade the Thatcher government to think again, the actual message emerging into the public domain was somewhat confused, and in danger of being seen as a series of protests engineered by the opposition Labour party rather than a serious cry for help.

There was indeed a case to be made for the retention of steel making in Corby. It was the only plant in the country capable of processing indigenous ore. Close Corby and the country becomes totally dependent on imported ore. Admittedly the Bessemer process was expensive but my understanding was that the Corby works were not unprofitable. I contacted one or two of my Conservative MP friends seeking their support if only to show some form of all party recognition of Corby's plight. Ken Lewis, MP for Melton Mowbray, and John Farr, MP for Market Harborough, came to my aid and made supportive noises in the House.

It was all to little avail as the truth was, of course, that the government had built two large works at Llanwern and Ravenscraig in anticipation of an increasing world demand for steel. In fact the reverse was happening and demand was declining fast as Third World countries, more often than not with British technical assistance, were now making their own, and new plastic materials were taking the place of steel in many fields. With the financial and social commitment that had been made in Llanwern and Ravenscraig it was inevitable that they should be used to satisfy such demand as existed and there was no place for Corby. In fact as it turned out their days were numbered too.

The authorities at county and at district level recognised the impossibility of retaining steel making at Corby and were anxious to set about attracting alternative employment to the town. Any suggestion that the campaign to retain steelmaking at Corby might not succeed was, however, regarded as an anathema by the unions and action groups, who accused the Councillors, many of whom were their members, of acting in bad faith. Feelings ran high and the resulting media reports of this in-fighting was not helping Corby's public image.

After two or three weeks of this I received a telephone call from Ron Hunt, the editor of the local paper, the *Evening Telegraph*, asking to come and see me.

'I am fed up with reporting all this discord in Corby,' he said. 'If only all these action groups and unions would get together and sort out their differences behind closed doors we might then be able to report more constructively on the situation. I have had a word with one or two of the leading players and they have agreed to do this if we can find a suitable chairman who is acceptable to all parties. I tried the Anglican vicar but the unions would not have him on account of his sermon the previous Sunday which had been seen as anti union. Your name was put forward and they all seem happy to serve under you. Would you be prepared to do it? The council will provide a secretariat.'

I was both surprised and flattered that I as a local landowner should be chosen for this role and without hesitation agreed to give it a trial.

We met in one of the committee rooms at Corby district council offices. Round the table sat representatives of the various trade unions involved in the steelworks, including the TGW, AUEW, GMB, ISTC and others such as the NUT. Then there were representatives of the district council, community groups, the various churches, the Chamber of Commerce, and the Industrial Group. We agreed that there should be no minutes and that nothing that passed should be officially recorded. We were to call ourselves the Corby Community Advisory Group and meet monthly or more frequently as required.

We then launched into a discussion on the industrial situation and the social problems flowing from it. At once areas of tension began to surface. The council on the one hand was trying desperately, almost at any price, to bring work into the town. The unions on the other hand were concerned that some of the incoming firms were cowboys with a bad health and safety record. Other issues emerged, and after a time when everyone had had their say and various hobby horses had been ridden round the room, I sensed a growing feeling that we were making progress and, if there was not total agreement on all the issues, at least they had had a good airing. One thing was clear and that was that each one of us was there to help Corby and its people through this time of crisis. We might differ over the method but that principle held firm throughout all our discussions.

The CCAG as it was known, continued in being for five years providing what I believe was a useful talking shop for disgruntled parties, and a clearing house for many good ideas. Meanwhile the government designated Corby as an Enterprise Zone to encourage industry into the town. The

British Steel Industry* was very actively converting areas of wasteland into potential industrial sites, and the county council with the district council were making progress. Within a remarkably short space of time the employment situation began to improve and, while the unskilled over-fifties had difficulty finding work, most of the skilled workers were back in employment within a year or so.

The redundancy pay was generous and most of the workers had their unemployment benefit made up to their original wage by the European Iron and Steel Community Fund. That lasted for a year and then, if they were still unemployed, they would have to fall back on supplementary benefit, with the rigorous conditions that were attached to it. One anomaly that I found particularly irritating was the need to show capital of less than £2500. This meant that the prudent man who put his redundancy money into savings or life insurance would not be able to draw supplementary benefit until he had surrendered his life policy, probably at a loss, and reduced his capital to that figure. Meanwhile the more profligate who had spent their redundancy money on trips abroad or white goods, could straightaway qualify for supplementary benefit. It seemed crazy for a Conservative government to encourage savings on the one hand while penalising them on the other. I wrote to the Chancellor about it and received a polite reply. In due course the threshold was raised to £3000 but that did not really answer the point which was as much one of principal as of cash.

The cessation of steel making at Corby meant the end of the open cast mining which has disfigured so much of the area. When in the 1930s the Scottish steel making firm, Stewarts and Lloyds decided to move their work force down to Corby, the agricultural recession was in full swing. So depressed was the farming community with the future prospects for agriculture that they greeted the agent for Stewarts and Lloyds with open arms and happily signed leases which could potentially take their land out of agriculture – certainly for their lifetime if not for all time. In return they were to receive a royalty of one shilling per ton of iron ore won from their land. The process involved huge diggers, or 'drag lines' as they were called, ripping off the top soil before reaching the ore which was then transported by a dedicated railway system to the Corby works .

The dragline left behind it a series of large artificial valleys, known as 'gullets', their steep banks consisting mainly of heavy blue clay subsoil. In the first instance no thought was given to restoration, and once the ore had been extracted, the practice was to plant the resulting hill and dale with conifers. With the onset of the second world war and the food shortages

---

* British Steel Industry, a subsidiary of British Steel was set up to rehabilitate and market the land no longer required by British Steel after closure of the steelworks

that followed, agricultural land was once more in demand and restoration of worked land became a priority. It was not a simple matter. There were problems finding adequate top soil, stabilisation and drainage and, of course, cost. Who was to pay? After much discussion it was agreed to set up a restoration fund to which the landowner, the operator, and the government through the local authority would all contribute a standing charge based on the royalties. In these negotiations, the landowners were represented by the Ironstone Royalty Owners Association (IROA) which was set up and chaired by my uncle. In due course I found myself in the chair after mining had ceased and our chief concern was the proper restoration of the remaining worked land when no more money was coming into the fund. By and large this was achieved and with the aid of Roger Freeman, MP for Kettering, I saw through the legislation to close down an original and unique initiative started by uncle Michael, the objective of which had been satisfactorily achieved. As the senior civil servant pointed out at the time, a rare occurrence in government.

If you live in a castle it is immediately assumed that you have time on your hands and you find yourself rapidly becoming swamped with requests to undertake voluntary work of one sort and another. At first it is rather flattering and it is much easier to say yes than no. Furthermore much of this work is both interesting and rewarding. Within two years of arriving at Rockingham I found myself a trustee of Oakham School, a governor of Lodge Park comprehensive school in Corby, a governor of St Andrew's Hospital in Northampton, chairman of the local Tourist Board's Commercial Members and Development Committees a member of the Country Landowners Association (CLA) Northamptonshire Branch Committee, a member of the Northamptonshire Small Industries Committee, and chairman designate of the Northamptonshire Association of Youth Clubs (NAYC). Each one of these was interesting and relevant but when they were superimposed on an already somewhat stressful life trying to make sense of Rockingham, something had to give.

I decided to limit my local voluntary work to those areas which directly affected Rockingham, such as the Tourist Board and CLA, and to concentrate the balance of my available time on doing something at district and at county level. For the former I focussed on Lodge Park School where I chaired the governors for five years, and for the latter I settled on the Northamptonshire Association of Youth Clubs with which I have been closely associated either as chairman or president for almost thirty years.

Founded in 1965 by a Baptist minister, Rev. Harry Whittaker, the Northamptonshire Association of Youth Clubs, or NAYC as it is more commonly known, is a remarkable demonstration of the power of faith put to practical effect. Both Harry and his son, John, who succeeded his father as chief executive, are committed Christians and through a combination of faith and sheer hard work they have presided over a charitable organisation dedicated to the training of youth leaders and the provision of facilities for young people which has seen its assets grow from zero to in excess of £7 million in forty-one years.

With bases in Northamptonshire, Shropshire, Wales and the Hebrides, hundreds of thousands of young people from all over the country have benefited from the challenging experiences on offer. It is particularly moving to watch some brash young lad from the back streets of Birmingham dithering at the top of a 40ft pole while his colleagues below urge him on to cross the high wire.

A feature of modern landownership which our ancestors would have found strange is the handover process. They would have expected to live and die in their property having made suitable arrangements for the succession in their will. Today, owners are encouraged by the tax system to hand as much as possible of the estate over in their lifetime, or *inter vivos* as it is called. Indeed the conscientious heir to a landed property needs to start thinking about his handover plan almost as soon as he takes possession. It is a complex and difficult process which can easily lead to bitter family feuds if not handled sensitively. The principal problem faced by the owner is to ensure that his heir has adequate funds to maintain the property, and that he himself has adequate funds for his personal requirements without incurring a 'reservation of benefit'.

I was fortunate in that I had an obvious heir. My eldest son, James, married to a capable and delightful girl, exhibited all the qualities and more required to run Rockingham. After ten years in the Royal Navy which included a degree in Systems Management at City University, he was now well established as a merchant banker. My game plan was to follow my uncle's example and hand over the estate in good time when we were both young enough to adapt to our new lives. In particular I wanted James's young family to enjoy the special experience of growing up at Rockingham. We therefore set a target date of 1994, my sixtieth year, for the main handover of the estate and 1999 for our move. In practice the actual handover started earlier and, when opportunities arose under the almost continuously changing legislation, I would arrange to hand over parcels of land which were not central to the estate's economy but which might have some future potential for sale or development. We also set up a pilot maintenance fund. While there was no need for this financially, it was useful to identify the land and property which could be included in the so-called 'heritage property' as a guide to possible conditional exemption should James have to claim it under inheritance tax on my death.

With all its various stages, the handover was a mammoth exercise and I am deeply indebted to Rupert West, our agent, for co-ordinating it and recording the final result in what has become known as the 'Bible'.

As we approached the date in 1994 when we were due to sign the documents handing the bulk of the estate and the castle over to James, we became increasingly conscious that we had not yet found a new home. There was no immediate panic as we were not due to move out of the castle for another five years and we had kept back from the handover Pastures House, a pretty 17th century farmhouse in the village, if all else failed. The village was too close, however, and while we wanted to stay in the same area we did not want to be on James and Lizzie's doorstep; nor did they.

A somewhat desultory search over two years had revealed a number of attractive houses but there was always some major snag. Either they were too close to the new A14, or the yard had been sold off for development, or someone had added on a monstrous wing at the back. Then one day I was driving through the village of Stoke Albany past the old manor house, a fine 14th century hall house which I had sold in 1974 to raise funds for the purchase of more agricultural land.[*] At that time it was virtually derelict and needed huge sums to put it in order. With rents controlled and taxed at 98 pence in the pound there was no point in doing it up even if we could have afforded to do so. Reluctantly therefore I sold it. Now of course it was just exactly what we wanted, but, alas, not as far as I knew on the market.

The very next morning however, at the rent audit, the wife of one of the tenants mentioned in passing:

'I hear that the Manor is coming back on the market again.'

My abiding memory is her look of surprise as I thanked her for this piece of information and leapt for the door. Almost equally surprised were the owners of the Manor when I burst in on them unannounced. Everything fell into place in a remarkable way and, by the time we signed the papers transferring the estate to James, we had secured our future home. Now, twelve years later as I write this, I marvel at the series of coincidences which led us to this lovely house in which we have been so happy for the past nine years.

James and I had agreed that I should continue to run the estate on his behalf up until the time of our move. In order to abide by the rules of the Provisionally Exempt Transfer or PET as it was known under inheritance tax, it was important that I avoided incurring a 'reservation of benefit'. In other words I could not be seen to benefit in any way from the property I had given to James. If I had died within seven years of the gift and the

---

[*] See Chapter 5

revenue found that I had reserved a benefit by, for instance, in their view paying insufficient rent for our accommodation in the castle, then they could claim the full rate of 40% tax on the gift. The tax bill could have necessitated the sale of the castle and spelt the end of all we had been trying to achieve. The situation was not helped by the revenue refusing to clear any arrangement in advance of a death.

In the event all was well. I survived the seven years, and remarkably the whole estate passed to James with no tax payable. A feat which would have seemed quite impossible in the 1970s.

Meanwhile my personal life had taken another turn and once again I was sailing in strange waters. Shortly after I left the British Library, I received a telephone call from a friend, John Robinson, who asked me whether I should like my name put forward as a candidate for the chair of Kettering General Hospital which was due to become a fourth wave NHS Trust later in the year. He was a candidate for Northampton General. Needless to say I had no idea what a hospital trust was, how a hospital was run, or how the NHS worked – but I now had plenty of experience of working for bodies whose functions involved me in a steep learning curve. I was indeed looking for something to take the place of my commitment to the British Library though nothing could have been further from my mind than a hospital!

I rang around various medical friends to sound out their views.

'You must be mad!' they said, 'You will be under constant pressure to meet ever higher expectations with inadequate funding. The worthiest of causes will have to be turned down and with the best will in the world you will never please everyone. It is a no-win job. Don't touch it.'

Not all my friends took this gloomy view and I did receive some encouragement. Furthermore I was attracted by the idea of spending the last years of my working life in something so completely different, with healthcare as it were rounding off my experience in heritage, education and information. It would certainly be a challenge. I gave John an affirmative answer.

A few days later I received another telephone call. This time it was from Stuart Burgess, the chairman of the Oxford Health Authority, arranging an interview. I had a pleasant half hour or so with Sir Stuart, as he subsequently became, after which there was silence. This is often what happens with public appointments. Your name is put forward to the Department concerned and you are then left in the dark, awaiting the ministerial pleasure.

After a month or two I received a third telephone call from Frank Collins, general manager of Kettering General Hospital, seeking to arrange a meeting so that he could brief me.

'Why?' I asked

'Oh,' he said, 'has no one told you? You are chairman designate of Kettering Hospital Trust. Congratulations!'

This was news to me. As far as I was concerned I had neither been offered nor accepted any such appointment. However there was no point in standing on my dignity and I went along to see Frank. He greeted me enthusiastically and gave me a detailed brief on the recent health service reforms illustrating everything he said with copious diagrams on flipcharts. This was my first encounter with the modern NHS manager and I was much impressed. I was also impressed with the scale of the reforms and the relative independence of the Trusts by comparison with other government bodies on whose boards I had served. Sadly this independence was whittled away as government after government sought to regain ever closer control.

Clearly working with Frank was going to be both stimulating and fun. Any reservations I may have had about spending my last working years in a hospital vanished, and I set to with enthusiasm to learn about the hospital and its role as an acute trust.

The view from my bed. The orthopaedic ward, Princess Alexandra Hospital, Paisley.

CHAPTER 14

Health, Hospitals and Happiness

Kettering General Hospital was founded in 1897 and built by local subscription on land given by the Duke of Buccleuch. The site was far larger than that required for the relatively modest building in order that the patients could be fed plenty of fresh fruit and vegetables grown in the hospital garden. Sadly in recent years the vegetable garden, orchard, and other facilities made possible by the generosity of the Duke, have succumbed to the need for more buildings as the hospital expanded, and to the ever-increasing demand for 'blacktop' car parking facilities of which there never seems to be enough.

The hospital serves a constituency of 280,000 people living in the northern half of Northamptonshire, including Corby, which has one of the highest death rates from heart disease in the country. The staff is stable and largely local which gives the hospital a special sense of identity. It is a friendly place and as the biggest single employer in Kettering, many patients have members of their family working there.

When I became involved in 1993, the wide ranging reforms introduced in the Health Service by the Thatcher Administration were in the process of being rolled out. The Local Health Authority was being disbanded and its functions were divided between two NHS Trusts, an acute trust which ran the hospital and a community trust which was responsible for all the remaining medical services in the north of the county.

Similar arrangements were made in the southern half of the county with the acute hospital in Northampton, and a Community Trust. A new Health Authority was to be set up as the principal purchasing body in Northamptonshire. It had no direct supervisory function as such but holding the purse-strings gave it considerable influence.

Our board consisted of a non-executive chairman and five non-executive members appointed by the Secretary of State, plus five executive members drawn from the hospital's management team led by the chief executive. As a board we were responsible for all aspects of running the hospital and in particular for meeting certain financial criteria. As chairman I reported to the chairman of the Oxford Regional Health Authority, Sir Stuart Burgess.

The hospital was then divided into functional directorates headed up by a consultant as clinical director who would have a sister as clinical nurse manager, and a business manager. Wards were allocated to the individual directorates, each of which became its own cost centre. Even I, with my very limited knowledge of the NHS, could see that this was a revolution in hospital management.

Coupled with this restructuring, the reforms introduced an 'internal market' in which hospitals, or acute units as they were known, competed with each other for all elective work 'purchased' by GPs with funds provided by the County Health Authority. The reforms were introduced by the Thatcher government in an attempt to make the NHS more efficient and cost conscious. Certainly it brought the staff, and in particular the consultants, into much closer contact with the financial situation but it introduced a number of problems which took up staff time and as a result was not universally popular. Like so much reforming legislation, it was introduced in a hurry, and a number of aspects had not been properly thought through.

To achieve trust status, all hospitals had to adopt the new structure which could clearly be upsetting and difficult. Fortunately for me by the time I arrived on the scene Frank had achieved it at Kettering and done so with such success that the medical staff recommended him for an NHS award.

My first task was to put forward seven names to the Regional Chairman as potential candidates for the five non-executive directorships. Frank Collins had a note of those who had applied for the post plus one or two more who had been recommended. We drew up a shortlist covering a spectrum of experience and geographical location within the catchment area of the hospital whom we interviewed and submitted our recommendations – to our delight they were all accepted almost without question. We thus had an excellent bunch of non-executive directors, all of whom were passionately interested in the hospital, bringing to the board a range of experience and in whose appointment politics played no part. This was in marked contrast to the complex procedures introduced for the appointment of non-executive directors in future years. The only snag was that for some strange reason the entire board, including the chairman, were appointed for two years. Not only is two years insufficient time for a non-executive director coming from outside the NHS to learn his way about and make his mark but, by failing to stagger the terms of appointment in the usual way, the authorities laid themselves open to having no board at all, as indeed very nearly happened.

The board was appointed in November to run as a 'shadow board' for six months before taking over from the Local Health Authority the following April. We thus had plenty of time to find our feet, get to know one another, or 'bond' as the expression goes.

Adopting the general principle that I had employed at the British Library, namely that a non-executive chairman should 'know everything and do nothing', I set about finding my way round the hospital and meeting as many of the staff as possible. I also arranged for board members to visit each directorate in turn, reporting back to the board at the next meeting. I made it a rule that whenever I visited the wards unannounced I would always be accompanied by a member of staff, generally in my case the director of nursing, Gina Pharaoh, and encouraged my non-executive colleagues to do likewise. Non-executive directors wandering about the hospital on their own can lead to embarrassing situations and create misunderstandings. If there was anything wrong it soon became apparent and I did not find it necessary to follow the example of another trust chairman who admitted himself to his hospital as a bogus patient in order to find out what was going on.

As I had found in the British Library the scope and variety of the activities in the hospital were legion. On one occasion I found myself sitting chatting in a group of nurses in the special care baby unit when I became aware of a strange noise by my right ear. What I had taken to be yet another piece of hospital machinery was a tiny baby in an incubator. This contrasted with a visit to the mortuary which with its crude instruments and bowls was reminiscent of a 17th century surgery in the days when the surgeon's principal job was that of ship's barber.

I witnessed a squint being corrected by an eye surgeon and was surprised at the undercurrent of noise in the theatre. I had expected a tense silence broken only by the surgeon calling for his forceps, and the anaesthetist juggling with his tubes. It was not as I had imagined at all. The test match was on the television in the corner, and everything seemed very relaxed. I then paid a visit to the general theatre.

'You are lucky,' said the surgeon rubbing his hands. 'You have got two operations in one today, a hernia and varicose veins.'

I was warned that I might feel ill at the sight of so much blood, but I felt sure that my curiosity would overcome any feelings of nausea I might have. I could not have been more wrong. I duly 'scrubbed up', and was taken into the theatre where the first thing that struck me was the mountain of flesh on the operating table. It was a lady and she was huge. The surgeon proceeded to explain what he was about to do, and plunged in his scalpel. That was enough for me. The room began to go round and I felt a firm hand on my shoulder guiding me out of the theatre and offering me coffee. I was not aware of any sensation of horror which might have precipitated my nausea, and felt rather a fool. I was assured that this was perfectly normal and most people felt ill on their first visit to theatre.

In common with many hospitals founded in the 19th century there was little or no development at Kettering until the end of World War II when the creation of the National Health Service, the advance of medical technology and, in the case of Kettering General, the rapid post war growth of Corby heralded a massive increase in facilities. The hospital grew like topsy during this period with successive buildings springing up all over the place, the one common factor being that in style and materials each building was a product of its age and bore no resemblance to any other. The result was a heterogeneous collection of buildings connected by long corridors of differing heights and levels, very difficult to keep clean, giving an overall impression of seediness. It was not an environment calculated to make a sick person feel better. Steps were however in hand to put this right and one of the first actions of the new trust board was to approve expenditure on lowering the ceilings and lining the walls of the corridors so that at least the place looked like a modern hospital.

There was also of course a new language to learn. Medical acronyms proliferate. On one occasion I was sitting in on a meeting which I thought was discussing ways of speeding up the clinics with a view to reducing patients' waiting time, when people started talking about DNA. I failed to see the connection between reducing waiting time for operations and genetics, and said so. There was much laughter. DNA was the acronym for 'did not attend' (a clinic).

I felt on stronger ground when it came to politics. As in any large organisation, especially one within government, there were a number of political strands emanating from different sections of the NHS which did not necessarily share the same objective. One of these concerned the pros and cons of specialisation. There was a strong school of thought, backed by medical research, which wanted to see hospitals specialise in particular areas, such as cancer, on the very reasonable basis that the more experience gained by the consultant in treating the disease, the more successful the outcome.

Taken to its logical conclusion this argument called for a range of large highly specialised hospitals strategically placed across the country with the district general hospital reduced to the role of a minor treatment centre. 'Is there a future for the District General Hospital?' was a favourite title for debates at NHS seminars and Northampton General cast greedy eyes in our direction. There were however two incontrovertible arguments for the retention of Kettering General in its present form. The first was geography and the ability of the local residents to attend for treatment. Kettering General is six miles from Corby which had the highest number of heart attacks and the lowest numbers of car owners per household in the country. For Corby patients to have to travel the twenty plus miles to Leicester or Northampton posed very real problems. The second was the continuing need for a generalised approach for the increasing number of elderly patients who could be suffering from a number of other ailments in addition to the one for which they have been hospitalised.

A typical example might be a patient admitted to hospital with, say, a fractured hip. At the same time they may have Parkinson's disease or some such chronic illness requiring special treatment which may or may not have been diagnosed. On the strength of the initial diagnosis, they will be placed in an orthopaedic ward which is unsuited to dealing with medical problems and they may well suffer as a result.

While there are strong arguments in favour of specialisation within, say, a region, there will always be a need for a general hospital geographically placed to serve a specific constituency. Kettering General was just this and, despite pressure to link up with Northampton, stoutly preserved its independence throughout my time in the chair and subsequently.

Another area of local health politics concerned the NHS Trust structure in Northamptonshire. The county was served by two acute trusts and two community trusts. The former ran the two general hospitals in the north and south of the county and the two community trusts were responsible for mental health, care of the elderly, district nurses and all other outlying areas of healthcare. The northern community trust was set up a month or so after KGH and chose to call itself The Rockingham Forest NHS Trust regardless of the fact that another trust using a similar but with very different objectives already existed. More importantly there were areas where our responsibilities overlapped. For instance, the physiotherapists came under the RFT but were treating KGH patients under our consultants. Our consultants held clinics in RFT buildings. Three of our wards were run by RFT – one mental and two geriatric. It was a recipe for muddle and waste.

Meanwhile the NHS was stressing the importance of a 'seamless' link between hospital and home. It seemed to me that these problems could be resolved with considerable saving in administrative costs, if the two trusts were brought together under the same head. I rang Stuart Burgess, the Regional Chairman, and put this idea to him but it received the thumbs down because it would create a health monopoly in the hands of KGH and undermine the principle of the internal market. I found this difficult to understand as both trusts were operating in different markets and while there might be overlap in administration there was no competition between us. All I was seeking to do was to streamline the management.

The internal market was a piece of Tory ideology which caused more problems than it solved. GPs for instance could become 'fundholders' which would enable them to 'purchase' elective work directly from the acute trust. They had to have suitable secretarial and accounting services and it was therefore an option limited to the larger surgeries. Those GPs who were not fundholders were financed by the Health Authority. The situation could arise where the Health Authority was short of funds and those patients whose GP was a fundholder found themselves on a fast track to the head of the queue.

The medical profession was not only facing great changes in their administrative arrangements, a process which continues to this day ten years later; there were also major technical advances, particularly in the surgical field, where it was becoming possible to carry out more and more procedures on a day-case basis using minimal intrusive techniques. This had the great advantage of greatly reducing, if not cutting out altogether, the trauma of a major operation, and reducing the patients' time in hospital accordingly. There was a transitional problem in that some of the most experienced senior surgeons understandably preferred to continue to use the traditional methods with the added pressure on beds and staff that this entailed.

The traditional role of the consultant was under attack from another direction. The workhorses of a hospital are without doubt the junior doctors who, as part of their training, spend some time in a hospital before pursuing their chosen specialisation. During this time they act as the first port of call for the patient requiring medical assistance beyond the capabilities of a trained nurse. During the day they work in a directorate and at night they are on call for that directorate. When I joined Kettering General they were working ridiculously long hours sometimes up to thirty-six at a stretch. When doing night rounds with the nursing director, Gina Pharaoh, we used to come across these zombie-like creatures staggering down the corridors, exhausted with lack of sleep and in no fit state to attend a patient. Then in the morning they were expected to join the procession of white-coated colleagues following behind the consultant as he did his rounds.

This was the traditional system under which most of our consultants had been trained and, while it may have had some training merit, it was unacceptable in human terms. The authorities therefore set a limit on the hours that junior doctors were permitted to work.

This was all very well in the short term but as there were no more junior doctors and the work still had to be done, it fell to the consultants to carry out the duties they thought they had left behind long ago. The shortening of junior doctors' hours without any increase in complement affected staff at all levels but while it may have been the first it was by no means the only factor contributing to the general increase in pressure on hospital staff during my last years at Kettering General.

The nursing complements of hospitals such as Kettering General were based on an assumption of 80% occupancy. It was further assumed that in any ward one third of the patients would require a high degree of nursing attention, one third would be well on the way to recovery requiring less attention while the remaining third would be getting ready for discharge and require little or no nursing.

This arrangement worked well provided the flow of patients remained constant which was the case during my first three years as chairman. The situation changed dramatically, however, with the arrival of the new Labour government, committed to reducing hospital waiting lists. While this was undoubtedly an admirable objective as waiting lists for certain elective procedures were far too long, it could only be met by increasing the throughput of elective patients which was not as simple as it sounds.

First, the hospital needed more beds to accommodate the additional patients who would be coming forward for treatment. More beds meant more staff to look after them. Then clinics would have to be speeded up; consultants would have to see more patients in a given time, which meant either more consultants, or reducing the amount of time taken for each consultancy. More theatre staff would be required with the corresponding backup in pathology, and diagnosis. The knock on effect was considerable and while close investigation showed up a number of administrative improvements that could be made, essentially the hospital's ability to deliver on reducing waiting lists turned on having the additional staff and bed space.

Not surprisingly this was not forthcoming, but targets were nevertheless set and had to be met. By a superhuman effort the targets were met and waiting lists were reduced but the cost in staff morale and standards of care was very high. In order to make space on the wards patients were discharged before they had been properly cured. The proportion of very sick patients correspondingly increased and the shortage of beds seriously compromised the hospital's ability to handle emergency cases. The state known as 'Red Alert', meaning that the hospital is full and cannot accept any more emergency cases, which was unheard of in my early days, became a common occurrence.

What struck me most forcibly at this time was the way that edicts, of which the reduction in waiting lists was but one of many, were handed down from on high without any apparent understanding or appreciation of their implications at the coalface. For instance at a regional chairman's meeting following the successful achievement of the waiting lists target, we were duly congratulated by the chairman who then said words to the effect that:

'...Now we have the tourniquet tightened, do not let it slip.'

To which I could not resist the response:'I am not a medical man, but I do know something about first aid, and it is my understanding that if you do not release a tourniquet within a certain amount of time, the limb falls off.'

The point was not taken and we moved onto the next item on the agenda.

As at the British Library, I found it easier to identify with the people with whom I worked rather than those for whom I worked. I saw our loyal hardworking nurses in despair on the wards because they were unable to give the patients the level of care that they felt was necessary and worse, they were having to send patients home before they were ready. To expect nursing staff to work at this pressure for ever was asking for trouble.

I had a feeling that our able and energetic chief executive, Frank Collins, would not be with us for long. Having guided the hospital and its new board into trust status so successfully he was clearly ready to move onwards and upwards and it came as no surprise when he told me that he had been offered a challenging job in the NHS with considerably better pay. Ultimately, as with all good chief executives, he found his way into the private sector. He was replaced by David Loasby, a local lad born in Kettering, who came with a very good write-up from Leicester General.

He looked so young at our first interview that I had doubts whether he would be able to command the respect of some of our more senior consultants. I was wrong. He was one of the few people I know who seldom open their mouths unless they have something useful to say. Where Frank bounced around the place bursting with enthusiasm and energy, David was quiet and thoughtful. He was a delight to work with and a first-class chief executive. As his reputation grew he became much in demand by the region as a trouble shooter and he too ended up in the private sector.

We were also fortunate at Kettering in having a financial wizard as our finance director. Gill Scoular did not have the proper financial qualifications to be a finance director of a Hospital Trust and had to spend her first six months sitting examinations which she passed with flying colours, and proceeded to manage the hospital's complex financial arrangements with supreme confidence and aplomb. This was great relief to me as the finances were very finely balanced and could easily have gone wrong.

The board worked well with each non-executive member bringing his or her particular experience to bear on the many and varied issues which we discussed. They were all enthusiastically committed to the hospital and gave it a very considerable amount of their time. By the time our two-year appointments were coming to an end we were just starting to be really effective. Some of us had been informed of our re-appointment. Others had heard nothing. When the day on which their appointments ended came and went with no word as to whether they were to retire or be reappointed, we were left in a quandary. It was not possible to appoint new directors until we knew the fate of their predecessors, and the board was barely quorate without them.

The problem was that the ministers of the new incoming Labour government arriving too late on the scene insisted on vetting all the appointments themselves, regardless of the delays this caused, and then did not have the courtesy to inform people what was happening.

Despite these and other setbacks which were not of our making, I found my time at Kettering General stimulating and enjoyable. I felt very privileged to work with people so committed to helping others. There were other advantages of working in a hospital such as immediate access to specialists. From my naval days I had suffered from an arthritic complaint known as Ankylosing Spondilitis (AS). It involved a stiffening at the base of the spine and while it remained dormant for many years every so often it would surface in some form or other. I had been feeling rather stiff and slow which was particularly noticeable when I walked. Furthermore my left hand showed a tendency to lie across my chest when at rest. Thinking this was my old friend, AS, I went to see the Rheumatologist, Ian Morris. He gave me various tests and then said:

'I don't think this is my department, I think you should see Richard Abbott, the Neurologist. I think you have got Parkinson's disease.'

A short walk up and down the consulting room was enough for Richard Abbott to confirm the diagnosis. People have reacted in varying ways when receiving the news ranging from shock to relief that it was not something worse. In my case I was in the latter category. Georgina's reaction when I told her was, 'What a bore!'

And indeed it was. I set out to learn as much as I could about the disease. I read the medical handbook which spared the reader nothing in its description of the horrors to come. The principal symptom was fatigue accompanied by general slowing down of the muscles. Medication can alleviate but not cure the symptoms. It took me some time to find the right level of medication, but once that had been achieved my life settled down into a workable routine. The disease was diagnosed in June 1996, though I probably had it as least six months before. At the time of writing in October 2007, eleven years later, the disease has undoubtedly progressed. I get tired very easily, my mind is not as sharp as it used to be and I am very absent-minded. For all that life is still very good.

We moved out of the castle in July 1999 almost twenty-eight years after we moved in and with relief I handed over the reins to James. My term of office in the hospital came to an end three months later in November 1999 and brought to a close twenty-five years of public work during which I had the opportunity of observing the working of government and Parliament from a variety of vantage points. As a lobbyist for the HHA. I was an outsider looking in and using the political machine to achieve specific objectives. As chairman of HWG, I was inside the system looking out; and as chairman of the British Library and Kettering General Hospital, I was appointed by and working for the government, but with responsibilities which went beyond the immediate government agenda.

While there were areas of frustration and misunderstanding in my relations with ministers and civil servants which have surfaced in the text of this memoir, I enjoyed my time in the public sector and would not have missed it for anything. A common complaint which I endorse is that ministers seldom spend long enough in their ministries to get on top of the job; and as a result they are heavily dependent on their civil servants whose experience is often contained within the ivory tower in which they work and are themselves wily politicians. For instance, when I was working in the DES I think I identified at one time at least three agendas running on the HWG within the Department

The other feature of work in the public sector which used to irritate me was the atmosphere of constant change, generally coinciding with the arrival of a new minister. My niece, who works for famine relief in Africa, told me of a very primitive tribe whose system of government involved elections once every six years. Regardless of who won the election the incoming government was bound by law to continue with the policies of its predecessor for three years before they could introduce their own. Maybe we could learn something from them.

With the end of my time as Chairman of Kettering General came total retirement, and an empty diary. For a moment I had a brief spell of apprehension as I contemplated that diary which had once been so full. I then took up painting in watercolours and the diary soon began to fill again but this time mainly with nice things.

Hospitals continued to dog my life and I now boast a replacement hip which dislocated itself when I was securing my boat in Scotland and had to be put back manually in Princess Alexandra's Hospital, Paisley. That was an horrific experience due to the shortage of staff generally and trained staff in particular. A few years later I had a pacemaker fitted. So all in all with my plethora of pills, to combat Parkinson's, I owe much to modern medicine, its technology and its practitioners.

Looking back over my seventy odd years I have been extraordinarily lucky. I have had a wonderfully varied and exciting life most of which I have shared with Georgina, my beloved wife of almost fifty years, three fine children – all of whom have found their way in life – and a close extended family which assembles for weddings, funerals, etc.

If life is likened to a game of Snakes and Ladders, there have been some snakes, but these have been heavily outnumbered by the ladders. The worst snake was giving up my command but it was more than compensated for by the ladders opened up in the challenge of securing the future of Rockingham with which I was entrusted by my uncle and in my work for the heritage which would not have been possible if I had remained in the Navy. I watch with admiration the flair with which my son, James, now runs Rockingham, and I am a happy man. If this story requires an epitaph, it is written on the beams of the great hall:

THIS HOWSE SHAL BE PRESERVED AND NEVER WILL DECAYE WHEARE
THE ALMIGHTIE GOD IS HONOURED AND SERVED DAYE BY DAYE

To which I can only add – Amen.

Index

Individuals are listed with their rank and title at the time these events took place

THE WATSONS
OF ROCKINGHAM

[Actual holders of Rockingham Castle are shown in purple type]

EDWARD ⊤ DOROTHY, dau. of
WATSON │ Sir Edward Montagu
c. 1511-1584 │ of Boughton

Sir EDWARD ⊤ ANNE, dau. of
WATSON │ Kenelm Digby
d. 1617 │ of Stoke Dry

(1) ⎯ **Sir** LEWIS WATSON, ⊤ (2) ELEANOR
Hon. CATHERINE │ **1st Lord** │ MANNERS,
BERTIE, dau. of 12th │ **Rockingham** │ sister of 8th
Lord Willoughby │ *1584-1652* │ Earl of Rutland
d'Eresby

EDWARD WATSON, ⊤ Lady ANNE
2nd Lord │ WENTWORTH
Rockingham │ dau. of 1st Earl
1630-1689 │ of Strafford

CATHERINE, ⎯ LEWIS WATSON,   Hon. THOMAS ⊤ ALICE,
dau. of Sir │ **3rd Lord Rockingham,** WATSON-WENTWORTH │ dau. of Sir Thomas
George Sondes │ **created Viscount Sondes** *1665-1722* │ Proby of Elton, Hunt
of Lees Court, │ **and 1st Earl of**
Kent, created │ **Rockingham**
Earl of Feversham │ *1655-1724*

THOMAS ⊤ Lady MARY
WATSON-WENTWORTH, │ FINCH, dau.
6th Lord Rockingham │ of 6th Earl of
1693-1750, created Marquis │ Winchelsea an
of Rockingham │ Earl of Nottin

Lady CATHERINE ⊤ EDWARD WATSON, ⎯ Lady ⊤ 1st
TUFTON, dau. of │ Viscount Sondes │ MARGARET │ Lord
5th Earl of Thanet │ *1687-1722* │ WATSON │ Monson

CHARLES   ANNE ⊤ 3rd Earl Fitzwillian
WATSON-WENTWORTH, │
2nd Marquis of Rockingham │ THE EARLS FITZWILLIAM C
1730-1782, Prime Minister │ WENTWORTH WOODHOU
1765-6 and 1780-2
d.s.p. 1782

LEWIS WATSON, ⎯ CATHERINE,   THOMAS WATSON,   **Hon.** LEWIS ⊤ GRACE, dau.   2nd
2nd Earl of │ dau. of   **3rd Earl of** MONSON-WATSON, │ of Rt. Hon.   Lord
Rockingham │ Sir Robert   **Rockingham** **1st Lord Sondes** │ Henry   Monson
1712-1745 │ Furnese, Bt.   *1715-1746* *1728-1795* │ Pelham
d.s.p. *d. unm.*

THE LORDS MONSON

[continued on next page]